Choice of Law in International Commercial Arbitration

CHOICE OF LAW IN INTERNATIONAL COMMERCIAL ARBITRATION

OKEZIE CHUKWUMERIJE

Q
Quorum Books
Westport, Connecticut • London

Library of Congress Cataloging-in-Publication Data

Chukwumerije, Okezie.
Choice of law in international commercial arbitration / Okezie Chukwumerije.
p. cm.
Includes bibliographical references and index.
ISBN 0–89930–878–3 (alk. paper)
1. Conflict of laws—Arbitration and award. 2. Arbitration and award, International. I. Title.
K7690.C48 1994
341.5'22—dc20 93–49035

British Library Cataloguing in Publication Data is available.

Library of Congress Catalog Card Number: 93–49035
ISBN: 0–89930–878–3

First published in 1994

Quorum Books, 88 Post Road West, Westport, CT 06881
An imprint of Greenwood Publishing Group, Inc.

Printed in the United States of America

The paper used in this book complies with the Permanent Paper Standard issued by the National Information Standards Organization (Z39.48–1984).

10 9 8 7 6 5 4 3 2 1

To my parents,
Uto and Mgbeke

Contents

Preface

International commercial arbitration tribunals typically encounter choice of law problems at three levels. They may need to determine the laws applicable to the arbitration agreement, to the arbitral procedure, and to the substance of the dispute. In determining and applying the applicable laws, they also have to moderate the impact of contending national public policies on the arbitral process. This book analyzes the various possible solutions to the choice of law problems faced by international commercial arbitrators at these three levels. It focuses primarily on international arbitral practice and international conventions on arbitration. It also surveys judicial and legislative practices in selected jurisdictions, and examines existing juristic opinions on the issue.

Chapter One, the general introduction, examines the characteristics and theories of arbitration, and the role of conventions in international commercial arbitration. Chapter Two analyzes the laws relating to the arbitration agreement: the law applicable to the arbitration agreement, and the laws applicable to subjective and objective arbitrability. Chapter Three examines the law governing arbitral procedure, with a particular focus on the attempt to delocalize arbitral procedure. Chapter Four explores the law governing substantive issues, while Chapter Five considers particular issues in the law applicable to State contracts. Chapter Six deals with the role of mandatory rules of law in international commercial arbitration; it also examines the role of transnational public policy. Chapter Seven, the conclusion, is a reflection on the major trends in approaching choice of law issues in international commercial arbitration.

The perspective informing this book is eclectic; it stresses the dynamic interaction between the will of the arbitrating parties and the interest of various national legal systems in ensuring the fairness of the arbitral process and its respect for vital and appropriate national interests. This book suggests that the survival of international commercial arbitration as a legitimate system of dispute resolution depends not only on its responsiveness to the wishes and needs of the participants, but, perhaps more crucially, on its respect for vital juridical interests.

I wish to acknowledge my debt of gratitude to Ben Geva, Tom Johnson, Brian Slattery, and Mary Schaufele, all of Osgoode Hall Law School, Canada; to Jacob Ziegel of the University of Toronto; to Judy Freedberg of the TMC Asser Institute at The Hague; and to my colleagues at the University of Sydney Law School. I remain eternally grateful to my extended family and friends.

Choice of Law in International Commercial Arbitration

CHAPTER ONE

General Introduction

> Of all mankind's adventures in search of peace and justice, arbitration is among the earliest. Long before law was established, or courts were organized, or judges had formulated principles of law, man had resorted to arbitration for resolving of discord, the adjustment of differences and the settlement of disputes.[1]

INTRODUCTION

The objective of this introductory chapter is to identify the characteristics of arbitration, to examine what makes an arbitration international, and to outline the reasons for the increasing use of arbitration. The chapter also analyzes the various theories that seek to explain the nature and functioning of arbitration, and concludes by examining the role that international conventions have played and continue to play in the growth and regulation of international commercial arbitration. The following discussion relates to international commercial arbitration, which is the focus of this book; some of the points made are not necessarily applicable in the area of national (domestic) arbitrations.

CHARACTERISTICS OF ARBITRATION

The question, what is arbitration? often engenders an urge to define the concept. We will shrug off this urge; instead, we will examine some definitions of arbitration proffered by learned writers and extract from these definitions the essential characteristics of the process of arbitration.

R. David defines arbitration as

> a device whereby the settlement of a question, which is of interest for two or more persons, is entrusted to one or more other persons—the arbitrator or arbitrators—

who derive their powers from a private agreement, not the authority of a State, and who are to proceed and decide the case on the basis of such an agreement.[2]

Arbitration has also been defined as a mechanism for the settlement of disputes between parties, either by a person appointed by themselves or by relying upon procedures or institutions chosen by the parties.[3] In his definition of arbitration, J. Robert highlights the similarity between arbitration and litigation: "Arbitration means instituting a private jurisdiction by which litigations are withdrawn from the public jurisdictions, in order to be resolved by individuals vested, for a given case, with the powers to judge such litigations."[4]

From the above definitions it is possible to outline certain essential characteristics of arbitration. One of the cornerstones of arbitration is its consensual nature.[5] The power and jurisdiction of arbitrators are determined by the intention of the parties as reflected in their contractual agreement. Thus, the scope of an arbitrator's power is circumscribed by the wording of the arbitration agreement.[6] The consensual nature of arbitration has led one writer to contend that arbitration is a private system of adjudication and that it is the parties, not the State, that control the powers and duties of arbitrators.[7] This view is accurate to the extent that it underlines the private character of arbitration. However, it is misleading in suggesting that parties to an arbitration have the exclusive right to assign powers and duties to the arbitrators. Although arbitration is essentially a private process, the assistance of national legal systems is in some cases sought to assist the arbitration proceedings or to enforce an ensuing award. Furthermore, the effectiveness of the arbitration process is guaranteed by the assistance of national courts.[8]

The fact that the process of arbitration at some point draws assistance from national legal systems suggests that the latter could demand and ensure that the arbitration process meets minimum standards of fairness and justice. One way of ensuring this is by imposing on arbitrators a positive duty to maintain due process in the conduct of arbitrations, a duty that is indirectly enforced by national courts refusing to enforce awards made by arbitrators who do not follow due process in the conduct of arbitration.[9] It is therefore misleading to suggest that parties to an arbitration have exclusive right to assign the powers and duties of arbitrators. However, the point should be made that, unlike litigators before a national court who have very little control over the judge's powers and duties, parties to an arbitration, together with the relevant national legal systems, regulate the powers and duties of arbitrators.

Arbitration is also characterized by the fact that the arbitrator is appointed by the parties themselves. The parties may delegate this responsibility to an arbitration institution.[10] Equally, they may select a few arbitrators and mandate them to appoint other arbitrators.[11]

The parties to an arbitration also determine the procedure to be followed in the conduct of the arbitration. They may do this by enumerating detailed procedural rules as part of their arbitration agreement or by adopting the in-house rules of an established arbitration institution, such as the International Chamber of Commerce. It is disputed to what extent they can exclude certain procedural rules of the place of arbitration, especially those that are considered mandatory.[12]

Another important feature of arbitration is that awards made by arbitrators, in contrast to the decision or recommendations of conciliators and mediators, are binding on the parties. Arbitrators perform the "judicial function" of settling the parties' dispute based on their determination of the rights and obligations of the parties. Under narrowly defined situations, international arbitral awards could be appealed against in appropriate courts.[13]

The essential elements of an international arbitration are thus its consensual and binding nature, and the active role played by the participants in choosing the arbitrators and determining the procedure for resolving their disputes. However, the role of national law in international arbitrations is noteworthy, although, as we shall see in subsequent chapters, the scope of national law interventions in international arbitrations is continuously being circumscribed and streamlined.

WHEN IS AN ARBITRATION INTERNATIONAL?

The determination whether an arbitration is international or national (domestic) is often significant because most countries have different legal regimes to govern each type of arbitration. The word "international" is used to distinguish domestic arbitrations from those that in some way transcend national boundaries.[14] International arbitrations usually contain a foreign element and most countries treat such arbitrations much more liberally than they do arbitrations with purely domestic elements. The liberal treatment of international arbitrations includes greater respect for the expressed intentions of the arbitrating parties and far less judicial intrusion in the arbitration process than is the case in domestic arbitrations.

There are two main methods used in determining whether an arbitration is international: the identity of the parties and the nature of the dispute.

Identity of the Parties

The first method focuses on the identity of the arbitrating parties: their nationality or habitual place of residence, if they are individuals; or their place of incorporation or the seat of their management and control, if they are corporate entities. This approach is exemplified by the European Convention on International Commercial Arbitration,[15] which applies to "arbitration agreements concluded for the purpose of settling disputes arising from international trade between physical and legal persons having, when concluding the agreement, their habitual place of residence or their seat in different Contracting States."[16] The Swiss law governing international commercial arbitration also incorporates this approach. Article 176(1) of the Swiss Private International Law Act limits the application of the chapter on international arbitration to cases where the seat of arbitration is situated in Switzerland and, at the time the arbitration agreement was concluded, at least one of the parties had neither its domicile nor its habitual residence in Switzerland.[17]

This method of defining international arbitration is very limiting in that it excludes some situations where the dispute being arbitrated has a foreign element. For example, parties resident in the same country may have a dispute about a subject matter located in a foreign country. Focusing on the identity of the parties in cases like this obscures the fact that the nature of the subject matter in dispute imports an international element into the dispute, an element that may be crucial in the resolution of the dispute. This method also categorizes as domestic cases involving a foreign party who has a representative place of business in the country of the other party. For example, a transnational corporation based in the United States may have a representative office in Sydney through which it deals with its Australian customers. To characterize an arbitration between such a corporation and one of its Toronto customers as domestic fails to recognize the fact that the dealings between the parties are, as a practical matter, of an international nature.

Nature of the Dispute

The second criterion examines the nature of the dispute between the parties and categorizes the arbitration as international if the dispute implicates international commercial interests. The International Chamber of Commerce (ICC) was the first to adopt this criterion. Article 1.1 of the ICC Rules defines the function of the Court of Arbitration of the ICC as the provision of a forum for the "settlement of arbitration of business disputes of an international character." According to an ICC publication:

> The international nature of the arbitration does not mean that the parties must necessarily be of different nationalities. By virtue of its object the contract can nevertheless extend beyond national borders, when for example a contract is concluded between two nationals of the same State for performance in another country, or when it is concluded between a State, and a subsidiary of a foreign company doing business in that State.[18]

This test is adopted by French law. The French Code of Civil Procedure provides that "an arbitration is international if it involves international commercial interests,"[19] although it does not define what international commercial interests are.

The nature of the dispute test is less artificial than the identity of the parties test because it concentrates on the attributes of the dispute, thereby embracing cases where parties resident in the same country engage in international business transactions.

The Model Law on International Commercial Arbitration,[20] which is aimed at harmonizing State practice in relation to international commercial arbitration, rejected the idea of a single formula, and provides four alternative tests for determining when an arbitration is international:

An arbitration is international if:

(a) the parties to an arbitration agreement have, at the time of the conclusion of that agreement, their places of business in different States; or

(b) one of the following places is situated outside the State in which the parties have their place of business:

  (i) the place of arbitration if determined in, or pursuant to, the arbitration agreement;

  (ii) any place where a substantial part of the obligations of the commercial relationship is to be performed or the place with which the subject matter of the dispute is most closely connected; or

(c) the parties have expressly agreed that the subject matter of the arbitration agreement relates to more than one country.[21]

The definition adopts both the identity of the parties and the nature of dispute tests, in addition to two other ones: the "situs test" (the situation of the arbitration proceedings outside the place of business of one of the parties) and the "opt-in test" (the parties expressly agree that the subject matter of the arbitration agreement relates to more than one country). This definition effectively expands the test of internationality, although the opt-in provision may create some difficulties.

The opt-in clause gives the parties the opportunity to internationalize an arbitration with exclusively domestic elements merely by stating that "the subject matter of [their] arbitration agreement relates to more than one country." This provision is objectionable in that nationals of the same State seeking to benefit from the liberal treatment of international commercial arbitration may find tenuous grounds for proclaiming that their agreement relates to more than one country, and thereby internationalize their arbitration proceedings. There is evidence that the drafters of the Model Law were aware of this possibility:

> It was understood [by those who participated in drafting the Model Law], that the States will be prepared to allow the "opting-in" only if an element of internationality is present. Such elements should have been that not all of the following places are situated in the same State: place of offer of contract containing the arbitration clause

or of separate arbitration agreement; place of corresponding acceptance; place of performance of contract or of location of subject matter; place of registration or incorporation or nationality of each party; place of arbitration.[22]

However, the final draft of the Model Law fails to incorporate the above requirements, with the result that arbitrating parties could declare an otherwise domestic arbitration to be international. In response to this point, two commentators assert that "domestic arbitration laws tend to provide protections that are not needed by sophisticated parties likely to use the opt-in provision."[23] This observation misses the point: the issue is not the sophistication of the parties, but their ability to circumvent mandatory rules that are specifically designed to regulate domestic arbitrations—a category into which their arbitration may otherwise fall. No doubt many countries will find it difficult to accept a situation where parties might internationalize an arbitration that is otherwise purely domestic.[24] Under the framework of the Model Law, there exist possible avenues for dealing with parties who abuse the opt-in provision. Under Article 8, courts may refuse to refer such cases to arbitration, or exercise the power to set aside or refuse enforcement of any resultant award as being contrary to public policy under Articles 34 and 35. More simply, national courts could read into the opt-in clause a requirement that the subject matter of the dispute should *in fact* relate to more than one country, quite apart from the declaration of the parties.

In summary, the identity of the parties and the nature of the dispute are the two main methods of determining when an arbitration is international, although the Model Law introduces additional methods. It is crucial to remember that the answer to the question whether an arbitration is domestic or international is always to be found in the provisions of the relevant national law.

REASONS FOR THE INCREASING USE OF ARBITRATION

The post–World War II era has witnessed a considerable expansion in the level of international trade and commerce. This process has been tremendously aided by the General Agreement on Tariffs and Trade,[25] which led to a substantial reduction in tariff barriers to trade, with a resulting increase in the level of international trade in goods. International trade in services has also benefited from the globalization of economic activity. In relation to developing countries, there is a continuing, if often sporadic, inflow of foreign investments, such as capital, joint ventures, turnkey projects, and technology transfer agreements.[26]

In a sizable number of these commercial relations, the parties choose arbitration as a means of resolving any disputes that may arise.[27] In the words of one commentator, arbitration clauses "not only predominate but are nowadays almost universal" in international commercial contracts.[28] What reasons account for the increasing use of arbitration as an alternative to litigation of international commercial disputes? A variety of reasons have been suggested, some plausible, others far-fetched.[29] These reasons are encapsulated in the following statement by J. Meason and A. Smith:

> Advocates within the business community believe that arbitration is preferable over litigation because arbitration is thought to be informal, faster, less costly, equitable, a way to avoid unfavourable publicity, relatively conciliatory, absorbs less management time. . . . Most importantly, arbitration is seen as providing the best chance to save the underlying business relationship.[30]

Some of these reasons for the increasing use of arbitration are now considered.

Speed

To a businessperson time is a very important commodity. Unnecessary delays in the process of resolving a commercial dispute are inimical to the proper formulation of business policies and the efficient pursuit of business activities.[31] Litigation of disputes has usually been associated with protracted delays, a fact on which considerable juristic ink has flowed.[32]

For a long time arbitration has been marketed as a speedy system of dispute resolution.[33] If this view is correct, arbitration would afford a viable alternative to those who view delays in litigation as one reason why public legal systems have proved inefficient in handling the problems of businesspeople.[34]

However, it is not invariably true that arbitration is more expeditious than litigation. In most cases the same factors that make the process of litigation protracted are also present in arbitration. The taking of evidence consumes time, and where the arbitrators reside in different countries they have to coordinate their time so as to be available for hearings. Furthermore, judicial interventions in the process of arbitration or in the enforcement of awards (as allowed under the Model Law)[35] ensure that some of the delays inherent in litigation sometimes filter into arbitration.[36] A clear example of how protracted an arbitration may be is the arbitration involving Yugoslavia and SEE. The award in that case, which was rendered more than three decades ago, continued to attract litigation until recently.[37] It is true the SEE arbitration is not typical of the dispatch with which disputes are resolved in arbitration, but it exemplifies how resolution of disputes through arbitration could become protracted in cases where incessant recourse is made to the court system.

Cost

It is not unusual to hear the suggestion that arbitration is cheaper than litigation. One rationale for this view is that the speedy nature of arbitration curtails the costs incurred in the arbitral process. However, as noted above, arbitration is not always speedier than litigation. Moreover, the additional costs that have to be borne by the parties to an arbitration may result in the process being more expensive than litigation. In an arbitration, unlike in a litigation, the parties have to pay the salaries or fees of the arbitrator(s) and other personnel, such as secretaries, used during the arbitration. Additionally, they have to pay for facilities, such as the conference rooms, that are provided by the State in a litigation. Furthermore, where the arbitration is conducted under the auspices of an arbitral institution, the parties have to pay administrative fees that may be substantial when they are based on the amount of money in dispute.[38] Travel costs of the parties, their lawyers, the arbitrator(s), and witnesses to the site of arbitration may further compound the cost of arbitration. International arbitrations are not inexpensive; they are usually suitable for disputes involving large sums of money or where the parties are willing to pay top price for the benefit of selecting those they deem competent to resolve their dispute.

Privacy

The issues involved in a commercial dispute may be of such a sensitive nature that it would not be in the interest of the parties (or one of them) to litigate it in open court. Issues involving trade secrets, poor quality, or defective products are better settled outside the view of the public. In such cases the parties may opt for a private dispute resolution system.[39]

Arbitration is private in that the parties may decide to keep the award confidential, and the proceedings are conducted in a private arena free from the intrusive inquisitiveness of the press and other outsiders. The parties could also, as part of their agreement, decide to keep any ensuing award confidential between themselves. In recent times there has been a proliferation of books and reports that publish arbitration awards,[40] but parties to an arbitration retain the right to preclude their award from publication or to require that any published award does not contain any reference that may aid in identifying them. Arbitration thus provides participants the opportunity to resolve their disputes without unneeded publicity that might poison the dispute resolution process.

Neutrality of Forum

Where parties to an international commercial dispute are from different countries, they may be reluctant to submit their dispute to the national courts of one of the parties. This may arise from nationalistic sentiments or fear of bias. This is even more so where the dispute involves a State party. States are usually reluctant to submit to the jurisdiction of courts of another nation, and foreign parties normally lack confidence in the ability of the national court of the State party to do justice in such cases. This has led a commentator to state that in such situations "arbitration imposes itself for lack of an acceptable alternative."[41] Arbitration enables parties from different nationalities to avoid submitting their dispute to the national courts of either of them. It offers such parties the opportunity to select their own "judges," thereby avoiding the fear of biased judgment.[42]

In summary, speed and reduced cost are not necessarily benefits that accrue from every arbitration. Indeed, arbitration may in some cases, especially where judicial intervention occurs, be far slower and costlier than litigation. The reason for the increased use of arbitration would be found in the neutrality of the arbitral forum, the confidentiality of the process, and the relative informality of the arbitral process, in comparison to litigation. Parties to an arbitration are able to select their own rules of procedure, which are most often not as adversarial as the procedure applied in most national courts. Commercial relations are built over a period of time, and when disputes arise between commercial partners they often do not wish such disputes to permanently rupture their relationship.[43] The adversarial process of litigation in some jurisdictions is inimical to the smooth and healthy resolution of disputes. Arbitration affords such parties an opportunity to resolve their disputes in a private arena, devoid of the combativeness and aggression that litigation has come to epitomize.[44]

THEORIES OF ARBITRATION

We have seen that one of the essential characteristics of arbitration is its consensual nature.[45] Does the consensual attribute of arbitration fully explain the nature of the arbitration process? By focusing on the contractual nature of arbitration, can one clearly picture the functioning of arbitration and the way in which it interacts with other social phenomena?

An understanding of the nature of arbitration is crucial in this study because the way one classifies or qualifies arbitration has an impact on the manner in which applicable rules in arbitration are determined and their scope delimited.[46] It is also true that the attitude of national courts to the arbitral process depends on the nature of arbitration and its relationship with national legal systems.[47] In most cases judicial decisions concerning the scope and limits of the powers of arbitrators could be predicted by reference to the theory of arbitration accepted in the particular jurisdiction.[48]

Various theories of arbitration have been advanced by different schools.[49] These theories include the contractual, the jurisdictional, the mixed or hybrid, and the autonomous.

The Contractual Theory

The contractual theory emphasizes the contractual nature of arbitration. The jurisdiction and powers of an international arbitrator are, as noted above, dependent on the mutual intention of the parties as reflected in their agreement, and without their agreement there can be no valid arbitration. By mutual agreement, the parties design the procedure for settling their dispute:

> Arbitration is wholly voluntary in character. The contract of which the arbitration clause is a part is a voluntary agreement. No law requires the parties to make such a contract, nor does it give one party power to impose it on another. When such an arbitration agreement is made part of the principal contract, the parties voluntarily forego established rights in favour of what they deem to be the greater advantages of arbitration.[50]

The classical version of the contractual theory contends that arbitration is wholly a product of the consent of the parties and argues against State intervention in the process.[51] It also considers the arbitrator an agent of the parties: in rendering an award the arbitrator acts as the parties' agent and the award becomes binding on them as the principals:

> An arbitral decision rendered in a foreign country, is it anything other than a contract? Is it not the consequence of the agreement to arbitrate, as a result of which the arbitrators have rendered it? Is it not tied essentially to this arbitration agreement? Does it not form with the arbitration agreement a single entity? . . . It is the arbitration agreement that gives it its existence; it is from the arbitration agreement that it derives all its substance; it has, then, like the arbitration agreement, the character of a contract . . . it is, to put it precisely, only an agreement to which the parties have bound themselves by the hands of the latter (the arbitrators).[52]

Critiquing the classical version of the contractual theory, A. Samuel points out[53] that an arbitrator cannot be regarded as an agent of the parties for a variety of reasons. First, unlike an agent, the authority of an arbitrator can be made irrevocable and the duty of the arbitrator to render an impartial and unbiased award is inconsistent with an agent's obligation to conform with the wishes of the principal. Second, since no agent could do something that the principal is incapable of doing, an arbitrator cannot be acting on behalf of the parties in conducting an arbitration because the parties are not in a position to judge impartially the merits of their dispute.

The modern version of the contractual theory repudiates the idea that the arbitrator is an agent of the parties as understood in the law of agency and disowns the belief that an award is primarily a contractual document. However, it emphasizes the contractual nature of arbitration; it stresses the fact that the arbitral process is a product of the consent of the parties, and that the parties should be given a free hand in adapting the process to their particular needs. It thus recognizes the competence of the parties to choose the law to govern the arbitral process, free from the interference of national legal systems.[54]

The main weakness of the contractual theory of arbitration is that it presents a warped and incomplete picture of the arbitration process. No doubt, consent is cardinal to the understanding of arbitration. The efficacy of the arbitration agreement and the attendant award flow directly from the agreement of the parties to utilize the arbitration mechanism and their implicit undertaking to respect the award as an absolute and final determination of the disputes between them. But it is a limited view of arbitration that projects the consensual nature of arbitration as the most fundamental essence of the process. It should not be forgotten that arbitration, as a method of dispute resolution, is a process that is ultimately regulated in some form by society to ensure that it meets society's notions of fair play and justice. In the context of international arbitration, this regulation is done in the course of the procedure for the recognition and enforcement of the award or in cases where an application for the annulment of the award is made. Thus, the consensual nature of arbitration can only help in explaining the nature of arbitration when it is viewed within the context of the national legal systems that allow the consent of the parties and the award of the arbitrator(s) to be productive of legal consequences.[55]

The Jurisdictional Theory

The jurisdictional theory focuses on the authority of a State to regulate all arbitrations conducted within its territory. The theory maintains that the validity of the arbitration agreement, the powers of the arbitrators, and the enforcement of the arbitral award all derive from a particular national legal system.[56] In this sense an arbitration cannot be carried on without the regulation of a national legal system.[57]

One of the best known advocates of this theory is F. A. Mann, who argues that every State has the right to supervise and regulate any activity occurring within its territory.[58] Thus, the country where an arbitration is conducted regulates the arbitral proceedings and the efficacy of the process.[59] The arbitration agreement is binding on the parties not just because of their mutual consent, but because a national legal system decides to attach some legal consequences to their agreement. It follows then that the intentions of the parties as reflected in their agreement can only be binding to the extent they are sanctioned by the laws of the place where the arbitration is conducted. As Mann puts it,

No one has ever or anywhere been able to point to any provision or legal principle which would permit individuals to act outside the confines of a system of municipal law; even the idea of autonomy of the parties exists only by virtue of a given system of municipal law and in different systems may have different characteristics and effects.[60]

He further contends that the term "international arbitration" is a misnomer because all private arbitrations are invariably national in character. In his view, every system of private law is a system of national law. Consequently, arbitration, as a system of private law, necessarily derives its legitimacy from a national legal system.[61] Also, international conventions governing arbitration apply only by virtue of their incorporation into national law.[62]

One implication of this theory is that arbitrators are constrained to follow the conflicts of law rules of the seat of arbitration in trying to select the law to apply to the arbitration proceedings and the substance of the dispute. Also, an award may be set aside if the arbitration does not comply with the law of the seat of arbitration. As A. Hirsch notes, "What should be undisputed . . . is the fact the parties and arbitrators are to be governed by the *lex arbitri*. If they adopt a solution that is not allowed by the *lex arbitri*, the award may be set aside."[63]

This theory is useful because it stresses the importance of national laws in the conduct of arbitration. Unlike the contractual theory, it underscores the fact that national laws are an essential component in the process of understanding the nature of arbitration. However, just like the contractual theory, it overemphasizes what is at best a singular, albeit significant, consideration in the arbitration process: that is, the role of national legal systems. It does not give sufficient regard to the role of the parties' agreement. Much as it is correct to state that it is national law that confers legitimacy and efficacy to arbitration, it is also valid to state that there can be no arbitration without the agreement of the parties, except in cases of compulsory arbitration.[64]

It is a recognition of the significance of the parties' agreement, and the need to respect their desire to resolve their dispute privately and outside the confines of national judicial systems, that explains the current trend toward limiting judicial interference in the arbitration process. This trend is evident in the UNCITRAL Model Law on international commercial arbitration.[65] Therefore, a theory of arbitration that ignores the significance of the will of the parties to an international commercial arbitration is unsatisfactory.

The Mixed or Hybrid Theory

The previous critique of the contractual and jurisdictional theories of arbitration has centered on the fact that both theories are essentially a one-dimensional evaluation of the nature of arbitration. While the one looks at arbitration from a narrow contractual viewpoint, the other concentrates almost entirely on its jurisdictional character. The reality is that an understanding of the concept of arbitration must acknowledge the interaction of both its consensual basis and the legitimacy and support conferred on the process by national legal systems. Whereas arbitration is a product of the consent of the parties and the parties decide on the manner in which to conduct the proceedings, the legality and efficacy of that choice is guaranteed by national laws.

The mixed or hybrid theory recognizes the dual influence that defines the nature of arbitration. As its originator, G. Sauser-Hall, points out, "[a]lthough deriving its effectiveness from the agreement of the parties as set out in the arbitration agreement, it [arbitration] has a jurisdictional nature involving the application of the rules of procedure."[66] He indicates that it is not possible for arbitrations to be unbound—that is, to be carried out beyond the control of every national legal system—and contends that arbitration should be submitted to the law of the seat of arbitration.[67] The application of the law of the seat of arbitration and the use of its courts, according to him, works efficiently and justly in a majority of cases.[68] Proponents of the theory, however, recognize the need for the wishes of the parties to be respected and not unduly frustrated.[69]

This theory presents a fuller picture of the nature of arbitration. It clearly demonstrates that much as an arbitration agreement is a contract and must be treated as such, the arbitration proceedings remain subject to some national law.[70]

The Autonomous Theory

Arbitration developed in response to the need of businesspeople for a private and flexible means of resolving their disputes.[71] The business community has played a considerable role in the evolution of arbitration, which led to the development of yet another theory of arbitration.

The autonomous theory of arbitration insists that arbitration should be viewed in a broad context: rather than emphasizing the structure of the institution, emphasis should be placed on its goals and objectives. A complete picture of arbitration can only be presented by considering its use and purpose, and the way in which it responds to the needs of the business community.[72] The autonomous theory, breaking away from the trend to focus on either the contractual or jurisdictional nature of arbitration, examines the arbitration process itself—its role, its objectives, its methodology.

The autonomous theory also suggests that unhindered party autonomy is crucial to the full development of arbitration.[73] Respect for the parties' freedom of choice, the theory maintains, will fulfill the aspirations of those who use arbitration and also help in the development of arbitration as an institution.[74]

This view approaches that of those who contend that arbitration should be delocalized or unbound from the laws of the seat of arbitration.[75] It implies that the intention of the parties should be predominant in determining the law to be applied both to the arbitral proceedings and the substance of the dispute.

It is true that an understanding of the goal and purpose of arbitration is useful in appreciating the character of arbitration. Those who realize the fact that parties who consent to arbitration consciously intend to opt out of the judicial resolution of the dispute by national courts in favor of a private and flexible arena are more apt to appreciate the need for minimal judicial interference in the arbitration process. Parties to an arbitration do not expect the arbitration process to be frustrated by unrestricted judicial intrusion into the process. However, the autonomous theory is inadequate in underscoring the need for some form of, if only basic, national law regulation of arbitration. Without the regulation of arbitration by national law how can the integrity of the process be guaranteed? Indeed, how can it be ensured that arbitrators respect the expressed intentions of the parties?

Conclusion

The theories of arbitration discussed above illuminate the various and often conflicting pressures that affect the arbitration process. Is more prominence to be given to the contractual nature of arbitration than to its jurisdictional nature? Or should the above factors be entirely jettisoned in favor of an exclusive emphasis on the aims and objectives of arbitration?

It is clear that the answer to the above questions directly affects the way we view what role the legal process should play in arbitration. A contractual theorist would necessarily advocate unhindered party autonomy, whereas a jurisdictionalist would argue for substantial judicial supervision of arbitration. An adherent of the mixed or hybrid theory is likely to favor an effective mixture of autonomy and regulation, whereas an autonomist would focus on what is necessary to ensure that arbitration meets the needs and objectives of the parties.

In the end, each legal system must struggle to reconcile these conflicting interests. As argued above, no one approach is entirely satisfactory. Each represents a way of looking at arbitration. A fuller and richer view must, of course, contemplate its object from all possible perspectives. In this regard, the law should reflect a blend of the above theories so as to ensure that arbitration meets the larger needs of society. The mixed or hybrid theory meets this objective by focusing on both the contractual and the jurisdictional basis of arbitration. This theory cautions us always to remember that international arbitrations cannot be entirely divorced from the legal systems with which they come into contact. For as J. Robert and T. Carbonneau remind us, "the validity of arbitral adjudication is directly dependent upon the recognition by the legal system that the arbitral process responds to the felt needs of society."[76]

THE ROLE OF INTERNATIONAL CONVENTIONS

During the early stages of the twentieth century, when international commercial arbitration was still in its infancy, the regulation of international arbitration was essentially left to national jurisdictions. With the development of better means of transportation and communication, and the attendant increase in the volume of international trade and commerce, the practice of arbitration was increasingly embraced in international trade. In no time it became obvious that domestically cultivated laws of arbitration—which mostly reflected attitude and policy amenable to the needs of the domestic community—was ill-suited for the regulation of international arbitration. This realization argued the need for the development of effective international regimes that would not only unify the law relating to international arbitration, but also formulate rules that are appropriate in an international arena.

The first of the modern conventions dealing with arbitration was the 1889 Montevideo Convention,[77] a regional convention that provided for the recognition and enforcement of arbitration agreements between certain Latin American countries. On the initiative of the International Chamber of Commerce, the first truly international convention on arbitration—the Geneva Protocol on Arbitration Clauses of 1923[78]—was concluded under the auspices of the League of Nations. The objectives of that convention were to provide for the international enforcement of arbitration agreements, and to ensure that any resulting award could be enforced in the State where the award was made. It enjoined contracting parties to enforce arbitration agreements, except in situations where the arbitration agreement "cannot proceed or becomes inoperative,"[79] and to grant recognition and enforcement of awards made in their territory.[80] This territorial limitation on the enforcement of awards was a crucial shortcoming of the convention, because it meant that the convention was not applicable where enforcement of an award was sought outside the territory in which the award was made, a factor that rendered the convention unhelpful in promoting the international enforcement of awards. A further limitation of the convention was that it applied only to arbitration agreements between "parties subject respectively to the jurisdiction of Contracting States."[81] This provision not only limited the range of the application of the convention, but its vagueness was a constant source of controversy. The phrase was variously interpreted as referring to nationality, domicile, residence or the usual place of business of the parties.[82]

The next international convention on arbitration was the Geneva Convention on the Execution of Foreign Arbitral Awards of 1927,[83] which was also concluded under the auspices of the League of Nations. As the name indicates, the convention dealt exclusively with the recognition and enforcement of foreign awards made pursuant to an arbitration agreement to which the 1923 convention applied. Unlike the 1923 convention, which limited recognition and enforcement of awards to those made in the state where enforcement was sought, the 1927 convention provided for recognition and enforcement of awards made in the territory of any of the contracting parties.[84] Nonetheless, the 1927 convention contained several significant shortcomings that were to reduce its role and value in the enhancement of international arbitration. First, it required that the award should be "final" under the law of its place of rendition.[85] This requirement produced difficulties because in some countries an award could only become final if the local court granted leave to enforce it. The implication of this was that it became necessary to seek recognition of the award both in the country where it was rendered and in the country where execution of the award was sought. Second, an award was only enforceable under the convention if the constitution of the arbitral tribunal and the arbitral procedure were in conformity with the law of the place of arbitration. This provision restricted the flexibility of the arbitration process by subjecting international arbitrations to all provisions of the national law of the place of arbitration, some of which may have been specifically designed for domestic arbitration. Finally, the grounds upon which recognition and enforcement of an award could be challenged were wide and nonexclusive, thereby affording ample grounds for the losing party to frustrate the realization of an award.

The Geneva conventions were adhered to by a significant number of States, although their shortcomings exposed them to constant attack by commentators. In the words of one such commentator, "The formidable amount of highly qualified labour which went into their preparation has not been rewarded by any perceptible progress in international commercial arbitration."[86] However, regardless of their defects, the conventions marked the beginning of a continuing trend toward the harmonization of rules dealing with arbitration.

Owing to the deficiencies of the Geneva conventions, the International Chamber of Commerce initiated another move toward the formulation of a new convention that would improve on them. The ICC identified as the most fundamental defect of the old conventions the requirement that the award must conform with the rules of the place of arbitration.[87] It formulated a draft convention whose primary characteristic was that it freed arbitral procedure from the trappings of national law. Party autonomy was given primacy in the constitution of the arbitral tribunal and in the determination of arbitral procedure. In a sense, the draft convention presaged the debate, which has continued since then concerning truly a-national (or delocalized) arbitrations.

The draft convention was submitted to the United Nations Economic and Social Council (ECOSOC), which established an ad hoc committee of governmental experts to consider the draft. The committee, made up of representatives from eight countries,[88] came up with a draft convention that differed from that of the ICC in some respects, including its rejection of the concept of a-national arbitrations.

ECOSOC submitted the draft convention to governments as well as non-governmental and intergovernmental organizations for their comments. As a result of a positive response, a conference on international commercial arbitration was convened in New York in 1958 to draft the final convention and to "consider . . . measures for increasing the effectiveness of arbitration in the settlement of private law disputes and to make such recommendations as it may deem desirable."[89] The conference drafted the Convention on the Recognition and Enforcement of Foreign Arbitral Awards (the New York Convention).[90] Although drafted in 1958, it was not until the 1970s that many countries began to ratify the convention.

The objectives of the New York Convention were to unify the laws regarding the enforcement of awards and to enhance the procedure for enforcement. It established international rules of law that favored the utilization of arbitration.[91] It focused on two important stages of the arbitration process: recognition and enforcement of arbitration agreements and of awards. These two stages comprise the vital phases of potential interface between arbitration and national judicial systems. The convention contains a standardized and relatively flexible regime to guide national courts in the handling of issues arising from international commercial arbitration.

The New York Convention is an improvement on the Geneva conventions in several respects.[92] Its field of application is much broader: it applies to awards made in another State, dispensing with the need for the parties to be subject to the jurisdiction of different contracting States.[93] It also abrogates the prerequisite for enforcement of awards under the 1927 Geneva Convention, which required that the constitution of the arbitral tribunal and the arbitral procedure should be in accordance with the law of the place of arbitration.

The 1927 Geneva Convention placed on the petitioner the burden of proving that an award met all the requirements for recognition and enforcement. The New York Convention shifts this burden to the party against whom enforcement is sought. This makes it easier for awards to be enforced. Also, by narrowing the grounds on which the recognition and enforcement of awards could be rejected and making those grounds exclusive,[94] the convention aids the international enforcement of awards, thereby encouraging the growth in the utilization of arbitration.[95]

The New York Convention represents one of the boldest attempts to enhance the practice of arbitration and to achieve unification in state practice with respect to the recognition and enforcement of arbitration agreements and awards, goals that it attains with a great degree of success.[96] It has been suggested that the international acceptance of the convention results from its codification of existing and emerging international consensus on arbitration, and its reception by national legal systems that seek to affirm and integrate the convention's content and underlying intent.[97]

The next significant convention on international arbitration was the Convention on the Settlement of Investment Disputes between States and Nationals of Other States (the ICSID Convention).[98] It arose out of the efforts of the International Bank for Reconstruction and Development (the World Bank) to create an international machinery that would be available on a voluntary basis for the conciliation and arbitration of investment disputes between States and foreign private parties. The World Bank viewed the creation of such an international machinery as a giant step toward promoting an atmosphere of mutual confidence, thus stimulating a larger flow of private capital into those countries that wish to attract it.[99]

By a resolution adopted on September 10, 1964, the World Bank mandated its executive directors to "formulate a convention establishing facilities and procedures which would be available on a voluntary basis for the settlement of investment disputes between Contracting States and nationals of other Contracting States."[100] This process led to the formulation of the convention.

The convention came into force on October 14, 1966, and it is the only convention that deals with issues arising from arbitration between a private party and a sovereign state. It establishes an International Centre for the Settlement of Investment Disputes (the ICSID) as an autonomous international institution whose purpose is to provide facilities for conciliation and arbitration of investment disputes.[101] The ultimate objective of the convention is to depoliticize investment disputes and to promote the flow of investments that would contribute to economic development.[102]

The facilities of the ICSID have not been greatly utilized, although the number of arbitrations carried out under the auspices of ICSID has increased mildly in recent times. The lukewarm response is partly explained by the fact that ICSID to an extent duplicates the functions of other arbitration institutions, such as the International Chamber of Commerce, which also provide facilities suitable for the arbitration of investment disputes.

The ICSID Convention contains provisions both for the enforcement of arbitration agreements and awards and the conduct of arbitration proceedings. This is a significant departure from the New York Convention, which focuses only on the enforcement of arbitration agreements and awards. The incorporation of provisions dealing with the conduct of arbitration proceedings in the ICSID Convention was useful in that it harmonized the law governing procedural matters in arbitrations conducted under the ambit of the convention. However, the limitation of the scope of the convention to disputes arising from investment meant that the benefit of this harmonization could not reach the great majority of arbitration that fell outside the convention.

The arbitrations that fell outside the convention were subject to the procedural rules of the place of arbitration that were often not well developed to handle international arbitrations. Several countries still had arbitration laws dating from the period when national courts were hostile to arbitration. Additionally, the divergence in national arbitration laws complicated the ability of arbitrators to familiarize themselves with arbitration laws and procedures. The above factors underscored the need for the modernization and harmonization of national laws relating to international commercial arbitration.[103]

On the initiative of the Afro-Asian Legal Consultative Committee (AALCC), the United Nations Commission on International Trade Law (UNCITRAL) commenced a study aimed at the formulation of a model law that if enacted by member countries of the United Nations would modernize and harmonize the law relating to international commercial arbitration. UNCITRAL is the "core legal body within the United Nations system in the field of international law, [with a mandate] to coordinate legal activities in this field in order to avoid duplication of effort and to promote efficiency, consistency and coherence in the unification and harmonization of international trade law."[104]

A draft text of the model law formulated by the UNCITRAL Working Group on International Contract Practices was considered and amended by representatives and observers from 60 states and 18 international and intergovernmental organizations. On December 11, 1985, the United Nations General Assembly adopted a resolution approving the Model Law on International Commercial Arbitration (the Model Law). The resolution recommended that States give due consideration to the Model Law "in view of the desirability of uniformity of the law of arbitral procedures and the specific needs of international arbitration practice."[105]

The Model Law deals, *inter alia*, with arbitration agreements (chapter II), the composition of arbitral tribunals (chapter III), the jurisdiction of arbitral tribunals (chapter IV), the conduct of the arbitral proceedings (chapter V), the making of awards and the termination of proceedings (chapter VI), recourse against awards (chapter VII), and the recognition and enforcement of awards (chapter VIII). It thus covers virtually all aspects of arbitration, including those dealt with by other conventions, such as the New York and the Washington conventions. Article 1 of the Model Law provides that the Model Law is subject to treaty law. In areas of conflict between the Model Law and any other treaty dealing with international arbitration, the former is subservient to the latter. The New York Convention remains, therefore, the ultimate reference point for the recognition and enforcement of awards. The main domain of the Model Law are those stages preceding the phase for the recognition and enforcement of awards.[106]

The strength and utility of the Model Law lie in the fact that it is designed to refurbish and harmonize national laws dealing with international commercial arbitration, and the fact that it was elaborated by arbitration experts and representatives from various countries and international agencies who strove to reach an acceptable consensus. The Model Law has been described as the "most remarkable development and influential accomplishment in the field of commercial arbitration in the eighties."[107]

The Model Law has been adopted with some modifications in Australia, Bulgaria, Canada, Cyprus, Nigeria, and several states in the United States.[108] Its adoption has been opposed in countries that regard the consensus embodied therein as inconsistent with their policy objectives. For instance, the Mustill Committee in the United Kingdom[109] recommended against the adoption of the Model Law in England, Wales and Northern Ireland on the ground that one-third of its provisions were either of debatable benefit or detrimental when compared with English law.[110]

Apart from the above conventions, there are regional conventions dealing with arbitration. These include the European Convention on International Commercial Arbitration (the Geneva Convention),[111] and the Inter-American Commercial Arbitration Convention (the American Convention).[112]

It is hardly useful to stress that the above conventions and the Model Law apply only in those countries that have either ratified or enacted them into law. Despite this fact, this book makes constant reference to these conventions and the Model Law because they embody an emerging consensus on how the practice of international arbitration should be organized and regulated.

NOTES

1. F. Kellor, *American Arbitration: Its History, Functions and Achievements* (New York: Harper and Brothers, 1948) at 3.

2. R. David, *Arbitration in International Trade* (Deventer, The Netherlands: Kluwer Law and Taxation Publishers, 1985) at 5.

3. H. van den Horen, "Commercial Disputes and Their Settlement: A Factor in Business Planning" in *International Arbitration: 60 Years of ICC Arbitration—A Look at the Future* (Paris: ICC Publishing, 1984) at 35.

4. J. Robert, *Arbitrage: Civil et Commercial* (Paris: Dalloz, 1967) at 9.

5. A. Redfern and M. Hunter, *Law and Practice of International Commercial Arbitration* 2d ed. (London: Sweet and Maxwell, 1991) at 6.

6. It should, however, be noted that some jurisdictions have provision for compulsory arbitration, although this phenomenon is limited to domestic arbitration. See A. Walton and M. Victoria, *Russell on Arbitration* 20th ed. (London: Stevens, 1982), Chap. 2.

7. J. Lew, *Applicable Law in International Commercial Arbitration: A Study in Commercial Arbitration Awards* (Dobbs Ferry, NY: Oceana Publications, 1978) at 12.

8. A. Redfern and M. Hunter have very graphically illustrated this fact:

Arbitration tribunals have no sovereign powers equivalent to those of the state with which to enforce their awards; nor do they always have adequate powers to ensure the proper and efficient conduct of arbitration proceedings. For this reason, it has long been recognised that the effectiveness of the arbitral process is dependent upon a defined relationship, often described as a "partnership," between arbitration and the courts.

International Commercial Arbitration, supra note 5, at 306. The UNCITRAL Model Law (adopted by the United Nations Commission on International Trade Law on June 21, 1985) recognizes this fact by calling upon each state adopting the Model Law to entrust a particular "court" with the performance of certain functions of arbitration assistance and supervision. These functions relate to the appointment of arbitrators (article 11), decisions with respect to the termination of an arbitrator's mandate (articles 13 & 14), control of the arbitral tribunal's jurisdiction (article 16), and the setting aside of awards (article 34).

9. A. J. van den Berg, *The New York Convention of 1958: Towards a Uniform Judicial Interpretation* (Deventer, The Netherlands: Kluwer Law and Taxation Publishers, 1981) at 296.

10. See W. Craig, W. Park, and J. Paulsson, *International Chamber of Commerce Arbitration*, 2d ed. (Dobbs Ferry, NY: Oceana Publications, 1990) at 206.

11. For example, in *Benteler* v. *Belgium* [1985] European Economic Cases 101, the arbitration agreement provided that in the event of a dispute each party would name an arbitrator of its own nationality, and the two arbitrators so named would choose a chairman of a third nationality.

12. See J. Paulsson, "Arbitration Unbound: Award Detached from the Law of Its Country of Origin (1981) 30 *I.C.L.Q.* 358; W. Park, "The Lex Loci Arbitri and International Commercial Arbitration" (1983) *I.C.L.Q.* 21; H. Smit, "A-National Arbitration" (1989) 63 *Tulane L.R.* 629; A. Hirsch, "The Place of Arbitration and the Lex Arbitri" (1979) 34:3 *Arb. J.* 43. This issue is examined in Chapter 3.

13. See, for example, Article 34 of the Model Law. Infra note 105.

14. A. Redfern and M. Hunter, supra note 5, at 14.

15. A discussion of the role of international conventions, including the European Convention, in international commercial arbitrations is made in the last section of this chapter.

16. Article 1(1)(a).

17. A similar approach is adopted in England, albeit in an indirect manner. See A. Redfern and M. Hunter, supra note 5, at 12.

18. *The International Solution to International Business Disputes—ICC Arbitration* (ICC Publication No. 301, 1977) at 19.

19. Article 1492.

20. The Model Law project and its place in international arbitration is discussed in the last section of this chapter.

21. Article 1(3).

22. I. Szasz, "Introduction to the Model Law of UNCITRAL on International Commercial Arbitration" in P. Sanders (ed.) *UNCITRAL's Project for a Model Law on International Commercial Arbitration* (Deventer, The Netherlands: Kluwer Law and Taxation Publishers, 1984) at 43.

23. H. Holtzmann and J. Neuhaus, *A Guide to the UNCITRAL Model Law on International Commercial Arbitration: Legislative History and Commentary* (Deventer, The Netherlands: Kluwer Law and Taxation Publishers, 1989) at 32.

24. See I. Szasz, supra note 22, at 45.

25. General Agreement on Tariffs and Trade, October 30, 1947; T.I.A.S. No. 1700; 55 U.N.T.S. 194 (entered into force in January 1, 1948).

26. J. Cherian, *Investment Contracts and Arbitration* (Leyden, The Netherlands: A. W. Sijhoff-Leyden International Publishing Company, 1975) at 8.

27. Sometimes an institution may be geared toward the arbitration of all disputes that arise within its framework. This helps to keep things within the control of the institution and its participants. An example is the Society for Worldwide Interbank Financial Telecommunication Co-operative Society (SWIFT), an organization that facilitates the conduct of electronic banking. Clause 10 of the General Terms and Conditions of SWIFT provides:

> All relations between the company and each user shall be governed by Belgian law.
>
> Any dispute arising in connection with these General Terms and Conditions, failing amicable settlement, shall be finally settled under the rules of conciliation and arbitration of the International Chamber of Commerce by one or more arbitrators appointed in accordance with these rules.

28. Mr. Justice Kerr, "International Arbitration v. Litigation" (1980) *J. Bus. L.* 164 at 165. The statement, although hyperbolic, captures the growing utilization of arbitration. See (1990) 5 *Mealey's Int'l Arb. Rep.* 15.

29. See Mr. Justice Kerr, id. See also A. Redfern, "Arbitration: Myth and Reality" (1976) 4 *Int'l Bus. L.* 450; R. David, supra note 2 at 10; R. Stevenson, "An Introduction to ICC Arbitration" (1980) *J. Int'l L. & Econ.* 381; J. Wetter, "The Present Status of the International Court of Arbitration of the ICC: An Appraisal: Reasons for Prescribing Arbitration in Lieu of Litigation" (1990) 1 *American Rev. Int'l Arb.* 91.

30. J. Meason and A. Smith, "Non-Lawyers in International Commercial Arbitration: Gathering Splinters on the Bench" (1991) 12 *Northwestern J. Int'l L. & Bus* 27 at 27–28.

31. C. Taeusch, "Extrajudicial Settlement of Controversies; The Business Man's Opinion: Trial at Law v. Non Judicial Settlement" (1934–35) 83 *U. of P. L. Rev.* 150.

32. See, for example, M. Rosenberg, "Court Congestion: Status, Causes and Proposed Remedies" in H. Jones (ed.) *The Courts, the Public and the Law Explosion* (Englewood Cliffs, NJ: Prentice-Hall, 1965) at 32.

33. S. Lazarus et al., *Resolving Business Disputes* (New York: American Management Association, 1965) at 45.

34. See W. Evan, "Public and Private Legal Systems" in W. Evan (ed.) *Law and Sociology* (New York: The Free Press of Glencoe, 1962) at 180.

35. See supra note 8.

36. A handicap is imposed on commercial arbitration when the parties resort to the courts either before or during and after the arbitration. Here the various advantages of arbitration . . . are lost when the validity of the arbitration clause and its binding effect is tested in court, when the arbitrability of the issue is challenged, when the qualification of the arbitrator is questioned, and when these determinations may further be appealed in lengthy and expensive court proceedings.

M. Domke, *Commercial Arbitration* (Englewood Cliffs, NJ: Prentice-Hall, 1965) at 15.

37. See J. Paulsson, "The Extent of the Independence of International Arbitration from the Law of the Situs" in J. Lew (ed.) *Contemporary Problems in International Arbitration* (London: Centre for Commercial Law Studies, 1986) 141 at 142. See also *Tracomin S.A.* v. *Sudan OilSeeds Co. Ltd.* [1983] 2 Lloyds R. 624 at 625–626.

38. A. Redfern and M. Hunter, supra note 5 at 24.

39. W. Jone, "Three Centuries of Commercial Arbitration in New York: A Brief Summary" (1956) *Wa. U.L.Q.* 212.

40. See, for example, S. Jarvin and Y. Derains (eds.) *Collection of ICC Arbitral Awards: 1974–1985* (Deventer, The Netherlands: Kluwer Law and Taxation Publishers, 1990).

41. W. Park, "Arbitration of International Contract Disputes" (1984) 39 *Bus. Law* 39. J. T. McLaughlin has also echoed the same opinion: "In the context of international trade, the discordant parties will be from different parts of the world, with correspondingly different world views, culture and legal systems. Ideally arbitration provides a flexible, mutually acceptable means of conflict resolution." J. T. McLaughlin, "Arbitration and Developing Countries" (1979) 13 *Int'l Law.* 211 at 212. See also L. J. Bouchez, "The Prospects for International Arbitration: Disputes between States and Private Enterprises" in A. Soons (ed.) *International Arbitration: Past and Prospects* (Dordrecht, The Netherlands: Martinus Nijhoff, 1990) at 111–113.

42. According to W. Park, "the role of arbitration in the process of global wealth creation normally is justified by neither speed nor cost, but rather because its neutrality of forum and delocalized procedure provides a means of avoiding the 'hometown justice' of the other party's judicial system." W. Park, "National Law and Commercial Justice: Safeguarding Procedural Integrity in International Arbitration" (1989) 63 *Tulane L. Rev.* 647 at 702. The point is sometimes made that the fear of bias may be unjustified in countries with established commercial traditions such as England. This viewpoint ignores the crucial difference between established commercial law practice and the impartiality of judges who apply these laws.

43. In the construction industry, where each contractor not only wishes to complete his present job, but, more important, wishes to continue to be utilized for future jobs, arbitration is well accepted. In the textile industry, where a firm must come back each year to do business with the same suppliers, or with the same market, arbitration is customary.

R. Coulson, "Management Arbitration in Action" (1965) 3 *Am. Bus L. J.* 34.

44. For an in-depth analysis of the limitations of litigation, see E. Miller, "The Adversary System: Dinosaur or Phoenix?" (1984) 69 *Minn. L.R.* 1; S. Landsman, "The Decline of the Adversary System: How the Rhetoric of Swift and Certain Justice has Affected Adjudication in American Courts" (1980) 29 *Buffalo L.R.* 487; R. Pound, "The Causes of Popular Dissatisfaction with the Administration of Justice" (1906) 40 *Am. L.R.* 729.

45. With the obvious exception of compulsory arbitration.

46. See R. David, *Arbitration in International Trade*, supra note 2 at 77.

47. I. Wilner, "Determining the Law Governing Performance in International Commercial Arbitration: A Comparative Study" (1965) 19 *Rutgers L. Rev.* 646 at 650.

48. See A. Samuel, *Jurisdictional Problems in International Commercial Arbitration: A Study of Belgian, Dutch, English, French, Swedish, Swiss, U.S. and West German Law* (Zurich: Schulthess Polygraphischer Verlag, 1989) at 32. This part of the thesis has benefited from the author's study.

49. The debate about the nature of arbitration has mainly been predominant in continental Europe. See R. David, supra note 2 at 76.

50. F. Kellor, *Arbitration in Action* (New York: Harper and Brothers, 1941) at 8.

51. J. Foelix, *Traité du droit international privé*, 2d ed. (Paris: Joubert, 1847) at 461.

52. M. Merlin, *Recueil alphabetiqué de questions de droit*, 4th ed. (Brussels: Tarlier, 1829) vol. 9, at 145. Quoted by A. Samuel, supra note 48 at 34.

53. A. Samuel, supra note 48 at 36 et seq.

54. J. Lew, supra note 7 at 56.

55. Arbitration is, more or less, liberation from the court jurisdiction and substantive law of the sovereign state. Each sovereign state is, however, by itself something like a microcosm and the ultimate regulator of social life within its own territory, at least, at the present stage of historical development. In any event, there is no society that is not subject to legal regulation. It is no wonder that each state has its own statutory or common law regulating the arbitration proceedings.

K. Titigawa, "Contractual Autonomy in International Commercial Arbitration" in P. Sanders (ed.) *International Arbitration: Liber Amicorum for Martin Domke* (The Hague: Martinus Nijhoff, 1967) 133 at 135.

56. J. Lew, supra note 7, at 52.

57. Some writers have, however, argued that arbitration may be delocalized from the law of the seat of arbitration. See J. Paulsson, supra note 12, at 359. For a contrary opinion, see W. Park, supra note 12, at 21. This theory is discussed in Chapter 3.

58. Is not every activity occurring on the territory of a state necessarily subject to its jurisdiction? Is it not for such state to say whether and in what manner arbitrators are assimilated to judges and, like them subject to the law? Various states may give various answers to the question, but that each of them has the right to, and does, answer it according to its own discretion cannot be doubted.

F. A. Mann, "Lex Facit Arbitrum" in P. Sanders (ed.) *International Arbitration: Liber Amicorum for Martin Domke*, supra note 55, 157 at 162.

59. W. Park concedes that an arbitration should be controlled by the law of the seat of arbitration, although he suggests that such control be limited to ensuring respect for traditional standards of fairness, the limits of the arbitral mission and the rights of third parties. Supra note 57 at 51.

60. F. A. Mann, supra note 58 at 160.

61. Id. at 159.

62. Id.

63. A. Hirsch, "The Place of Arbitration and the Lex Arbitri" (1979) 34:3 *Arb. J.* 43 at 45.

64. A. Samuel, supra note 48 at 59. The process of compulsory arbitrations is, however, mainly found in domestic arbitration laws.

65. Supra note 8. The Model Law allows the parties to tailor the arbitration process to meet their particular needs, allowing only minimal court interference when required to aid the arbitration proceeding and to ensure that it meets the minimum standards of justice. See G. Hermann, "The UNCITRAL Model Law—Its Salient Features and Prospects" in N. Antaki and A. Prujiner (eds.) *Proceedings of the First International Arbitration Conference* (Montreal: Wilson and Lafleur, 1986) at 351.

66. G. Sauser-Hall, "L'Arbitrage en droit international Privé" (1952) 44–1 *Ann. Inst. Dr. Int'l* 469 at 471. Quoted by A. Samuel, supra note 48 at 60.

67. Id. at 531.

68. Id. at 533.

69. See W. Park, supra note 42. A. Redfern and M. Hunter have also submitted that an international commercial arbitration is a hybrid that begins as a private arrangement between the parties and ends with a legally binding award that, in appropriate cases, the courts of most countries would be prepared to recognize and enforce. See their *International Commercial Arbitration,* supra note 5 at 8.

70. See J. Lew, supra note 7 at 58.

71. M. Mustill, "Arbitration: History and Background" (1989) 6:2 *J. Int'l Arb.* 43.

72. Lew, supra note 7 at 59.

73. A. Samuel, supra note 48 at 72.

74. Id.

75. See supra note 57.

76. J. Robert and T. Carbunneau, *The French Law of Arbitration* (New York: Matthew Bender, 1983) at 1: 1–6.

77. Done at Montevideo on January 11, 1889. Published in *Register of Texts of Conventions and Other Instruments Concerning International Trade Law*, vol. 2 (United Nations, 1973) at 5.

78. Done at Geneva on September 24, 1923; entered into force on July 28, 1924. (1924) 27 *League of Nations Treaty Series* 158.

79. Article 4.

80. Article 3.

81. Article 1.

82. A. Redfern and M. Hunter, supra note 5 at 456.

83. Done at Geneva on September 26, 1927; entered into force on July 25, 1929. (1929–30) 92 *League of Nations Treaty Series* 302.

84. Article 1.

85. Article 1(d).

86. A. Nussbaum, "Treaties on Commercial Arbitration: A Test of International Private Law Legislation" (1942) 56 *Harv. L.R.* 219 at 234.

87. UN Doc. E/C2 372/Add 1; reproduced in G. Gaja, *International Commercial Arbitration* (Dobbs Ferry, NY: Oceana Publications, 1978) at Part III A. 1.2.

88. Australia, Belgium, Ecuador, Egypt, India, Sweden, USSR, and the United Kingdom.

89. G. Gaja, *The New York Convention* (Dobbs Ferry, NY: Oceana Publications, 1978) vol. I at A. 4.1.

90. Done at New York on June 10, 1958. 330 U.N.T.S. 38; 21 U.S.T. 25, T.I.A.S. No. 6997.

91. T. Carbonneau, *Alternative Dispute Resolution: Melting the Lances and Dismounting the Steeds* (Urbana: University of Illinois Press, 1989) at 65.

92. The Geneva conventions cease to have effect and are superseded by the New York Convention to the extent that the latter convention is ratified by contracting parties. See Article VII(2) of the New York Convention.

93. Article 1(3), however, allows contracting states to limit the applicability of the convention to awards made in other contracting states.

94. See Article V.

95. The easy enforcement of awards on a global basis is a fundamental element in the effectiveness and security of international arbitration. Barring it, businesspeople will be reluctant to engage in the process. As A. Redfern emphasizes,

> the ultimate purpose of a resort to arbitration is to arrive at a decision which is final and binding and which, if not carried out voluntarily, is capable of international recognition and enforcement. If such a result is not obtained, the time and care of the parties and of the arbitral tribunal (to say nothing of the money spent) is simply thrown away.

A. Redfern, "International Commercial Arbitration: Jurisdiction Denied, The Pyramid Collapses" (1986) *J. Bus. L.* 15 at 21.

96. See P. Sanders, "A Twenty Years' Review of the Convention on the Recognition and Enforcement of Foreign Arbitral Awards" (1979) 13 *Int'l Law.* 269.

97. T. Carbonneau, supra note 91 at 67.

98. Done at Washington on March 18, 1965. 575 U.N.T.S. 159; 17 U.S.T. 1270, T.I.A.S. No. 6090.

99. Report of the Executive Director on the Convention on the Settlement of Investment Disputes between States and Nationals of Other States (1965) 4 *I.L.M.* 524 at 525.

100. Id. at 524.

101. Article 1(2).

102. I. Shihata, "Towards a Greater Depoliticization of Investment Disputes: The Role of ICSID and MIGA" (1986) 1 *ICSID Review* 1.

103. M. Hunter urges us not to forget that "when we are working abroad—whether as arbitrators, expert witnesses or representing a party—we normally operate within the ambit of the local law and there must surely be an enormous practical advantage for us if that law is not only familiar but known to be effective." M. Hunter, "UNCITRAL Model Law: Which Road Should London Take?" (1984) 49 *Arbitration* 295.

104. United Nations General Assembly Resolution 40/71, 40 GAOR Supp. No. 53, A/40/53 at 307.

105. Id. at 308. Reproduced in H. Holtzmann and J. Neuhaus, supra note 23, at 1.

106. See G. Hermann, "The UNCITRAL Model Law on International Commercial Arbitration: Introduction and General Principles" in P. Sarcevic (ed.) *Essays on International Commercial Arbitration* (London: Martinus Nijhoff, 1989) at 3.

107. C. Fleischhauer in his Foreword to *A Guide to the UNCITRAL Model Law*, supra note 23, at V.

108. See R. Goodman, "UNCITRAL Model Law on International and Commercial Arbitration: Divergent Approaches in England and Scotland—A Question of Appeal?" (1990) 18 *Int'l Bus. Law* 250.

109. *A New Arbitration Act? The Response of the Departmental Advisory Committee to the UNCITRAL Model Law on International Commercial Arbitration.* Summarized in (1990) 6 *Arb. Int'l* 3.

110. See R. Goodman, supra note 108 at 252. For a critique of the Model Law from a developing country perspective, see M. Sornarajah, "The UNCITRAL Model Law: A Third World Perspective" (1989) 6:4 *J. Int'l Arb.* 7.

111. 484 U.N.T.S. 349.

112. 14 I.L.M. 339.

CHAPTER TWO

The Arbitration Agreement

INTRODUCTION

The arbitration agreement is the cornerstone of arbitration because it embodies the consent of the parties to arbitration. It is in the arbitration agreement that the basis for the jurisdiction and powers of an international commercial arbitrator can be found. The necessity of examining the laws relating to arbitration agreements is therefore self-evident.

The laws relating to the arbitration agreement are those that determine whether or not the parties consented to arbitration and the legal implications of the arbitration agreement. When reference is made to the law relating to arbitration agreements, it should be noted that this does not necessarily refer to one body of law; it is possible for different laws to apply to different areas of the arbitration agreement. For example, the law governing the capacity of the parties to enter into an arbitration agreement may differ from the law governing the arbitrability of the subject matter.

There are two types of arbitration agreements. The first, the submission, is an agreement to refer existing disputes to arbitration. This is known in continental parlance as a *compromis*. The second, the arbitration clause, is an agreement to refer any future dispute to arbitration. In continental parlance it is known as the *clause compromissoire*. The arbitration clause, which is usually part of a large commercial agreement, is the more common source of arbitration.[1]

The distinction between an arbitration clause and a submission agreement is reflected in some national laws. Article 1442 of the French Code of Civil Procedure, for example, states that an arbitration clause is "an agreement by which the parties to a contract undertake to submit to arbitration a dispute which may arise with respect to the contract." Article 1447 of the same code also defines a submission as "an agreement by which the parties to an existing dispute refer the matter to arbitration by one or more persons." Arbitration clauses are not fully recognized in some countries. To illustrate, in France the general rule is that an arbitration clause is not binding on the parties, except where it relates to commercial matters or if it is part of an international contract.[2]

Submission agreements in international contracts are generally recognized by most States and international conventions. One such convention is the New York Convention on the Recognition and Enforcement of Foreign Arbitral Awards (the New York Convention),[3] which provides that "each contracting State shall recognize an agreement in writing under which the parties undertake to submit to arbitration all or any differences which have arisen or which may arise between them."[4]

An arbitration clause is significantly different from the substantive agreement in which it is contained. While the latter outlines the rights, duties, and obligations of the parties, the former contains the procedure for resolving any disputes that have arisen or may arise under the substantive agreement. Thus the one may be described as substantive and the other procedural.

This chapter examines the law applicable to arbitration agreements and to the arbitrability of disputes. It focuses on the questions: (1) What law applies to an arbitration agreement? (2) Who can arbitrate (subjective arbitrability)? and (3) What matters can be arbitrated (objective arbitrability)? The principle of the autonomy of the arbitration agreement is also considered in order to highlight the distinction between the arbitration clause and the substantive contract in which it is contained, and to illustrate the effect of this distinction on the law relating to the arbitration agreement.

JURIDICAL AUTONOMY OF THE ARBITRATION AGREEMENT

The issue may arise whether or not an arbitration clause survives the invalidity of the substantive agreement in which it is contained. Does the invalidity of the main contract adversely affect an arbitration clause contained therein?[5] If the question is answered in the affirmative, an arbitrator cannot assume jurisdiction in situations where one of the parties contends that the substantive agreement containing the arbitration clause is invalid, at least until the validity of the substantive agreement is determined (perhaps by a national court).

It does not take much effort to see that if the validity of the arbitration clause is dependent on the validity of the main contract, a party seeking to frustrate or delay the arbitration process need only plead that the main contract is invalid in order to preempt the arbitrator's jurisdiction and seek a court resolution of that preliminary objection. The principle of the autonomy of arbitration agreements is designed, in part, to prevent the use of this kind of tactic in stalling the process of arbitration.

The principle of the jurisdictional autonomy of the arbitration agreement proclaims that an arbitration agreement is autonomous in relation to the contract from which it originates.[6] In this sense, an arbitration clause is independent of the commercial agreement in which it is contained, and cannot be automatically affected by the fortunes of the substantive contract. One effect of the principle is that the arbitration clause survives the invalidity of the substantive contract unless it is shown that the cause of the invalidity also specifically applies to the arbitration clause.[7]

The principle is recognized in many countries. Swiss courts have recognized the principle for a long time.[8] In the Swiss case of *K.K.S. c. M.S.A.*,[9] the court, relying on the juridical autonomy of the arbitration agreement, dismissed a challenge to the validity of an arbitration clause that was based on the ground that a fundamental mistake prevented the parties from reaching an agreement on the substantive contract.[10] In France, domestic and international arbitration are treated differently in this regard. The French judicial attitude toward the autonomy principle in international arbitration is most clearly demonstrated by the *Gosset* case,[11] where the court stated: "In the matters of International arbitration, the arbitration agreement, whether a separate agreement or included in the juridical act to which it refers, always represents, save in exceptional circumstances which are not alleged in the instant case, a complete juridical autonomy, excluding the possibility of its being affected by the eventual invalidity of the main contract."[12] The decision has been followed in subsequent cases.[13] French courts have, however, not applied the principle to domestic arbitrations.[14] Courts in Sweden,[15] Holland,[16] and the United States[17] also recognize the principle.

However, it has yet to be fully accepted in England. English law draws a distinction between the autonomy of the arbitration agreement in the sense that it continues to exist where the main contract has come to an end due to performance or frustration, and the autonomy according to which an arbitration agreement survives the invalidity of the main contract. In the latter case, the traditional English position was that where the main contract is invalid *ab initio*, the arbitration agreement contained therein is also invalid *ab initio*: "[I]n English law, no arbitrator can have jurisdiction, however wide the wording of the arbitration clause which the parties or alleged parties insert into their contract, to decide a dispute as to the initial existence or validity of the alleged contract in which the arbitration appears."[18] The English courts have therefore held that, absent a subsequent agreement to arbitrate, an arbitration agreement and the main contract must be tested in court in situations where it is alleged that the main contract was invalid as a result of its illegality[19] or due to the incapacity of one of the parties.[20] On the other hand, where the contract comes to an end as a result of its performance or frustration, the arbitration clause is regarded as being executory as long as there are outstanding disputes between the parties with respect to any obligation under the main contract.[21]

Although the autonomy principle continues to gain wide acceptance, [22] there is still a sound legal basis for the traditional English[23] reluctance to completely embrace it. Conceptually, an arbitration clause contained in a substantive contract derives its juridical basis from the efficacy of the substantive contract of which it is after all an integral part. Thus, where the facts and circumstances indicate that there never existed a valid contract between the parties, there exists no legal or factual basis on which to found the arbitration. Nevertheless, the approach of referring all challenges of the validity of an arbitration agreement to national courts could be faulted on two grounds. First, it is a ready tool to a party who wishes to stall an arbitration proceeding. By alleging invalidity of the arbitration agreement, such a party can effectively stall the proceedings, thereby causing inordinate delays and adding additional costs to the party who instituted the arbitration proceedings.[24] Furthermore, the parties are in no way prejudiced by the arbitral tribunal deciding its own jurisdiction. An arbitral award is still subject to being set aside by the court of the place of arbitration if the arbitrators lacked jurisdiction to hear the case, and the enforcement of the award may be resisted on that ground.[25]

The autonomy principle accords with practicality in that it frees an arbitration clause from allegation of invalidity of the substantive contract in which it is contained. The principle is founded more on practical needs than any credible theoretical basis,[26] because logic suggests that where the invalidity of a contract is alleged, all provisions of the alleged contract be held in abeyance until the question of validity is resolved by the courts, as opposed to an arbitral tribunal to be constituted under the disputed agreement.

The juridical autonomy of arbitration agreements has led to a trend toward the acceptance of the powers of an arbitral tribunal to determine its jurisdiction. The *Kompetenz-Kompetenz* rule empowers arbitral tribunals to determine their jurisdiction. The practical implication of the rule is that whenever the jurisdiction of an arbitral tribunal is challenged, the tribunal itself has to determine its jurisdiction, without the need to immediately refer the matter to a national court.[27]

It has been suggested that this trend is a product of the "inherent power" of arbitrators to determine their own jurisdiction.[28] This argument is preposterous, for how can an arbitral tribunal exercise its so-called 'inherent power' if the foundation for its exercise of jurisdiction, the arbitration agreement, is called in question. The better view is that the rule is a product of practical necessity, in that without it a party may stall the arbitration process by raising jurisdictional objections that can only be resolved by potentially lengthy court proceedings.[29]

This trend (that is, the acceptance of the *Kompetenz-Kompetenz* rule) is reflected in international conventions and treaties dealing with arbitration. Article 16(1) of the Model Law, for example, provides that "The arbitral tribunal may rule on its own jurisdiction, including any objection with respect to the existence and validity of the arbitration agreement. . . . A decision of the arbitral tribunal that the contract is null and void shall not entail *ipso jure* the invalidity of the arbitration clause."[30] The rule is also contained in the arbitration rules of institutional arbitration bodies. These bodies pride themselves as places where parties can resolve commercial disputes with limited interference by, or recourse to, national courts. Article 8(4) of the ICC Rules, for example, provides that:

> Unless otherwise provided, the arbitrator shall not cease to have jurisdiction by reason of any claim that the contract is null and void or allegation that it is inexistent provided that he upholds the validity of the agreement to arbitrate. He shall continue to have jurisdiction, even though the contract itself may be inexistent or null and void, to determine the respective rights of the parties and to adjudicate upon their claims and pleas.

The *Kompetenz-Kompetenz* rule is also accepted in some States.[31] According to the Supreme Court of Hong Kong, "[a]rbitrators should not pull down the shutters on the arbitral process as soon as one party objects to the jurisdiction of the tribunal. The arbitrator can rule on the question as to whether he [or her] has jurisdiction. . . . "[32] However, a number of states do not accept the rule in cases where the validity of the arbitration agreement itself is in dispute.[33] The argument is that where the validity of the arbitration agreement itself is questioned by one of the parties, the consensus of the parties needed for a valid arbitration is lacking, and that it is only a court that could then determine the consensual basis of the agreement.[34] This point was made by the English House of Lords in *Heyman* v. *Darwins Ltd.*:[35] "If the dispute is as to whether the contract which contains the clause has ever been entered into at all, that issue cannot go to arbitration under the clause, for the party who denies that he has ever entered into the contract is thereby denying that he has ever joined in the submission."[36] This position could promote the use of dilatory tactics by parties who wish to frustrate an arbitration.

What is needed is a kind of compromise that allows the arbitral tribunal to determine its jurisdiction while reserving to the parties the right to challenge such ruling in court if they are not satisfied with the tribunal's award. This type of compromise is contained in the Model Law, which reconciles the need for arbitral autonomy with the demands of those who insist on an avenue for judicial rectification of an arbitral tribunal's excess of jurisdiction.[37] It allows the arbitral tribunal to determine its jurisdiction subject to the possibility of appeal to a national court. It checks the prospect of unnecessary delays by limiting the time for such appeal, making the court decision final, and giving the arbitrator the discretion to continue with the proceedings while the court review is in progress.[38]

Another aspect of the autonomy principle is that the substantive agreement and the arbitration clause may be governed by different laws. Even where the parties expressly subject the substantive contract to the laws of a particular country, the autonomy principle ensures that the arbitrator does not necessarily have to apply such a law in relation to the arbitration agreement.[39] This point was made by the arbitrators in *Dow Chemical France* v. *Isover Saint Gobain*:[40]

> [T]he source of law applicable to determine the scope and the effects of an arbitration clause providing for international arbitration does not necessarily coincide with the law applicable to the merits of a dispute submitted to such arbitration. Although this law or these rules of law may in certain cases concern the merits of the dispute as well as the arbitration agreement, it is perfectly possible that in other cases, the latter, because of its autonomy, is governed—not only as to its scope, but as to its effect—by its own specific sources of law, distinct from those that govern the merits of the dispute.[41]

The arbitrators then went on to hold that the scope and effect of the arbitration agreement in the instant case was not intended to be governed by the law that the parties had chosen to govern the merits of the dispute. Rather, they relied on the common intention of the parties as evidenced in the conclusion and performance of the contract, and usages conforming to the needs of international commerce.[42] National courts also recognize that the law applicable to the substantive contract and the arbitration clause may differ.[43]

The juridical autonomy of the arbitration agreement helps us to view an arbitration clause as a regime independent of the substantive contract. Viewing the arbitration clause as separate from the substantive contract enables us to understand that the legal regime applicable to the former may differ from that applicable to the latter, although this is not invariably the case.

LAW APPLICABLE TO THE ARBITRATION AGREEMENT

The law applicable to the arbitration agreement should be distinguished from the law governing the capacity of the parties to arbitrate (subjective arbitrability) and the amenability of the subject matter of a dispute to arbitration (objective arbitrability).[44] The law governing the arbitration agreement applies to limited issues of consent (such as whether or not the agreement was induced by fraud, misrepresentation, or undue influence);[45] and the interpretation, effect, and scope of an arbitration agreement.

An anomaly in the present state of judicial and arbitral practice on the law governing arbitration agreements is that the determination of the applicable law depends on the stage at which the issue arises. Thus, the answer to the question of the law applicable to arbitration agreements depends on whether the issue arises: (1) when enforcement of an arbitration agreement is sought before a national judge, (2) when a jurisdictional objection is raised before an arbitrator, (3) when an application is made to set aside an award, or (4) when the recognition and enforcement of an award is requested. A common denominator in all of the above instances is that the intention of the parties predominates. Whenever parties expressly select a particular law to govern their arbitration agreement, this choice is respected by both judges and arbitrators. However, where the parties do not express their intention, the determination of the applicable law may vary according to the above four stages.

When Enforcement of an Arbitration Agreement Is Sought before a National Judge

Obviously, the determination of applicable law in cases where the issue arises before a national court depends on the national conflict of law rules of the court involved, because a national court is bound to apply the conflict rules of its *situs*. Under the law of most jurisdictions the law applicable to an arbitration agreement is that chosen by the parties.[46] In the absence of an express choice by the parties, there is generally a presumption that the applicable law is the law of the place where the arbitration is held.[47] For example this position is adopted under Egyptian law,[48] and a somewhat similar view was echoed by the Australian High Court, which noted that "[e]xcept for the parties' capacity to conclude the arbitration agreement, its validity or invalidity must, failing an agreement of the parties to the contrary, be judged under the law of the country in which the award is made."[49]

The primacy granted to the choice of the parties in determining the law applicable to the arbitration agreement is consistent with the consensual nature of arbitration. However, it is submitted that it is somewhat artificial to utilize the law of the place where an arbitration is to be held as an alternative and determinative test in determining the law governing arbitration agreements. Where the parties choose the place of arbitration themselves, there is reasonable basis for using the law of the place of arbitration as an alternative test, as the place of arbitration is closely connected to the parties' agreement. However, in cases where the place of arbitration is chosen by third parties (as is often done in institutional arbitrations in instances where the parties fail to make an express choice), application of the law of the place of arbitration would amount to granting third parties the power to designate the law governing an arbitration agreement to which they are not parties.[50] More importantly, in some cases the place of arbitration may not be known at the time when enforcement of an arbitration agreement is sought. For example, the agreement may provide for the arbitrators to select the place of arbitration. Clearly the rule is not helpful where enforcement of the arbitration agreement is sought before the arbitrators are even selected.[51]

When a Jurisdictional Objection Is Raised before an Arbitrator

The need to determine the law governing an arbitration agreement may arise where a jurisdictional objection is raised before an arbitral tribunal—for example, where a party alleges that his or her consent was the product of a fraudulent misrepresentation, or that the agreement was void under a given law. Arbitrators generally respect the parties' express choice of law to govern their arbitration agreement. In the absence of an express choice by the parties, arbitral practices diverge. There are four identifiable methods used by arbitrators to determine applicable law.

One group of arbitrators holds that in the absence of the parties' choice of applicable law, the arbitration agreement is governed by the law of the place of arbitration. In a ruling by the Arbitration Court of the Bulgarian Chamber of Commerce and Industry,[52] the tribunal held that an arbitration agreement is governed by the law of the place of arbitration, and not the law governing the merits of the dispute. This view was followed in another case where the arbitrators held that U.S. law governed the validity of an arbitration agreement because the arbitration was carried out in New York.[53]

Another group of arbitrators views the law governing the substance of the dispute as equally applicable to the arbitration agreement. In one case[54] the parties' contractual agreement, governed by Swiss law, provided that all disputes were to be arbitrated under the auspices of the International Chamber of Commerce. In determining the validity of the arbitration clause, the arbitrators relied on the law governing the substance of the dispute. In yet another claim, the arbitrators found that the choice of law applicable to the substance of the contractual agreement also applied to the validity of the arbitration clause.[55]

Some arbitrators believe that the rules of the arbitral institution chosen by the parties govern the arbitration agreement. In ICC Case No. 5486,[56] a joint-venture agreement between Belgian and Spanish companies contained an arbitration clause that provided for arbitration in either Madrid, Paris, or New York, depending on the identity of the party who instituted the proceedings. In determining the law governing the arbitration clause, the arbitrators said:

> [F]or the purpose of this arbitration proceeding the parties have expressly agreed to apply the ICC Rules of Arbitration rather than a specific national procedural

law . . . and such specific reference to the rules of an international arbitration institution converts such rules into the source of law governing the arbitration agreement, . . . therefore the appraisal of the validity of the arbitration clause must be made in accordance with the ICC Rules of Arbitration.[57]

Finally, in one claim the arbitrators placed reliance on "internationally accepted principles governing contractual relations."[58] One must wonder what these internationally accepted rules are, especially given the divergent approaches adopted by both judicial and arbitral authorities.

To say the least, the divergence in arbitral practices in this area is unhelpful and, as shall be argued in the conclusion to this section, there is need for the adoption of a single test in determining the law applicable to arbitration agreements.

When an Application Is Made to Set Aside an Award

When an application is made to set aside an award on the ground that the arbitration agreement from which the award arises is invalid, the law governing the arbitration agreement is determined in accordance with the laws of the country where the application is made. The Model Law, which hopes to harmonize legislative practices in countries that adopt it, gives primacy to the law chosen by the parties, and, in the absence of the parties' choice, to the law of the place where the application to set aside the award is made.[59] This provision differs markedly from the position in cases where the enforcement of an arbitration agreement is sought. In the latter case, the relevant law in most jurisdictions is the law of the place of arbitration.

When the Recognition and Enforcement of an Award Is Sought

The New York Convention is the focal point for the recognition and enforcement of awards. It provides that recognition and enforcement of an award may be refused, *inter alia*, if the arbitration agreement is "not valid under the law to which the parties have subjected it or, failing any indication thereon, under the law of the country where the award was made."[60] This provision, which has been described as "quite arbitrary,"[61] is also adopted by the Model Law.[62] Thus, at the recognition and enforcement stage, the relevant law is that chosen by the parties or, in the alternative, the law of the country where an award was made. The arbitrariness of the alternative test is revealed by the decision in *Hiscox* v. *Outhwaite*,[63] where the House of Lords held that an award is made where it is signed. Thus, under the alternative test, the validity of an arbitration agreement may be governed by the law of the country where the arbitrator signs the award, a location that can only be identified at the end of the arbitral process.

Conclusion

It is hardly satisfying that the law governing an arbitration agreement should depend on the stage at which the issue is raised. As seen above, several standards—such as the law of the place of arbitration, the law of the place where the award was made, and the law governing the substance of the dispute—are used. This divergence of practice is definitely not conducive to the development of a definite set of principles to govern international arbitrations.

The primacy at present granted to the will of the parties in the determination of the law applicable to arbitration agreements should be preserved, because it allows the parties to select a law that would give effect to their expectations in utilizing the arbitration process.[64] However, where the parties do not expressly choose a law to govern the arbitration agreement, it is suggested that a "close connection test" should be used. Under this test, in the absence of an express choice, the arbitration agreement would be governed by the law most closely related to the arbitration agreement. In this regard, the law of the place of arbitration would be viewed as being closely connected to the arbitration agreement only in cases where the parties themselves selected the place of arbitration. In cases where the place of arbitration is not selected by the parties, or where the place of arbitration has not even been selected before the issue of the applicable law arises, reference should be made to other connecting factors. For example, where parties choose to arbitrate under the auspices of an institutional arbitration body, they should be taken to have implicitly adopted the rules and regulations of that body to govern their agreement, except in cases where they expressly reject the application of the rules. For example, where the parties choose to arbitrate under the auspices of the ICC, they would be bound by the ICC rules of arbitration.[65]

SUBJECTIVE ARBITRABILITY

The traditional notion of arbitrability distinguished arbitrability from capacity on the grounds that while the former answered *what* can be arbitrated, the latter dealt with *who* can arbitrate.[66] This distinction is now considered impractical and unreal because essentially the result of both inquiries is the same: the answer to the questions can in either case preempt an arbitration. The result in situations where an issue cannot be arbitrated and where a party cannot arbitrate are identical—there can be no valid arbitration. This book therefore treats capacity as a branch of arbitrability. Capacity is designated as subjective arbitrability because the issue of capacity is subjective to the respective parties; this contrasts with questions regarding what matters can be arbitrated, an inquiry that can be determined only on an objective basis. Although the issue of authority is different from that of capacity, the former issue is also considered here it is very closely related to the latter, both are relevant in deter whether there is a valid arbitration agreement between the parties.

Arbitration, it should be remembered, derives from the mutual co of the parties. Party autonomy and the specific rights of the parties derived therefrom to choose arbitration instead of national courts to settle their commercial disputes are the cornerstones of international arbitration. The jurisdiction of arbitrators is as much dependent on the scope of the dispute covered by the arbitration agreement as on the capacity of the parties to authorize such arbitration. The absence of consent of one of the parties is thus a bar to the jurisdiction of an arbitrator to settle the dispute. It follows that capacity and authority are very crucial considerations in analyzing the jurisdiction of international commercial arbitrators. Absent one of the two factors, a party can dispute its consent to arbitration. The discussion focuses on the issues of capacity and authority as they relate to State parties because a great majority of the cases where these issues have arisen in arbitral practice involved State parties.

Capacity

The law applicable to the merits of a dispute is not necessarily the same as the law applicable in determining the capacity of the parties.[67] While parties to a commercial agreement can as a general rule choose the law to govern their contractual relationship,[68] it would be unrealistic to use such law in determining the capacity of the parties, because that would imply that in choosing the proper law of their contract, the parties could effectively confer capacity on themselves.[69] The proper law chosen by the parties to govern their contractual agreement may therefore differ from the law governing their capacity to contract.

The two major projects on international arbitration, the New York Convention and the Model Law, contemplate that the capacity of parties to arbitrate should be resolved under the conflict rules of the forum where the issue arises. Article V(1)(a) of the New York Convention provides that a State may refuse to recognize or enforce an award where the parties to the agreement were "under the law applicable to them, under some incapacity." The Convention does not provide any guidance as to how the law applicable to the parties could be determined. It is therefore open to the court where enforcement of an award is sought to utilize its conflict rules in resolving the issue.[70] Article V(1)(a) has been criticized on the grounds that it is incomplete and misleading in that it could be taken to refer to any of a variety of laws: the residence of the parties, their domicile or their nationality.[71]

Article 34(2)(a) of the Model Law provides that an award may be set aside if a party to the arbitration agreement was "under some incapacity."

The removal of the words "under the law applicable to them" contained in the New York Convention was supposed to remove the vagueness inherent in those words.[72] However, the court of the forum is still thrown back to its conflict rules in determining the capacity of parties to arbitrate.

Thus, under both the New York Convention and the Model Law, the capacity of parties to arbitrate is determined by the conflict of law rules of the forum in cases where the issue arises before the courts. This could be the forum where application for enforcement of an arbitration agreement is sought, where an action is brought to set aside the award, or where recognition and enforcement of the award are requested.

How should arbitrators approach the issue of capacity? Are they, like national judges, bound by the conflict of law rules of the forum? This writer believes that arbitrators are not bound to apply the conflict of law rules of the forum[73] as they are not instrumentalities of national legal systems in the same way that national courts are. This does not mean that arbitrators should deny themselves of the assistance of national conflict rules; on the contrary, in determining the issue of capacity, they should search national rules and international conventions for general trends. Thus, an arbitrator called upon to determine the capacity of a party need not feel constrained to apply the conflict rules of the place of arbitration, but should be guided by general trends, in particular the answer that is provided by the national laws of the parties. In regard to the issue of the capacity of States and their agencies to arbitrate—an issue to which we will turn—it shall be argued that arbitrators should apply the emerging rules of international arbitral practice.

States and Their Agencies. In spite of the increasing acceptance of arbitration as a means of resolving international commercial disputes, not all States favor it as a method of resolving State contract disputes. While some do not have any restrictions on the arbitrability of State contract disputes,[74] others, due to reasons of history or adverse experience with international arbitration, are reluctant to accept arbitration of such disputes.[75] States that fall within the latter category enact laws aimed at prohibiting or restricting the capacity of State organs to enter into arbitration agreements.

The idea behind these restrictions is normally that these entities should solve their disputes in national courts and that commercial arbitration is "too private" to be accepted by such State parties.[76] This antagonism toward arbitration further derives from a fear that arbitrators may be more susceptible to external influences than judges.

National law restrictions on arbitration of State contract disputes are usually of two kinds. The first is an outright denial of capacity. The usual approach is the promulgation of legislation prohibiting the State or its agencies from entering into arbitration agreements with private individuals. This relates to the capacity of the State and its organs to arbitrate. To the extent that such laws purport to preclude State contract disputes from the arbitral process, they are connected to the question of arbitrability, since their ultimate goal is to make State contract disputes nonarbitrable.

The second aspect of possible restriction with respect to arbitration of State contract disputes deals with the question of authority. A State may lay down detailed procedure that must be followed before a valid arbitration agreement can be concluded. It may, for example, provide that only a certain category of public officials can conclude binding arbitration agreements on its behalf. If the procedure laid down under the national law is not complied with, the State party cannot deny its capacity to arbitrate, rather it will contend that it was not in fact a party to the arbitration agreement in question. This argument will be anchored on procedural irregularities, an example of which may be the absence of those special powers that may be required under domestic law for the signing of arbitration undertakings. The implications of limitations on the authority of State officials to bind it or its agencies in valid arbitration agreements is discussed in the States and Their Agencies subsection of the next section, "Authority."[77] The following discussion focuses on the first aspect—that is, a purported lack of capacity to arbitrate on the part of a State or its agency.

Are arbitration agreements invalid because they are concluded in contravention of laws denying capacity to arbitrate to a State or its agency, or are such laws to be interpreted as incapable of invalidating an international commercial agreement? To put the question differently, do national laws denying a State or its agency the capacity to arbitrate have potency within the realms of transnational commerce? Before addressing this question, let us examine some of the attempts that have been made to deny capacity to arbitrate to States and their agencies.

An example of a national law prohibiting State agencies from entering into arbitration agreements was a Saudi Arabian law that provided that "it is prohibited for all government bodies to accept arbitration as a method for settlement of disputes which may arise between it and contracting individuals and companies."[78] In France there is a restriction on the arbitrability of State contract disputes. The rationale for this rule appears to be that State contract disputes should be settled by the French judiciary as opposed to private arbitration. The French courts have refused to apply this principle to international arbitrations. In *San Carlo*,[79] the plaintiff, a French government agency, brought an action in the French court against the captain of a vessel. The defendant requested the court to dismiss the action on the grounds that the parties had an arbitration agreement. The court of first instance denied the motion because under French law the plaintiff could not validly consent to arbitration. On appeal, the Court of Cassation reversed the lower court's decision:

> [A]lthough the prohibition [to submit to arbitration] resulting from Article 83 and 1004 of the Code of Civil Procedure is a matter of domestic policy, it is not a matter

of public policy in the international sense and does not bar a public agency from submitting, as could any other contracting party, the private law agreement to which it is a party to a foreign law recognizing the validity of the arbitral compact, when the agreement is one which should be characterized as an international contract.[80]

This decision was affirmed in the *Galakis case*,[81] which stressed that the rule of nonarbitrability of State contracts disputed in France does not apply to international arbitration. A new French statute now expressly provides that State and other public entities may submit to arbitration disputes arising out of contracts with foreign private parties.[82]

In Belgian law there was a restriction on the capacity of public law entities to conclude arbitration agreements. The State could only conclude such an agreement when a treaty authorized it to have recourse to arbitration.[83] This limitation on Belgian State entities' capacity to enter into arbitration agreements was a perpetuation of the French Code of Civil Procedure of 1806, which was applicable in Belgium until the adoption in 1972 of the Code Judiciare.[84] Belgian administrative law courts consistently enforced this limitation.[85]

The reach of these laws to international arbitration is disputed by many commentators who argue that international arbitrators are free to discount these national law restrictions. They argue that a State or its agency can not rely on these national law restrictions as grounds for challenging its consent to international arbitration. However, even among these commentators, there is no unanimity as to the law by reference to which such national law restrictions should be held inapplicable to international arbitrations. The laws suggested include the *lex arbitri*,[86] the proper law of the contract, and "the common law of international arbitration."[87]

F. A. Mann has suggested that where a State is under its own law precluded from submitting to arbitration, the *lex arbitri* will pronounce upon the scope and effect of such disability.[88] This view would seem to presuppose that the *lex arbitri* has a more justifiable interest in regulating the capacity of agencies of foreign States to enter into arbitration agreements than any other law. The fallacy inherent in this assumption is revealed by the fact that the forum may have no real connection with the underlying commercial agreement.[89] Very often the forum is chosen for reasons of convenience. Equally, the forum may not be known until a dispute arises, and in some cases the arbitrators may sit in various places during the duration of the arbitration. It seems reasonable to suggest that the *lex arbitri* should not affect either the capacity of the parties or the substance of the contract, unless the forum has a substantial and real connection with the underlying contract, which is sometimes not the case.

Another view is that the capacity of a State or its agencies should be determined by reference to the proper law of the contract.[90] This view adopts the common law approach in determining capacity.[91] The use of the proper law in determining the capacity of a State to arbitrate may, however, be inappropriate in cases where the parties themselves selected the proper law. This is because an arbitration agreement, together with the underlying commercial agreement, are only effective in law if the parties had the capacity to enter into the contract *ab initio*.[92] Therefore, the proper law chosen by the parties cannot be the basis for the validity of the agreement as the choice of the proper law derives its existence from the efficacy of the agreement in question.[93] Furthermore, using the proper law to determine capacity of State parties will result in varying results depending on the content of the proper law in question. As Paulsson points out,

> the concept that capacity of a State or a State entity should be governed by the proper law of the contract rather than the law of the State is open to the criticism that it may create a vast and unintended distinction between agreements subjected to a neutral law and those that are in fact governed by the law of the State party.[94]

Some writers suggest that the common law of international arbitration precludes a State from denying its capacity to enter into an arbitration agreement. By common law of international arbitration is meant those practices that are generally accepted and applied in international arbitral practice. These include respect for maintenance of due process in the conduct of arbitral procedure. It is argued that the common law of international arbitration contains a substantive rule that precludes States and their agencies from pleading incapacity to arbitrate. This principle is anchored on the concept of "international public policy"[95] and, what is suggested as one of its derivatives, the fundamental principle of good faith:

> [I]nternational ordre public would vigorously reject the proposition that a State organ, dealing with foreigners, having openly, with knowledge and intent, concluded an arbitration clause that inspires the concontractant's confidence could thereafter, whether in the arbitration or in execution proceedings, invoke the nullity of its own promise.[96]

This view was reiterated by Judge Mbaye of the International Court of Justice:

> For a time the French-speaking countries of Africa, following the French, had thought that they could avoid arbitration by citing procedural rules forbidding them to agree to internal arbitration . . . it is a question of pure good faith. A State must not be allowed to cite provisions of its law in order to escape from an arbitration that it had already accepted.[97]

This view, which is widely accepted in arbitration circles,[98] holds that it is contrary to international public policy for a State to prohibit arbitration of State contract disputes. If appropriate State agents sign an arbitration agreement, it will be contrary to international public policy for the State to challenge the validity of the arbitration agreement based on the State's or its agency's incapacity under its national law.

The uncertainty concerning the content of public policy is one of its essential characteristics.[99] It is said to reflect the fundamental economic, legal, moral, political, religious, and social standards of every society or extranational community.[100] Public policy is reflective of the fundamental norms of a given society; it is thus dependent on the judgment of the particular community, with the result that what is considered a part of the public policy in one society may not be seen as fundamental enough to constitute part of the public policy in another society with different political, religious, economic, and legal systems. Thus, the basic element of public policy is its embodiment of the fundamental norms of a given society.

A court within a municipal legal system is bound to apply the public policy of its country, so far as such policy is enforceable in law. When a State legislates that State entities lack capacity to enter into international arbitrations, such legislation becomes part and parcel of the public policy of the State. If the issue of the State's capacity to arbitrate arises before its municipal courts, the court is obliged to enforce the municipal law, provided it does not infringe the fundamental law of that society.

The issue then is whether an international commercial arbitrator is equally obliged to enforce domestic public policy of this nature. An arbitral tribunal derives its power from the consent of the parties and is neither an agent of any State nor is it obliged to uphold the public policy of any particular country in the same manner as national judges are. The responsibility of an arbitral tribunal is toward the parties in particular and the international business community in general, although it is up to States to determine under what conditions they would recognize and enforce international arbitral awards. This is not to say that arbitral tribunals can totally ignore the public policies of national legal systems. As we shall see in Chapter 6, arbitrators in appropriate cases have to respect the mandatory rules of relevant national legal systems. Indeed, the survival of arbitration as a legitimate process of dispute resolution lies mainly in its recognition by States as a valid and acceptable mechanism for resolving disputes. Thus, to secure the legitimacy of arbitration, arbitrators generally apply relevant mandatory rules of national law. However, international arbitrators are not bound by all domestic public policy in the same way that national courts are. While a national court looks only to its domestic public policy, an international arbitrator has to ensure that domestic public policies have a legitimate claim to application in the international arena.

Domestic public policy is usually reflective of domestic concerns and its application in an international forum may in some cases be tantamount to the projection of purely domestic considerations into matters of international commercial dealing between private parties of different nationalities. An arbitrator would, therefore, in appropriate cases, apply a system of public policy that is consistent with the needs of international commerce. Such a system of public policy would be transnational in character as international commerce transcends municipal boundaries.[101] The concept of international public policy is seen as meeting this requirement. As the Court of Appeal of Paris notes, "the security of international commercial and financial relations requires the recognition of a public policy which is, if not universal, at least common to the various legal systems."[102]

International public policy is drawn from the fundamental rules of natural law, the principles of universal justice, *jus cogens* in public international law, and the general principles of morality and public policy acceptable to a generality of countries.[103] International public policy includes a synthesis of the fundamental presumptions and practices that underlie legislative and judicial practice in a broad selection of countries. It therefore includes such transnational principles as good faith, estoppel, and *pacta sunt servanda*, principles that are present in most legal systems.

International public policy would thus dictate that a State cannot rely on its national law to challenge its capacity to arbitrate, because to hold otherwise will be in breach of good faith and the principle of *pacta sunt servanda*.[104] A state, having concluded an arbitration agreement, cannot rely on its own legislation as a ground for questioning its capacity to arbitrate: The private party may have accepted the underlying contract in the confidence that the State party will uphold its obligation to arbitrate, and having led the private party into acting on the representation of capacity, the State is estopped from going back on its word:

> [T]here is an obvious moral reason for not allowing a State or public entity to invoke, after having signed an arbitration undertaking, its own domestic incapacity; on the other hand, such type of behaviour would gravely undermine the trust and security which are indispensable to the normal functioning of international trade.... By the nature of his function, the international arbitrator has to protect a certain basic "contractual morality" and the superior interests of international trade, and he is therefore called upon ... to resort to the concept of transnational public policy.[105]

If States and their agencies were to comply with prohibition of arbitration agreements under their national laws by not entering into such agreements, problems would not arise. But there is a certain element of bad faith in a State or its agency consenting to arbitration, only to turn back later and seek to deny the agreement by relying on its incapacity under its national law. Such approbation and reprobation is not conducive to the need for trust and reliability in international commerce. A State should be sovereign enough to abide by its promises. More important, reliance on incapacity would be inconsistent with the notion of good faith and the principles of *pacta sunt servanda*, which are embodied in the concept of international public policy. This writer endorses the position that a State or its agency should not be able to rely on its incapacity to arbitrate under its domestic law as grounds for invalidating an arbitration agreement to which it had willingly consented.

Some arbitral awards have addressed the issue of capacity of State agencies to arbitrate. In these cases, State agencies pleaded their incapacity under their national laws to enter into arbitration agreements as a bar to the jurisdiction of arbitral tribunals. The consensus among arbitrators was that such a plea is unacceptable.

In *ICC Case 1939*,[106] the arbitrator had to determine the effect of an Ethiopian provision that prevented the State or public entities from submitting to arbitration. He held that:

> In effect, if certain laws . . . prohibit the State or another public body from submitting to arbitration, it is admitted that this prohibition is without effect for international contracts. In effect, in that it concerns a rule of public policy, this prohibition can only be effective in internal public policy. International public policy would be strongly opposed to a State organ, dealing with foreign persons, with knowledge and intention, openly accepting an arbitration clause in which the contracting party placed his confidence and then, whether in the arbitration proceedings or in the enforcement proceedings, avail itself of the nullity [of] his oral undertaking.[107]

The effect of a State's capacity to arbitrate under its national law also arose in *Benteler* v. *Belgium*.[108] The case concerned an agreement on the industrial and financial reorganization of a public limited liability company (referred to in the award as ABC), which was made in Brussels between the Belgian State, ABC, and Benteler. The agreement contained a clause for ad hoc arbitration. A dispute arose between the parties and Benteler resorted to the arbitration agreement, whereupon the tribunal was faced with the argument by Belgium that it was not bound by the arbitration clause since it was forbidden by its domestic law to enter into arbitration agreements.[109]

Having disposed the objection in reliance on the Geneva Convention,[110] the arbitrators went on to state, *obiter*, that the principles establishing the capacity of "legal persons of public law" to submit to arbitration has come to be regarded as a principle of private international law that is required to be followed in international arbitration.[111] They found support for this view first in the decision in the *Galakis Case*,[112] and, second, in the approach adopted in France and some other countries to make the capacity of a State to enter into arbitration agreements subject to the proper law of the contract, and, third, in the principle of international public policy.

While supporting the conclusion reached by the arbitrators, it must be reiterated that reference to the proper law as a determinant of capacity may result in discordant results depending on the content of the applicable proper law. Even if the proper law is adopted as a suitable guide, it does not lead to the evolution of a single substantive rule on the capacity of States to arbitrate because the different approaches adopted by States on the issue of capacity to arbitrate preclude the extraction of a common principle from national laws. Refusal to recognize national laws denying capacity to States and their agencies should be founded on international public policy. The principles of good faith, *pacta sunt servanda*, and estoppel are common to most if not all legal systems. These principles coalesce into a substantive rule of public policy that precludes a State from relying on its national law to challenge its capacity to arbitrate.

Switzerland has enacted legislation that purports to regulate the capacity of States to enter into arbitration agreements. Article 177(2) of the Swiss Private International Law Act provides that "[a] State, or an enterprise owned by, or an organization controlled by a State, which is a party to an arbitration agreement, cannot invoke its own law in order to contest its capacity to arbitrate or the arbitrability of a dispute covered by the arbitration agreement."[113] The provision, which is meant to apply to international arbitrations conducted in Switzerland,[114] precludes a State or its agencies from relying on their incapacity to arbitrate under their national law. Thus, if an arbitration takes place in Switzerland, the law would require the arbitrators to presume the capacity of the State or its agencies to arbitrate State contract disputes.

The problem with this type of solution is that it begs the question. An arbitral tribunal can only seek recourse to such a law if it is convinced that the place of arbitration is the appropriate law for determining the capacity of States and their organs to arbitrate.[115] If it finds that a different system of law is applicable, the law of the place of arbitration does not come into play. An arbitral tribunal is bound to apply such a law only if there is a substantive principle of international arbitration that obligates it to determine issues of capacity by reference to the law of the place of arbitration. As we have seen, no such principle exists.

The issue of capacity may also arise within the context of arbitrations conducted under the auspices of the International Centre for the Settlement of Investment Disputes.[116] Article 25(4) of the ICSID Convention allows Contracting States to notify ICSID, either at the time of ratification or at any time thereafter, of the class or classes of disputes it would not consider arbitrable under ICSID's auspices. Saudi Arabia has indicated that it will not arbitrate disputes relating to "oil and pertaining to acts of sovereignty," while Guyana and Jamaica have excluded disputes concerning minerals and other natural resources. It would seem that a State may rely on this notification to challenge ICSID's jurisdiction to determine matters it has excluded under Article 25(4). The article may thus be construed as a limitation on the jurisdiction of the ICSID.

State signatories to the ICSID Convention are estopped from pleading incapacity to arbitrate because their adherence to the treaty is a representation of capacity to arbitrate investment disputes. The only option available to a State signatory in this regard is to plead that it has notified the ICSID that a given class of disputes is nonarbitrable within the meaning of Article 25(4). It is useful to note that under Article 25(3) of the convention, consent of a constituent subdivision or agency of a State party to ICSID arbitration "shall require the approval of that State unless that State notifies the Centre that no such approval is required." Thus, there is a presumption of incapacity with respect to State agencies, a presumption that is rebutted either by a specific authorization by the State concerned or a notification by the State to the ICSID that no consent is needed.

The effect of Article 25(4) arose in *Alcoa Mineral of Jamaica Inc.* v. *Jamaica*.[117] A construction agreement between Alcoa and Jamaica provided for ICSID arbitration of any dispute arising under the contract. Five years later, Jamaica notified ICSID under Article 25(4) that "legal disputes arising directly out of an investment relating to minerals or other natural resources" shall not be subject to the jurisdiction of the ICSID. When a dispute arose under the contract and Alcoa invoked the arbitration agreement, Jamaica sought to rely on this notification as a bar to the jurisdiction of the tribunal. The case turned on whether the Jamaican notification effected five years after the initial agreement with Alcoa adversely affected the prior agreement to arbitrate. The tribunal held that the notification was ineffective to abrogate Jamaica's prior consent to arbitration:

> In the present case the written consent was contained in the arbitration clause between the Government and Alcoa which has already been quoted. This consent having been given could not be withdrawn. The notification under Article 25 only operates for the future by way of information to the Centre and potential investors in undertakings concerning minerals and other natural resources of Jamaica.[118]

It appears that the tribunal would have declined jurisdiction if Jamaica's notification had been made before it entered into the arbitration agreement. It is, however, clear that where there is no notification under Article 25(4), a State party, as distinct from a State agency or a subdivision of a State, cannot plead incapacity under its national law. Under Article 25(1) the ICSID has jurisdiction in respect of investment disputes between a Contracting State and a national of another Contracting State which the parties consent in writing to submit to it. Once a State party gives its consent to ICSID arbitration, it cannot be heard either to plead incapacity or to unilaterally withdraw its consent.

Authority

The issue of authority is as vital as that of capacity in determining the validity of an arbitration agreement. Authority is a particularly crucial consideration when a corporation or a State (or State agency) is involved. It is one thing to find that a corporation or a State has the capacity to enter into arbitration agreements; it is a different thing to determine whether or not the corporation or State was represented by duly authorized officials.

This question arises because corporations and State agencies, as fictional entities, can only act through the intermediation of their officials.[119]

How should arbitrators determine the authority of agents to bind their principal in valid arbitration agreements? Once again, arbitrators should not feel bound by the national conflict rules of the forum in this respect, but should seek assistance in the general trends in national law and arbitral practice. In most jurisdictions, particularly in Europe, courts usually follow the principle of *locus regit actum* in determining the authority of company officials.[120] There is an attempt to treat the issue of the authority of State officials differently by erecting a separate standard for determining the authority of these officials to bind the State and its agencies in valid arbitration agreement. Let us consider this issue.

States and Their Agencies. Some States that do not prohibit arbitration of State contract disputes nevertheless lay down formalities to be complied with before such disputes can be arbitrated. As a nonnatural entity, a State can act only through agents. National laws regulate the conduct of such agents and stipulate the procedures to be followed before such agents can validly bind the State. The same goes for State agencies that act through their officials. The authority of State officials to bind the State or its agency in valid contracts is conferred and regulated by national laws and regulations.

Can a State rely on these national law restrictions to challenge the validity of its alleged consent to arbitration? This question relates to authority rather than to capacity. Here the State does not plead incapacity to consent to arbitration, but questions the regularity of its alleged consent to arbitration. That a State cannot challenge an arbitration agreement by pleading incapacity under its national law is one thing; whether the State did in fact consent to arbitration raises entirely different considerations.

It has been suggested that the principle of bona fides as well as the security of international transactions do not permit that a State or public entity be allowed to invoke, after the execution of a contract, alleged irregularities such as the absence of those special powers that would be required under its domestic law for the signing of arbitration undertakings.[121] The only exception, it is suggested, is where the claimant knew or should have known of the alleged irregularities.[122]

One wonders why a private party should not be required to take due diligence in determining the authority of State officials to enter into arbitration agreements. While it is clear that there is a certain element of bad faith in a State consenting to arbitration and thereafter refusing to arbitrate an ensuing dispute on the ground that it lacks capacity to arbitrate, when the issue is whether the State did *in fact* consent to arbitration, the considerations ought to be different. In the former case there is a direct repudiation of a contract entered into by competent representatives of the parties, whereas in the latter case the State party contends that appropriate procedures were not followed in entering into the arbitration.

Since the consent of the parties is a fundamental element of a valid arbitration agreement, the arbitrator ought to ensure that the agreement was signed by the competent representatives of each party.[123] In this respect a State should be able to challenge the authority of its agents to bind it, if such agents act in contravention of that State's national law.[124] This view is consistent with the English conflicts rules under which the authority of company officials to bind it is determined by the company's *lex domicili*.[125]

Requiring parties who contract with States or their agencies to ensure that the State party or agency is represented by duly authorized officials in no way endangers the security of international transactions as Professor Lalive would have us believe.[126] Just as in cases involving corporations, parties should ensure that they deal with properly designated officials. As one commentator puts it, "the control of authority, even if sometimes difficult for the other contracting party, should follow the general rules. Therefore if the signatory [for the State party] has no authority, it follows that the government is not committed, exactly as any natural person or legal entity."[127] This requirement conforms with the general practice under most national laws whereby a "contractor dealing with the government is chargeable with notice of all statutory limitations placed upon the power of public officers."[128] In most jurisdictions the private party has the obligation to verify the authority of the administrative agent acting on behalf of the government:

> The contractual power of the Administration must . . . be exercised by a competent agent within the scope of powers which the general principles of law, the statute or the regulations confer upon him or her. This is a principle which the courts interpret strictly; it is sanctioned by a finding of nullity or by a holding that there is no commitment to anyone whatsoever that can be made by an unauthorised agent.[129]

Exception should nevertheless be made for cases where the facts of a particular case make it inequitable for the State party to rely on the lack of authority of the person who contracted on its behalf. As Delaume notes,

> arbitrators are not inclined to allow a State party to renege on its contractual undertakings on the ground of lack of authority or non-compliance with legal requirements, when to do so would be contrary to the principles of good faith or when the State involved may have been guilty of misrepresentation or non-disclosure of information.[130]

The interests of the private party would be best protected by seeking a legal opinion from local counsel on the authority of State officials. Reliance by the State or its agency on the lack of authority on the part of its officials accords with the thinking behind the Vienna Convention on the Law of Treaties.[131] Article 46 of the convention provides that

1. A State may not invoke the fact that its consent to be bound by a treaty has been expressed in violation of a provision of its internal law regarding competence to consent unless that violation was manifest and concerned a rule of its internal law of fundamental importance.
2. A violation is manifest if it would be objectively evident to any State conducting itself in the matter in accordance with normal practice and in good faith.

Where there is no express legislation regulating the authority of agents of the State to bind it in arbitration agreements, the private party should be able to rely on the ostensible authority of the competent agents of the State.[132] This is akin to the solution adopted by Article 7(2) of the Vienna Convention, which introduced the presumption that certain agents of the State have the authority to represent their State for the purposes of all acts relating to the conclusion of a treaty. These are: heads of States, heads of Governments, and ministers of foreign affairs. Just as such persons who are mainly responsible for foreign affairs can bind their countries in a treaty, it would seem fair to expect that a minister or head of the relevant State organ has ostensible authority to bind the State or its agency in valid arbitration. However, this presumption should be subject to contrary legislative provision.

Southern Pacific Properties v. *Egypt*[133] addressed the issue of a State's consent to arbitration. The claimant and the Egyptian Tourism Organization (EGOTH) entered into a joint venture to develop the plain adjacent to the pyramids plateau into a tourist complex. The agreement provided for ICC arbitration, with the seat of arbitration in Paris. The Egyptian minister of tourism appended his signature to the last page of the agreement together with the words "approved, agreed and ratified." When a dispute arose, Egypt argued that it was not a party to the agreement and that the minister's signature was given in exercise of his supervisory powers over EGOTH. This objection was rejected by the arbitrators and an award was rendered against Egypt. Egypt then petitioned the Paris Court of Appeal for the award to be set aside on the ground that it was never a party to the arbitration agreement. The court held that the notation "approved, agreed and ratified" must be understood in accordance with Egyptian law. Since under Egyptian law this approval did not make the State a party to the agreement and the attendant ICC arbitration clause, Egypt had not consented to the arbitration and the award was annulled.[134]

This decision suggests that issues relating to the formal validity of a State's alleged consent to arbitration should be determined in accordance with that State's national law. Nonetheless, the principle inherent in this decision does not extend to the issue of capacity. Once appropriate officials of the government conclude an arbitration agreement on a State's behalf, international public policy prevents the State from using the provisions of its national law to challenge its consent to the arbitration. The decision should rather be read as suggesting that the authority of State officials to bind it in arbitration agreements can only be verified by reference to the national law of the State.

Conclusion

As we have seen, the general consensus is that a State cannot plead lack of capacity under its national law as a bar to the jurisdiction of the arbitral tribunal. International public policy repudiates the idea that a State, after consenting to arbitration and carrying into effect the underlying commercial agreement, can turn back to plead incapacity to arbitrate. Such an attitude is incompatible with the need for trust and reliability in the commercial world. The principle that a State cannot plead incapacity to arbitrate has crystallized into a rule of "common law of arbitration."[135]

While it amounts to bad faith for a State to plead incapacity to enter into an arbitration agreement, it will be contrary to the principle of party autonomy—that cardinal principle of arbitration—to impose arbitration on a State if it did not *in fact* consent to it. An arbitrator should as a preliminary step examine the consensual basis of the arbitration agreement. Unless a State conducted itself in a manner that makes it unconscionable for it to rely on its lack of consent to the arbitration, the writer knows of no reasons of policy why it may not challenge the arbitrator's jurisdiction on that ground. Private parties should ensure that they deal with authorized agents of the State. In the absence of any law regulating authority to bind the State, the private party may rely on the ostensible authority of appropriate State officials.

As arbitration continues to gain prominence as a method of resolving international commercial disputes, restrictions on the ability of States and their agencies to consent to arbitration will be gradually dismantled. Foreign investors will no doubt be skeptical about investing in a country that insists on resolving all contractual disputes under its own national legal system.

OBJECTIVE ARBITRABILITY

In the discussion of the advantages of arbitration, we outlined some of the reasons why the business community continues to embrace arbitration as an alternative to litigation. Arbitration has fulfilled the expectations of the business community largely as a result of its flexibility and adaptability. It is partly due to the discernible utility of arbitration to the business community and the need to reduce congestion in the court system that various countries have endeavored to remove obstacles that inhibit access to arbitration. Even in those countries that traditionally were antagonistic to the development of arbitration, there is a gradual, sometimes accelerated, change in attitude.[136] This is particularly so in connection with international commercial arbitration.[137]

However, there comes a stage when each country must reconcile the need for allowing parties to utilize the dispute resolution method best adapted to their objectives (e.g., arbitration), with the necessity of ensuring that public interests are protected. The line between these competing objectives is not very clear-cut, as it is often unclear when the public interests of a State may be undermined by fidelity to the parties' preferred method of dispute resolution.[138]

The doctrine of objective arbitrability is designed to draw the lines beyond which the cart of arbitration may not cross. It is the tool by which a State proclaims those interests that it considers so vital and sensitive as to be removed from the scope of private arbitration. Objective arbitrability, then, answers the question: What can be arbitrated?[139]

The decision as to what matters should be removed from the ambit of arbitration is evidently subjective to respective national legal systems. What is considered so fundamental as to be nonarbitrable in one country may be viewed as amenable to the process of private arbitration in another country. The permissible limit of arbitrable matters consequently varies among countries.

It has been suggested in some quarters that the New York Convention should be amended to include a list of nonarbitrable subject matters for each Contracting State or a list reflecting judicial and legislative practice in all member countries.[140] The suggestion is erroneous in implying that it is possible to distill a list of nonarbitrable matters reflective of the law in all Contracting States. Additionally, it is hardly helpful for the convention to list nonarbitrable matters in each Contracting State. Arbitrability encapsulates the present perception of each country as to matters that could be left to arbitration. The scope of arbitrable matters therefore varies according to the changing views of each country as to where the line between public interests and private adjudication should be drawn. A convention, which is not easily amenable to change, is therefore ill-suited to contain a synopsis of flexible national practice.[141]

This section examines the law that governs objective arbitrability of disputes. Arbitrability is governed by national law. In an international contract, there may be more than one national law that connects with the arbitration—for example, the law applicable to the agreement, the law of the place of arbitration, and the law of the place where enforcement of the agreement or award is sought. Where two or more laws are involved, an arbitral tribunal obviously has to select one of them in testing the arbitrability of the issue before it. This choice of law problem equally arises in proceedings before national courts when enforcement of the arbitration agreement is sought or when enforcement of the award is requested. In either case, the judge has to determine the law that governs arbitrability.

Both the New York convention and the Model Law recognize the doctrine of objective arbitrability. Article II of the New York Convention provides that each Contracting State shall recognize an arbitration agreement "concerning a subject matter capable of settlement by arbitration." Article V(2)(A) of the convention equally allows Contracting States to refuse recognition and enforcement of an award where "the subject matter of the difference is not capable of settlement by arbitration under the law of that country." Similarly, by virtue of Article 1(5) of the Model Law, the Model Law does not affect those laws of a Contracting State by virtue of which certain disputes "may be submitted to arbitration only according to provisions other than those of [the Model Law]." Under Article 34(2)(b)(i) of the Model Law, an award may be set aside if the subject matter of the dispute is not capable of settlement by arbitration under the law of the Contracting State involved. Similar provisions relating to arbitrability are contained in other conventions dealing with arbitration.

The critical issue here is to determine the law that governs arbitrability. As already noted, the issue of arbitrability may arise at any of four different stages: (1) before the arbitral tribunal, (2) before a judge from whom enforcement of the arbitration agreement is sought, (3) before a judge who is requested to enforce the award, and (4) before a judge to whom an application is made to set aside the award. Each stage will now be considered in turn.

When the Issue Arises before an Arbitral Tribunal

The jurisdiction and authority of arbitrators are founded on the arbitration agreement. It could well be argued that where a party contends that an arbitration agreement is void as a result of objective nonarbitrability, there is no basis for the arbitral tribunal to exercise jurisdiction, and that it must therefore refuse to hear the case. As we have seen, the separability doctrine, coupled with the *Kompetenz-Kompetenz* rule, enables the arbitral tribunal to determine its jurisdiction. Thus, an arbitral tribunal is entitled to hear any preliminary objection relating to the arbitrability of the subject matter and to rule on such an objection.

Some commentators have suggested that an arbitral tribunal should be guided by the law applicable to the arbitration agreement in making a ruling on arbitrability.[142] This view is said to be consistent with the trend toward the recognition of the doctrine of party autonomy and the need for contractual security.[143] The law applicable to the arbitration agreement would be a relevant standard in determining arbitrability in cases where it is the law of the country that is most closely connected to the underlying transaction. Where it is not so connected, one sees no compelling reason why the law applicable to the arbitration agreement should be considered relevant. As reiterated, objective arbitrability is a means by which countries delimit the scope of issues that can legitimately be the subject of private arbitration. Each State should be able to determine whether arbitration is an available option in resolving disputes that implicate its policy interest in a most direct way. Parties to an arbitration should not be allowed to circumvent the rules on arbitrability in jurisdictions in which their transaction has its closest connection. Thus it should be open to a tribunal to disregard the parties' choice of law applicable to the arbitration agreement if it is convinced that the law applicable to the arbitration agreement is unconnected with the underlying commercial transaction. For example, where parties are from the same country, and their transaction has an impact on their country, an arbitral tribunal should be justified in applying the law of that jurisdiction to the determination of objective arbitrability, as against the law of another jurisdiction chosen by the parties to apply to their arbitration agreement. The relevant test should be the law of the jurisdiction whose policy interests are most directly implicated by the parties' transaction by virtue of the jurisdiction's close connection with the underlying commercial agreement.

There is a problem in this regard. The law of the country most closely connected with the underlying agreement may be different from the law of the forum where the arbitration is conducted. Is an arbitral tribunal in such a case entitled to disregard the law of the forum? It should be remembered that an arbitral tribunal owes a duty to the parties to render an enforceable award.[144] This duty flows directly from the very goal and essence of the arbitration process, and the intention of the parties in utilizing the process. This duty should be juxtaposed against the fact that an award may be set aside under the Model Law where the subject matter of the award is not arbitrable under the law of the forum.[145] The implication of the award being set aside is far-reaching in that it constitutes a ground for other jurisdictions to refuse to recognize or enforce the award.[146] This result is regrettable because the seat of arbitration may not be substantially connected with the parties' transaction. For example, where a Canadian party and a French party enter into an agreement for the construction of an industrial complex in France, and an arbitration between them is held in Britain, it makes little sense for the arbitrability of the subject matter to be determined according to British law. Yet this was precisely the solution adopted in *ICC Case No. 6162 of 1990*,[147] where in a dispute between a French party and an Egyptian party, the arbitral tribunal used Swiss law—the law of the place of arbitration—in determining the arbitrability of the dispute. It is suggested in cases like these, where the transaction has no connection with the place of arbitration, that the law of the place of arbitration should not be used in determining arbitrability and that the courts of the place of arbitration should refrain from setting aside awards rendered in such cases on the ground that the subject matter is nonarbitrable in accordance with its national laws.

When the Issue Arises before a Judge to Whom an Application Is Made to Enforce an Arbitration Agreement

An application may be made to a judge to enforce an arbitration agreement either where one of the parties is reluctant to proceed with arbitration or where a party institutes a suit in contravention of an arbitration agreement.[148] The court could refuse to enforce the agreement to arbitrate if it considers that the subject matter of the dispute is not capable of settlement by arbitration.[149] Although Article 8 of the Model Law does not specifically refer to arbitrability as a ground for refusal to enforce an arbitration agreement, the general view is that the reference to an agreement that is "null and void" encompasses agreements whose subject matters are nonarbitrable.[150]

Neither the Model Law nor the New York Convention provide any guidance as to the law which a judge may apply in determining arbitrability in this kind of situation. A. van den Berg is of the view that the judge should apply the law of the forum (*lex fori*). He offers two reasons for his view. First, he contends that this approach enhances the internal consistency of the convention.[151] Second, he suggests that since the effect of an arbitration agreement is to exclude the competence of the court, the court should enquire under its law to determine whether the arbitration agreement effectively excludes its competence.[152]

His internal consistency argument is based on the ground that in the enforcement of an award the New York Convention provides for the law of *lex fori* to determine arbitrability.[153] In van den Berg's view, the utilization of the law of the forum to test arbitrability at the stage where enforcement of an arbitration agreement is sought would be in harmony with the convention's provision that recognition and enforcement of an award could be refused where the matter constituting the basis of an award is nonarbitrable in the forum where enforcement is sought.

It seems to this writer that the internal consistency argument is not a particularly strong reason to apply the *lex fori* in cases where enforcement of an arbitration agreement is sought. While at the stage of the enforcement of an award the court is required to take an action that may result in attachment of the assets of a party resident in its jurisdiction, the same effect does not necessarily result where enforcement of an arbitration agreement is sought. It may be that the arbitration agreement and the underlying commercial transaction have entirely no connection with the forum other than the fact that one of the parties is resident in that country. Furthermore, it could be the case that the rules of arbitrability in the *lex fori* are more restrictive than the law with which the commercial transaction is most closely connected. In these kinds of situations, it would be unfair to apply the *lex fori* that has neither a real nor a substantial connection with the commercial transaction.

The second argument that the court should use the *lex fori* in determining arbitrability because the effect of the arbitration is to exclude the jurisdiction of the court is objectionable on two grounds. First, the basis on which courts assume jurisdiction is sometimes so tenuous[154] that it would be irrational to use such assumption of jurisdiction to thwart the agreement of the parties, and to oust the application of the law with which the contract is most closely connected. Second, and more important, the fact that an arbitration agreement ousts the jurisdiction of the court should not be a vital consideration where the underlying contract does not significantly implicate the legitimate interests of the forum.

Most judicial decisions have tended to apply the *lex fori* in determining arbitrability where the enforcement of an arbitration agreement is sought. An illustration is the celebrated case of *Mitsubishi Motors Corp.* v. *Soler Chrysler-Plymouth Inc.*,[155] where the U.S. Supreme Court utilized U.S. law in determining the arbitrability of antitrust disputes.[156] It should be noted, however, that in *Mitsubishi* the commercial transaction had a significant link with the United States.

Another view is that arbitrability at this stage should be determined according to the law of the place of arbitration.[157] As indicated above, the court of the place (or seat) of arbitration may set aside the award if the subject matter of the award is not arbitrable under its law, and the effect may be far-reaching as it constitutes a ground for refusing to recognize and enforce the award in other jurisdictions.[158] This result is regrettable because not only is the place of arbitration often chosen due to reasons of convenience, but it may have no relationship at all with the underlying commercial transaction.[159]

Finally, the law applicable to the arbitration agreement has been suggested as being dispositive of the issue of subject matter arbitrability at the stage of the enforcement of the arbitration agreement. This view was very ably articulated in a decision of the Court of Appeal of Brussels.[160] A Belgian company and a Swiss company signed an exclusive distribution agreement which had effects, *inter alia*, in Belgium. The agreement contained an arbitration clause providing for the application of Swiss law. When a dispute arose under the agreement, the Belgian party brought a suit before the Tribunal de Commerce (Court of First Instance) of Brussels, but the Swiss party objected to the court's jurisdiction on the basis of the arbitration clause. The tribunal held that the clause was invalid because the subject matter of the dispute was not arbitrable under Belgian law. In reversing the lower court's decision, the Court of Appeal held that the criteria used in determining the arbitrability of disputes varies, depending on whether the question arises when dealing with the validity of the arbitration agreement, or when dealing with the recognition and enforcement of the arbitral award. In the former case, arbitrability is determined according to the law applicable to the validity of the arbitration agreement; and in the latter case, the law of the forum regulates arbitrability.[161] In the instant case, the court held that Swiss law, the law expressly chosen by the parties to govern their agreement, should determine the arbitrability of the dispute.

This writer believes that the laws of the country most closely connected to the underlying transaction should be the relevant standard in determining objective arbitrability. This view is grounded on the need to ensure that only the law of a forum that has some bearing with the commercial transaction determines which disputes are arbitrable, at least at the stage where enforcement of an arbitration agreement is sought.[162] It is therefore suggested that the court before which the enforcement of an arbitration agreement is sought should apply the law of the country most closely connected to the agreement in determining subject-matter arbitrability. A court should apply the law of its forum only in cases where the underlying transaction has an overwhelming connection with the forum.

When the Issue Arises before a Judge to Whom an Application Is Made for the Recognition and Enforcement of an Award

Under Article V(2)(a) of the New York Convention and Article 36(1)(b)(i) of the Model Law, recognition and enforcement of an award may be refused if the subject matter of the dispute is nonarbitrable under the law of the country where recognition or enforcement is sought. A judge before whom recognition and enforcement of an award is sought would therefore apply the *lex fori* in determining the arbitrability of the subject matter of the award.

This approach guarantees a forum the opportunity to ensure that its courts enforce only awards that are the product of matters considered arbitrable under the forum's law. The forum court can deny recognition and enforcement to an award if the subject matter of the arbitration is nonarbitrable under its law. The provision could be useful in protecting the legitimate interests of a forum in ensuring that certain sensitive or public-interest matters are removed from the scope of private arbitration.

However, this approach may be untenable in cases where enforcement proceedings are the only factor connecting the forum with the commercial transaction underlying the arbitration agreement. Where the commercial transaction impacts upon another country, it strains the imagination to conceive of any justifiable reason why the law of an enforcement jurisdiction should be capable of declaring the subject matter of the dispute nonarbitrable.[163] The primary reason why the jurisdiction of the enforcement court is invoked in instances like this is because the respondent has assets in the country that may be attached to fulfil its obligations under the arbitral award. It seems reasonable to suggest that the *lex fori* of the enforcement court should not have any impact on the arbitrability of the dispute, unless in situations where the subject matter of the dispute has a significant impact in the forum, thereby implicating the legitimate interests of the forum.

Reliance on the laws of the forum also encourages forum shopping in that the successful claimant has to seek an enforcement jurisdiction with favorable arbitration rules.[164] A better approach would be to apply the *lex fori* only in situations where it has a real and substantial connection with the commercial transaction that is the subject matter of the arbitration agreement, or where the effect of the award has a significant impact in the enforcing jurisdiction.

Where an Application Is Made to Set Aside an Award

The final instance where the issue of arbitrability may arise is before a judge to whom an application is made to set aside an award. Article 34(2)(b)(i) of the Model Law provides that an award may be set aside where "the subject matter of the dispute is not capable of settlement by arbitration under the law of the [enacting country]." The only country whose courts could be asked to set aside an award under this article is the country that is the seat of the arbitration. Courts in other countries cannot set aside awards made outside their jurisdiction; they can only refuse to recognize and enforce such awards.[165] It should be remembered, however, that a decision to set aside an award applies *erga omnes*.[166] Where the seat of arbitration is unconnected to the transaction between the arbitrating parties, it is illogical to use the law of the seat of arbitration in determining subject-matter arbitrability. In a lot of instances, the parties to an arbitration are from other jurisdictions, and the place of arbitration is chosen due to convenience and the ability to attract qualified arbitrators to such a location. What is more, in some cases the seat of arbitration is chosen, not by the parties, but by third parties, such as an arbitral institution or the arbitrators themselves. The parties may therefore not be aware of the seat of arbitration at the time the arbitration agreement is contracted and the underlying commercial transaction carried out. These factors clearly demonstrate that it is unrealistic to use the law of the seat of arbitration (the *lex loci arbitri*) in determining arbitrability in proceedings to set aside an award. The injustice in testing arbitrability by a *lex loci arbitri* that has no connection with the agreement and the underlying transaction is heightened by the fact that a decision of the court of the seat of arbitration to set aside the award has a potentially global effect.[167] This potential outcome strongly supports the suggestion that the law of fora unrelated to an arbitration agreement and its underlying transaction should not govern the arbitrability of a dispute, as their policy interests are not directly implicated. Arbitrability should be governed solely by the law with which the agreement is most closely connected.

Conclusion

In summary, this writer believes that the objective arbitrability of a subject matter should be determined according to the law of the country whose jurisdiction is most closely connected to the dispute. For example, if a transaction between a Canadian party and a French party involves the importation of automobiles into Canada and the transaction implicates issues of Canadian antitrust law, Canadian law should regulate the arbitrability of such a matter as the transaction impacts significantly on Canada. It makes little sense to determine the arbitrability of such a matter by reference to the law of the place of arbitration (say, Switzerland) which is not connected to the commercial transaction in question. Neither is it sound to rely on the proper law of the contract chosen by the parties, except in cases where the proper law is the law of the jurisdiction most closely connected with the agreement.

It should be noted that there is a discernible trend toward the dismantling of national restrictions on the arbitrability of international disputes.[168] For example, Article 177(1) of the Swiss Private International Law Statute, 1987,[169] provides that any dispute of "financial interest" is arbitrable. In England there is virtually no restriction on arbitrability except in relation to obligations under the EEC Treaty of Rome and except under the rule that the court may revoke an arbitration agreement where one of the parties must prove a fraud in order to establish his claim.[170] International arbitration has similarly received favorable treatment in U.S. courts; the courts recognize the fact that arbitration meets the needs of the international business community for a flexible and neutral dispute resolution mechanism.[171] This recognition translates into a presumption of arbitrability:

> The burden is on the party opposing arbitration . . . to show that Congress intended to preclude a waiver of judicial remedies for the statutory rights at issue. If Congress did intend to limit or prohibit waiver of a judicial forum for a particular claim, such an intent will be deducible from the statute's text or legislative history . . . or from an inherent conflict between arbitration and the statute's underlying proposes.[172]

The increasing reduction in the list of nonarbitrable matters in international arbitration is explained by various factors. There is a tendency to distinguish between domestic and international transactions.[173] In the former case, the parties are usually resident in, and the transactions occur within, the same country. Clearly, there is a pervasive need for that country to regulate transactions that not only involve their residents, but that also impact exclusively on its jurisdiction. In the latter case, however, the transaction may occur in or impact on different countries. Here there is less reason for a particular country to insist on regulating the entire transaction, since this may in practice have extra-territorial ramifications.[174] This consideration is one of the reasons why most countries are apt to treat international contracts less stringently than their domestic counterparts.

The liberal treatment of international arbitration has also been justified on the basis of comity and the special needs of international commerce.[175] In *Scherk* v. *Alberto-Culver Co.*,[176] the court, swayed by the "truly international (character of the) agreement," disregarded the fact that securities disputes could not be arbitrated domestically, and held that such disputes were arbitrable in international disputes. The same consideration influenced the *Mitsubishi* court,[177] and the French courts in the *San Carlo*[178] and *Galakis*[179] cases.

Recognition of the fact that international arbitration is amenable to the needs of the international business community has made arbitration attractive as a means of decongesting the court system. The more the process is utilized, the less the pressures on the overcrowded court system.[180] The doctrine of objective arbitrability is nonetheless a means by which States declare what they consider the outer limits of private arbitration and the proper scope of matters that fall within the exclusive jurisdiction of national courts. Arbitrators should respect the rules on arbitrability of those jurisdictions whose policy interests are directly implicated by the parties' commercial transactions.

CONCLUSION

In this chapter we examined the law relating to arbitration agreements. The chapter outlined the doctrine of the juridical autonomy of arbitration agreements, and its corollary principle that the law applicable to an arbitration agreement is not necessarily coterminous with that applicable to the substantive contract. It was noted that it is spurious to utilize the law of the seat of arbitration as an alternative test in determining the validity of arbitration agreements, and the formulation of a "close connection test" was advocated.

It was argued that different considerations applied in determining the law relating to the capacity of States to arbitrate and the authority of their officials to bind them in valid arbitration agreements. It was submitted that the efficacy of national law restrictions should be different in either case. Whereas international public policy precludes a State or its agency from relying on its incapacity under its national law as grounds for challenging an arbitration agreement, private parties should be required to verify the authority of State officials—under the national law of the State concerned—to bind the State or its agencies in a valid arbitration agreement.

Finally, it was suggested that objective arbitrability should be determined in accordance with the law of the country whose national interests are most directly implicated by the commercial transactions underlying the parties' agreement. It was argued that reliance on the law of the forum (either that where enforcement of the arbitration agreement or the arbitration award is sought), could lead to the use of a law totally unconnected with the commercial transaction in determining arbitrability, a result that was considered objectionable because the country whose national interests are directly implicated by the commercial transaction has a more legitimate claim in regulating objective arbitrability.

NOTES

1. W. Craig, W. Park, and P. Paulsson, *International Chamber of Commerce Arbitration*, 2d ed., (Dobbs Ferry, NY: Oceana Publications, 1990) at 49; J. Lew, "Arbitration Agreements: Form and Character" in P. Sarcevic (ed.) *Essays on International Commercial Arbitration* (London: Martinus Nijhoff, 1989) 51 at 52.

2. Y. Derains, "France" (1981) 6 *Y. Comm. Arb.* 1 at 4; R. David, *Arbitration in International Trade* (Deventer, The Netherlands: Kluwer Law and Taxation Publishers, 1985) at 171.

3. 330 U.N.T.S. 38; T.I.A.S. 6997; 21 U.S.T. 2517.

4. Article II(1). There is provision to the same effect in the Model Law. Article 7(1) of the Model Law defines arbitration as "an agreement by the parties to submit to arbitration all or certain disputes which have arisen or which may arise between them in respect of a defined legal relationship."

5. It should be noted that this issue does not arise in submission agreements that are independent arbitration agreements entered into in relation to existing disputes. The question of autonomy arises only in cases where the arbitration agreement is a clause in a larger commercial contract.

6. The main advantage of this principle is that it constitutes a serious bar for a party who desires delay or wishes to repudiate the arbitration agreement or to subvert the arbitration clause by questioning in court the existence and validity of the agreement to arbitrate. See T. Szurski, "Arbitration Agreement and Competence of the Arbitral Tribunal" in P. Sanders (ed.) *UNCITRAL's Project for a Model Law on International Commercial Arbitration* (Deventer, The Netherlands: Kluwer Law and Taxation Publishers, 1984) 53 at 76. See also J. Robert and T. Carbonneau, *The French Law of Arbitration* (New York: Matthew Bender, 1983) at 11: 2–19.

7. See W. Craig et al., supra note 1, at 66. In their view, if the invalidity of the substantive contract reaches the arbitration agreement,

> it is presumed that even though the parties may have signed an invalid contract (because, for example, it is contrary to competition law) they nevertheless expressed a separate and valid intent that any dispute arising in connection with the contract should be resolved by arbitration. That intent is then viewed as extending to cover the consequences of the invalidity of the contract (assuming the arbitral tribunal in fact finds it to be invalid). Id.

8. See Tobler c/ Justizkommission des Kantos Schwyz (1933) ATF 59 I 177.

9. (1985) 3 ASA Bulletin 19.

10. This position is codified in the 1987 Swiss Private International Law Act. [A translated version of the legislation approved by the Swiss Arbitration Association is published in (1989) 14 *Y. Comm Arb.* 511.] Article 178(3) of the act provides

that the validity of an arbitration agreement cannot be contested on the ground that the main contract is not valid. It has been suggested that in Switzerland if the main contract is void, the arbitration clause only becomes void where the reason for the nullity also applies to the arbitration clause. See R. Briner, "Switzerland" (1989) 14 *Y. Comm Arb.* 1 at 13.

11. [1963] *Rev. Crit. Dr. Int'l Pr.* 615.

12. Id.

13. See, for example, *Société Impex* [1972] Dalloz 37.

14. R. David, supra note 2, at 193. A. Samuel, *Jurisdictional Problems in International Commercial Arbitration: A Study of Belgian, Dutch, English, French, Swiss, U.S. and West German Law* (Zurich: Schulthess Polygraphischer Verlag, 1989) at 164.

15. *AB NorrkÖppings Trikafabrik* v. *AB Per Persson* (1936) NJA 521. See also K. Hobér, "The Doctrine of Separability Under Swedish Arbitration Law" (1983) 68 *SvJT* 257.

16. [1964] Nederlandse Jurisprudentie, No. 43.

17. *Prima Paints* v. *Flood & Conklin* (1967) 388 U.S. 395; *Robert Muh* v. *Newburger Loeb Inc.* (1976) 540 F. 2d 970; *Sauser-Getriebe KG* v. *White Hydraulics Inc.* (1983) 715 F. 2d 348. See also R. Caulson, "Prima Paint: An Arbitration Milestone" (1967) *Arb. J.* 237.

18. *Dalmia Dairy Industries* v. *National Bank of Pakistan* [1978] 2 Lloyd's Rep. 233 at 286. For an indication of a change in the English position see note 20, below. See also A. Redfern and M. Hunter, *Law and Practice of International Commercial Arbitration*, 1st ed. (London: Sweet and Maxwell, 1986) at 134; J. Castel, "International Commercial Arbitration" in P. Emond (ed.) *Commercial Dispute Resolution: Alternatives to Litigation* (Ontario: Canada Law Book, 1989) 121 at 129.

19. *Overseas Union* v. *AA Mutual International* [1988] 2 Lloyd's Rep. 63.

20. *Slade* v. *Metrodent Ltd.* [1953] Q.B. 122. The English courts are beginning to relax their parsimonious version of the autonomy principle. In *Harbour Assurance Ltd* v. *International Assurance Ltd* the Court of Appeal held that the autonomy principle could give jurisdiction to an arbitrator to determine a dispute over the initial validity or invalidity, or illegality of a written contract provided the arbitration clause itself was not directly impeached. [1993] 3 All E.R. 897.

21. *Bremer Vulkan* v. *South Indian Shipping Corporation Ltd.* (1981) A.C. 909 (per Lord Diplock at 982).

22. The principle is equally acknowledged in arbitral practice. In *Elf Aquitaine Iran* v. *National Iranian Oil Company*, the arbitrator, Professor B. Gormard, stated that it is "a generally recognised principle of law of international arbitration that arbitration clauses continue to be operative, even though an objection is raised by one of the parties that the contract containing the arbitration clause is null and void." (1986) 11 *Y. Comm. Arb.* 97. See also ICC Case No. 1152 (1980) 5 *Y. Comm. Arb.* 171 at 173; *Texaco Overseas Petroleum Company* v. *Libya* (1979) 4 *Y. Comm. Arb.* 117 at 179; U.S.S.R. Maritime Arbitration Commission Award No. 24/1984 (1989) 14 *Y. Comm. Arb.* 209 at 210; ICC Case No. 5485 (1989) 14 *Y. Comm. Arb.* 156.

23. I say "sound *legal* basis" because the English position finds little support outside the arena of legal logic.

24. Indeed Devlin J. in *Christopher Brown Ltd.* v. *Holzwirtschaftbetriebe* ([1954] 1 Q.B. 8), recognized this potential avenue for delays and was prepared to allow,

albeit with some limitation, an arbitral tribunal to determine its jurisdiction where the invalidity of the substantive contract is pleaded:

> It is clear that at the beginning of any arbitration one side or the other may challenge the jurisdiction of the arbitrator. It is not the law that arbitrators, if their jurisdiction is challenged or questioned, are bound immediately to refuse to act until their jurisdiction has been determined by some court which has power to determine it finally. . . . They are entitled to enquire into the merits of the issue whether they have jurisdiction or not, not for the purpose of reaching any conclusion which will be binding upon the parties—because that they cannot do—but for the purpose of satisfying themselves as a preliminary matter whether they ought to go on with the arbitration or not.

25. Article 190 of the Swiss Private International Law Act, for example, provides that an award may be set aside where the "arbitral tribunal has wrongly declared itself to have or not have jurisdiction."

26. See S. Schwebel, *International Arbitration: Three Salient Problems* (Cambridge: Grotius, 1987) at 60.

27. It should be pointed out that countries that do not accept the autonomy principle would deny an arbitral tribunal the power to determine its jurisdiction in cases where the validity of the arbitration agreement is in question.

28. W. Craig, W. Park, and J. Paulsson, supra note 1 at 196.

29. H. Holtzmann and J. Neuhaus, *A Guide to the UNCITRAL Model Law on International Commercial Arbitration: Legislative History and Commentary* (Deventer, The Netherlands: Kluwer Law and Taxation Publishers, 1989) at 479.

30. See also Article V(3) of the European Convention on International Commercial Arbitration, 484 U.N.T.S. 349; Article 41(1) of the Convention on the Settlement of Investment Disputes between States and Nationals of Other States, 575 U.N.T.S. 159.

31. An example is Switzerland. Article 186 of the Swiss Private International Law Act provides that the "arbitral tribunal shall decide on its own jurisdiction." See also Article 1466 of the French Code of Civil Procedure.

32. *Fung Sang Trading Ltd* v. *Kai Sun Sea Products* (1992) 17 *Y. Comm. Arb.* 289 at 302.

33. H. Holtzmann and J. Neuhaus, supra note 29 at 479.

34. According to J. Castel, "if one party denies the existence of both the contract and the arbitration clause, the arbitration cannot proceed until this question has been settled by the relevant court." Supra note 18 at 129.

35. [1942] 1 All E.R. 337.

36. Id. at 342. Cf. *Paul Smith* v. *H & S International Holdings Co* [1991] 2 Lloyd's Rep. 127 at 130; *Harbour Assurance* v. *Kansa* [1992] 1 Lloyd's Rep. 81; and the Australian case of *QH Tours Ltd* v. *Ship Design & Management Pty Ltd* (1991) 105 Australian L.R. 371. For an analysis of the *Kompetenz-Kompetenz* rule, see P. Schlosser, "The Competence of Arbitrators and of Courts" (1992) 8 *Arb. Int'l* 189; P. Cross, "Competence of Competence" (1992) 8 *Arb. Int'l* 205; C. Svernlov, "The Evolution of the Doctrine of Separability in England" (1992) 9 *J. Int'l Arb.* 115.

37. See Holtzmann and Neuhaus, supra note 29, at 485.

38. Article 16(3) of the Model Law provides:

> The arbitral tribunal may rule [on its jurisdiction] either as a preliminary question or in an award on the merits. If the arbitral tribunal rules as a preliminary question that it has jurisdiction, any party may request, within thirty days after having received notice of that

ruling, the court specified in article 6 to decide the matter, which decision shall be subject to no appeal; while such a request is pending, the arbitral tribunal may continue the arbitral proceedings and make an award.

39. USSR Maritime Commission Award No. 24/1984 (1989) 14 *Y. Comm. Arb.* 209 at 210.

40. (1984) 9 *Y. Comm. Arb.* 131.

41. Id. at 133.

42. Id. at 134.

43. See *Black Clawson Ltd.* v. *Papierwerke* [1981] 2 Lloyd's L. Rep. 446; *James Miller Ltd.* v. *Whitworth* [1970] 2 W.L.R. 728. See also the decision of the Court of Appeal in Paris in *Dow Chemical* v. *Isover Saint Gobian,* extracted in (1984) 9 *Y. Comm. Arb.* 132.

44. It is possible, given the present state of arbitral practice, for different laws to govern the arbitration agreement and either aspects of arbitrability.

45. See A. van den Berg, "The New York Convention of 1958: Consolidated Commentary" (1989) 14 *Y. Comm. Arb.* 528 at 585.

46. For the position in England, see L. Collins (ed.) *Dicey and Morris on Conflict of Laws,* 11th ed. (London: Stevens and Sons, 1987) vol. 2 at 537. For the position in Spain, see B. Cremades, *Arbitration in Spain* (London: Butterworths, 1991) at 117.

47. See A. Samuel, "The Effect of the Place of Arbitration on the Enforcement of the Agreement to Arbitrate" in M. Storme and F. Ly (eds.) *The Place of Arbitration* (Ghent: Mys and Breesch, 1992) at 39. See also the English cases of *Tzortzis* v. *Monark Line* [1968] 1 W.L.R. 406; *Maritime Insurance Co. Ltd.* v. *Assecuranz-Union* (1935) 52 Lloyd's L.R. 16.

48. *Misr Insurance* v. *M.V. Dominion Trader,* June 13 No. 1259 (1983). See also the Indian case of *National Thermal Power Corp.* v. *The Singer Corp.* (1992) 7:6 Mealey's Int'l Arb. Rep. 3.

49. Decision of November 17, 1971, quoted in A. van den Berg, *The New York Convention of 1958: Towards a Uniform Judicial Interpretation* (Deventer, The Netherlands: Kluwer Law and Taxation Publishers, 1981) at 128. The European Convention of 1961, which has been adopted in some European countries, provides that, except for capacity of the parties, the validity of an arbitration agreement shall be determined, *inter alia,* "under the law of the country in which the award is to be made." Article VI(2). The country in which the award is to be made is generally the same country where the arbitration is held. But see *Hiscox* v. *Outhwaite,* infra note 63.

50. *Dicey and Morris* state that the presumption in favor of the law of the place of arbitration is inoperative in cases where the original agreement does not indicate a seat of arbitration, or where the seat of arbitration is chosen by the arbitrators or other third party (such as an arbitral institution). Supra note 46, at 537.

51. A. van den Berg is of the view that the conflict law of the forum should provide a solution in these kinds of cases. Supra note 49, at 127.

52. Case No. 52/65. Extracted in (1976) 1 *Y. Comm. Arb.* 123.

53. *Baques Centroamericanos* v. *Petroleo SA* (1988) 13 *Y. Comm. Arb.* 133.

54. First Interim Award in ICC Case No. 4145, extracted in (1987) 12 *Y. Comm. Arb.* 99.

55. The Award of the Arbitral Tribunal of the Netherlands Oil, Fats and Oilseed Trade Association, rendered on September 5, 1977; extracted in (1979) 4 *Y. Comm. Arb.* 218 at 219.

56. (1989) 14 *Y. Comm. Arb.* 156.

57. Id. at 161. The arbitrators in reliance on Article 13(5) of the ICC Rules, which obligated them to take account of international trade usages and practices, also tested the validity of the arbitration agreement of those basis. Pursuant to Article 26 of the ICC Rules, which required them to ensure that their award is enforceable at law, the arbitrators further tested the arbitration agreement under French law as the law of the place of arbitration. Id. at 162.

58. ICC Case No. 3572 of 1982, extracted in (1989) 14 *Y. Comm. Arb.* 111 at 116.

59. Article 43(2)(a)(i): "An arbitral award may be set aside . . . if . . . the said agreement is not valid under the law to which the parties have subjected it or, failing any indication thereon, under the law of this state. . . ."

60. Article V(1)(a). This provision was designed as an improvement on the Geneva Convention of 1927, which provides that the validity of an arbitration agreement is to be governed by the "applicable law," although the term is not defined in that convention. The European Convention echoes the provision of the New York Convention. The European Convention provides that the annulment of an award in a Contracting State shall not be a ground for refusal to recognize and enforce an award in another state unless the award was annulled on the ground, *inter alia*, that the agreement is "not valid under the law to which the parties submitted it or, failing any indication thereon, under the law of country where the award was made." Article IX(1)(A).

61. Robert and Carbonneau, supra note 6, at 11:8–22.

62. See Article 36(1)(a)(i).

63. [1991] 3 W.L.R. 297. For a critical review of the decision, see O. Chukwumerije, "Is an Arbitration Award 'Made' Where It Is Signed?" (1992) 20 *Canadian Bus. L.J.* 305.

64. This test is, however, obviously unsuitable in cases where the validity of the arbitration agreement is in question (for example, where fraud or misrepresentation is pleaded as negating the existence of an agreement). In instances like this, reference should be made to the law with which the alleged agreement is closely connected.

65. Indeed Article 8(1) of the ICC rules makes this very clear that "[w]here the parties agreed to submit to arbitration by the International Chamber of Commerce, they shall be deemed thereby to have submitted ipso facto to the present Rules."

66. K. Bockstiegel, "Public Policy and Arbitrability" in P. Sanders (ed.) *Comparative Arbitration Practice and Public Policy in Arbitration* (Deventer, The Netherlands: Kluwer Law and Taxation Publishers, 1987), 177 at 181.

67. See A. Jan van den Berg, supra note 49, at 277.

68. See L. Collins, supra note 46, at 1161. J. Castel, *Canadian Conflict of Laws*, 2d ed. (Toronto: Butterworths, 1986) at 530.

69. In *Cooper* v. *Cooper* [(1888) 13 App. Cas. 88 at 108.] Lord Macnaghten said "It is difficult to suppose that Mrs Cooper could confer capacity on herself by contemplating a different country as a place where the contract was to be fulfilled."

70. L. Quigley, "Convention on Foreign Arbitral Award" (1972) 58 *A.B.A.J.* 831 at 824; R. Springer, "The United Nations Convention on the Recognition and Enforcement of Foreign Arbitral Awards" (1968) 3 *Int'l Law* 320 at 323; L. Collins, supra note 46, at 585; A. van den Berg, supra note 49, at 276.

71. H. Holtzmann and J. Neuhaus, supra note 29, at 916.

72. Id.

73. See discussion in Chapter 4, section entitled "Choice by Arbitrators."

74. For example, Switzerland [R. Briner, "Switzerland" (1978) 3 *Y. Comm Arb.* 181]; United Kingdom [W. Gill, "United Kingdom" (1977) 2 *Y. Comm. Arb.* 90]; India [N. Krishnamurthi, "India" (1971) 2 *Y. Comm. Arb.* 31.]

75. A. van den Berg suggests that one of the reasons for prohibiting the arbitration of state contract disputes in Saudi Arabia was the result in the famous Aramco Arbitration, 27 I.L.R. 117 (1963), which Saudi Arabia lost. See A. van den Berg, "Saudi Arabia" IX *Y. Comm. Arb.* 7 at 14 (1984).

76. K. Bockstiegel, supra note 66 at 202.

77. See p. 49.

78. Saudi Arabia Council of Ministers Resolution No. 58. Quoted by A. van den Berg, supra note 75, at 7.

79. Cass, May 2, 1966, Clunet 1965, 646.

80. Id.

81. Clunet 1966, 648.

82. Law No. 86–972, Article 9. Reproduced in (1987) 2 *Int'l Arb. Rep.* 28.

83. Article 1672(2) of the Belgian Code Judiciare provides: "Apart from public law entities, any person who has the capacity or the authority to negotiate a settlement may conclude an arbitration agreement. The state may conclude such an agreement whenever a treaty authorizes it to have recourse to arbitration."

84. J. Paulsson, "May a State Invoke Its Internal Law to Repudiate Consent to International Arbitration?" (1986) 2 *Arb. Int'l* 90 at 91.

85. Id.

86. In this respect, the term is used to denote the law of the place of arbitration.

87. P. Lalive, "Transnational (or Truly International) Public Policy and International Arbitration" in *Comparative Arbitration Practice and Public Policy in Arbitration*, supra note 66, 257 at 295.

88. F. A. Mann, "State Contracts and International Arbitration" (1967) 42 *Brit. Y. Int'l L.* 1 at 36. By the *lex arbitri* he meant the law of the place of arbitration.

89. For example, in *Benteler* v. *Belgium* [1985] European Economic Cases 101, the contract provided that in the event of a dispute each party would name an arbitrator of its own nationality, and the two arbitrators so named would choose a chairman of a third nationality. The latter's domicile would become the seat of arbitration.

90. *Benteler* v. *Belgium*, id. at 109. See also A. von Mehren, "Draft Report on Arbitration between States and Foreign Enterprises" (1989) 63 *Yearbook Institute Int'l Law* 100 at 132.

91. *Charron* v. *Montreal Trust Co.* [1958] O.R. 597 (C.A.). See also A. Dicey and J. Morris, *The Conflicts of Laws*, 10th ed. (London: Sweet and Maxwell, 1980) at 778–783.

92. A. Simpson, *A History of the Common Law of Contract* (Oxford: Clarendon Press, 1975) at 539 et seq.

93. J. Castel suggests that only an objectively ascertained proper law can be used to determine the capacity of parties to enter into contractual relationships. See J. Castel, supra note 68 at 549.

94. J. Paulsson, supra note 84, at 102.

95. J. Lew, *Applicable Law in International Commercial Arbitration: A Study in Commercial Arbitration Awards* (Dobbs Ferry, NY: Oceana Publications, 1978) at 535. See P. Lalive, supra note 87 at 295; K. Bockstiegel, supra note 66 at 203.

96. *ICC Case 1939*. Cited by Y. Derains (1973) *Revue de L'Arbitrage* 145.

97. Commentary in *International Arbitration: 60 Years of ICC Arbitration—A Look at the Future* (Paris: ICC Publishing, 1984) 293 at 296.

98. See J. Paulsson, supra note 84; K. Bockstiegel, supra note 66 at 202; P. Lalive, supra note 87; E. Gaillard, "A Foreign View of the New Swiss Law on International Arbitration" (1988) 4 *Arb. Int'l* 25; M. Blessing, "The New International Arbitration Law in Switzerland" (1988) 5(2) *J. Int'l Arb.* 9; P. Lalive, "The New Swiss Law on International Arbitration" (1988) 4 *Arb. Int'l* 2.

99. J. Lew, supra note 95 at 531.

100. Id. at 532. See also M. Buchanan, "Public Policy and International Commercial Arbitration" (1988) 26 *Am. Bus L.J.* 511 at 529.

101. It is nevertheless recognized that an arbitrator may have to apply some of the public policy of the *lex contractus* as it relates to the merits of the disputes, and, as we shall see in Chapter 6, other relevant national mandatory rules. See generally, Y. Derain, "Public Policy and the Law Applicable to the Dispute in International Arbitration" in *Comparative Arbitration Practice and Public Policy in Arbitration*, supra note 66 at 227; O. Lando, "The Law Applicable to the Merits of the Dispute" in P. Sarcevic (ed.) *Essays on International Commercial Arbitration* (London: Graham and Trotman, 1989) 129 at 155.

102. Quoted by P. Lalive, supra note 87 at 278.

103. J. Lew, supra note 95 at 534.

104. As B. Cremades puts it: "My intuitive interpretation of this is that this [the issue of capacity of States and their organs to enter into arbitration agreements] is a question which should be perhaps resolved by the . . . principle of *'pacta sunt servanda'* which is the principle of good faith." "States and Public Enterprises as International Commercial Partners." Commentary in *International Arbitration*, supra note 97, 177 at 185. This view was reiterated by the arbitrator in *Soleh* v. *Uganda* [reproduced in S. Jarvin and Y. Derains, *Collection of ICC Arbitral Awards: 1974–1985* (Deventer, The Netherlands: Kluwer Law and Taxation Publishers, 1990) at 8]. An arbitrator stated:

> I most admit that I have found some difficulties to follow a line of reasoning that a State, just because of its supreme position and qualities, should be unable to give a binding promise. The principle of *pacta sunt servanda* is generally acknowledged in international law and it is difficult to see any reason why it should not apply here. Id. at 10.

105. P. Lalive, supra note 87 at 297.

106. Discussed by J. Lew, supra note 95 at 548.

107. Id. See also *Fermatome* v. *Atomic Energy Organisation of Iran* [1984] Clunet 58; *Elf Acquitaine Iran* v. *National Iranian Oil Company* [1984] *Rev. Arb.* 401.

108. Supra note 89. For a discussion of the award, see J. Paulsson, supra note 84.

109. See Article 1672(2) of the Belgian Code Judiciare, supra note 83.

110. Belgium is a signatory to the 1961 European Convention on International Commercial Arbitration (the Geneva Convention). Under Article 1(1)(a), the convention applies to international commercial arbitration between natural and legal

persons whose residence or seat at the time when the agreement is made are in different Contracting States. Article 11(1) of the convention provides that legal persons of public law have the capacity to conclude valid arbitration agreements. It was not disputed that the convention was applicable to the instant case as the claimant was from Germany (another Contracting State) and the dispute related to an international commercial transaction. The arbitrators, relying on Article 11(1) of the convention, held that Belgium had the requisite capacity to enter into the arbitration agreement in question.

111. Supra note 89 at 108.

112. Supra note 81.

113. For a review of this law, see M. Blessing, supra note 98; P. Lalive, "The New Swiss Law on International Arbitration" supra note 98, and E. Gaillard, supra note 98.

114. Article 176, which deals with the scope of application of the legislation, provides as follows:

1. The provisions of this Chapter [relating to international arbitrations] shall apply to all arbitrations if the seat of the arbitral tribunal is situated in Switzerland and if, at the time when the arbitration agreement was concluded, at least one of the parties had neither its domicile nor its habitual residence in Switzerland.
2. The provisions of this Chapter shall not apply where the parties have excluded its application in writing and have agreed to the exclusive application of the procedural provisions of the Cantonal law relating to arbitration.

115. See *ICC Case No. 6162 of 1990* (1992) 17 *Y. Comm. Arb.* 153.

116. The ICSID was established by the Convention on the Settlement of Investment Disputes between States and Nationals of other States, 575 U.N.T.S. 159. It provides facilities for the conciliation and arbitration of investment disputes.

117. ICSID Case ARB/74/2. Discussed by J. Schmidt in (1976) 17 *Harvard Int'l L.J.* 90. See also G. Delaume, "ICSID and the Transnational Financial Community" (1986) 1 *ICSID Review* 237.

118. Quoted by J. Schmidt, id. at 103.

119. In the words of Viscount Haldane L.C. in *Lennard's Carrying Co.* v. *Asiatic Petroleum Co. Ltd.* [1915] A.C. 705 at 713:

> My Lords, a corporation is an abstraction. It has no mind of its own any more than it has a body of its own, its active and directing will must consequently be sought in the person of somebody who for some purposes may be called an agent, but who is really the directing mind and will of the corporation, the very ego and centre of the personality of the corporation.

120. See W. Craig, W. Park, and J. Paulsson, supra note 1 at 63–64.

121. P. Lalive, supra note 87, at 297; B. Cremades, supra note 104, at 187.

122. Id.

123. According to W. Peter, "[i]t goes without saying that the investor should ascertain by appropriate means (e.g. legal opinion of local lawyers) the validity of a proposed arbitration clause or even have an express warranty in the contract that the arbitration is binding." W. Peter, *Arbitration and Renegotiation of International Investment Agreements* (Dordrecht, The Netherlands: Martinus Nijhoff, 1986) at 182.

124. See F. Garcia-Amador, L. Sohn, and R. Baxter, *Recent Codification of the Law of State Responsibility for Injuries to Aliens* (Dobbs Ferry, NY: Oceana Publications, 1974) at 70. See also G. Ray, "Law Governing Contracts between States and Foreign Nationals" in *Selected Readings on Protection by Law of Private Foreign Investments* (New York: Matthew Bender, 1964) 453 at 461.

125. P. North and J. Fawcett, *Cheshire and North Private International Law* (London: Butterworths, 1987) at 901.

126. See supra note 121.

127. M. Rubino-Sammartano, *International Arbitration Law* (Deventer, The Netherlands: Kluwer Law and Taxation Publishers, 1990) at 119.

128. *The Queen* v. *Woodburn* (1899) 29 S.C.R. 113 at 123.

129. R. Dessault and L. Borgent, *Administrative Law: A Treatise*, 2d ed. (Toronto: Carswell, 1985) at 501; H. E. Manning, "Contracts with the Crown" (1972) 2 D.L.R. 513 at 515; D. Foulkes, *Administrative Law*, 7th ed. (London: Butterworths, 1990) at 438. P. Hogg echoes the same view: "A contract within the power of a government representing the Crown will bind the Crown only if it is made by a servant or agent of the Crown, acting within the scope of his authority. The scope of a Crown's servant's authority will often be determined by statute or by regulation made under statutory authority." P. Hogg, *Liability of the Crown in Australia, New Zealand and the United Kingdom* (Melbourne: The Law Book Company, 1971) at 125.

130. G. Delaume, "ICSID Arbitration: Practical Considerations" (1984) 1 *J. Int'l Arb.* 101 at 106.

131. (1969) 8 I.L.M. 679.

132. R. Dessault and L. Borgent, supra note 129 at 502; *The Queen* v. *C.A.E. Industries Ltd.* (1986) D.L.R. (4th) 347 (C.A.).

133. (1983) 22 I.L.M. 752.

134. (1984) 23 I.L.M. 1048. On appeal to the Court of Cassation, the Court of Appeal's decision was affirmed: (1987) 26 I.L.M. 1004.

135. *Benteler* v. *Belgium*, supra note 89; P. Lalive, supra note 87, at 297.

136. For example, the English courts were traditionally hostile to arbitration, which they viewed as a competitor for adjudicatory power. Reviewing the historical development of arbitration, Lord Campbell noted that

> as formerly the emoluments of the judges depended mainly, or almost entirely, upon fees, and as they had no fixed salary, there was a great competition to get as much as possible of litigation into Westminster Hall . . . therefore they said that the courts ought not to be ousted of their jurisdiction, and that it was contrary to policy of the law to do that.

Scott v. *Avery* (1853) 25 L.J. Ex. 308. See M. Hunter, "Arbitration Procedure in England: Past, Present and Future" (1985) 1 *Arb. Int'l* 82 at 84. Cf. M. Mustill and S. Boyd, *The Law and Practice of Commercial Arbitration in England*, 2d ed. (London: Butterworths, 1989) at 5. For a review of the contemporary English judicial attitude toward arbitration, see W. Park, "Judicial Supervision of Transnational Commercial Arbitration: The English Arbitration Act" (1980) 21 *Hastings Int'l L.J.* 87. The initial hostility of English courts to arbitration was picked up by U.S. courts. See H.R. Rep. No. 96, 68th Cong., 1st Sess., 1,2 (1924); W. Sturges and I. Murphy, "Some Confusing Matters Relating to Arbitration Under the United States Arbitration Act (1952) 17 *Law & Cont. Prob.* 580.

137. See *Scherk* v. *Alberto-Culver Co.* 417 U.S. 506. In the words of the British Columbia Supreme Court, "there is a worldwide trend toward restricting judicial

control over international commercial arbitration awards." *Quintette Coal Ltd* v. *Nippon Steel Corp.* (1988) 29 C.C.L.R. (2d) 233 at 234.

138. See A. Samuel, supra note 14, at 125.

139. K. Bockstiegel, supra note 66, at 181.

140. I. Neslor, "Problems Concerning the Application and Interpretation of Existing Multilateral Conventions on International Commercial Arbitration and Related Matters" (1972) 3 *UNCITRAL Yearbook* 193 at 244.

141. See H. Holtzmann and J. Neuhaus, supra note 29, at 39.

142. See W. Craig, W. Park, and J. Paulsson, supra note 1, at 39. See also M. Jacobs, *International Commercial Arbitration in Australia: Law and Practice* (Sydney: The Law Book Company, 1992) at 2574.

143. Id. See also Article 6(2) of the European Convention on International Commercial Arbitration (the European Convention), done at Geneva on 21 April 1961. The article stipulates the law chosen by the parties as having priority in determining arbitrability.

144. Article 26 of the ICC Rules of Arbitration, for example, requires an arbitrator to "make every effort [to ensure] that the award is enforceable at law."

145. Article 34(2)(b)(i).

146. See Article V(1)(e) of the New York Convention and Article 36(1)(v) of the Model Law.

147. (1992) 17 *Y. Comm. Arb.* 153.

148. See Article 8 of the Model Law.

149. See H. Holtzmann and J. Neuhaus, supra note 29 at 303.

150. Id.

151. Although he was dealing with the New York Convention, his analysis is germane in discussing the Model Law because their provisions on the issue of arbitrability are broadly similar.

152. A. van den Berg, supra note 49 at 152.

153. Article V(2)(a).

154. Under the common law, a court may assume jurisdiction over persons who were within its territorial jurisdiction at the time of service of the writ. See J. Castel, supra note 68 at 190.

155. 105 S. Ct. 3346.

156. See also *Scherk* v. *Alberto-Culver Co.* 417 U.S. 505; *Impex* v. *Malteria* (French Supreme Court) [1971] JDI 62; *S.A. Agima* v. *Smith Industries Ltd.* (Court of First Instance of Brussels) (1983) 8 *Y. Comm. Arb.* 360.

157. See H. Holtzmann and J. Neuhaus, supra note 29, at 303.

158. See text accompanying note 145, supra.

159. See text accompanying note 89, supra.

160. Decision of 4 October 1985. Extracted in (1989) 14 *Y. Comm. Arb.* 618.

161. Cf. *Audi-NSU Auto Union A.g.* v. *S.A. Adelin, Petit & Cie* (1980) 5 Y. Comm. Arb. 257, where the supreme court of Belgium held that by virtue of the Belgian law of July 27, 1961, a dispute that had arisen out of the termination of an exclusive distributorship agreement between a Belgian distributor and a German car manufacturer could not be settled by arbitration in Zurich as provided in the arbitration clause contained in the distributorship agreement. See also, *S.A. Agima* v. *Smith Industries Ltd.*, supra note 156.

162. Under both the New York Convention and the Model Law, however, the forum where enforcement of an award is sought can refuse recognition and enforcement on the ground of subject matter nonarbitrability, irrespective of the fact that another forum had earlier enforced the arbitration agreement which resulted in the award.

163. J. Lew has criticized the approach as being "too restrictive considering that the place where enforcement is sought may be fortuitous." See J. Lew, "The Arbitration Act, 1975" (1975) 24 *Int'l & Comp. L.Q.* 875 at 876.

164. L. Quigley, "Accession by the United States to the United Nations Convention on the Recognition and Enforcement of Foreign Arbitral Awards." (1961) 70 *Yale L.J.* 1049 at 1070.

165. See comment by Mr. Broches during the negotiation of the Model Law, reported in H. Holtzmann and J. Neuhaus, supra note 29, at 974.

166. It constitutes a ground for other jurisdictions to refuse to recognize or enforce the award. Supra note 145.

167. See text accompanying note 145, above.

168. In the United States this trend culminated in the Supreme Court decision in *Mitsubishi Motors Corp.* v. *Soler Chrysler-Plymouth Inc.* 105 S. Ct. 3346, which held that antitrust disputes were arbitrable. See J. McClendon, "Subject-Matter Arbitrability in International Cases" (1986) *N.C.J. Int'l L. & Comm. Reg.* 81. Cf. W. Kuhn, "Arbitrability of Antitrust Disputes in the Federal Republic of Germany" (1987) 3 *Arb. Int'l* 226.

169. See P. Karrer and K. Arnold, *Switzerland's Private International Law Statute, 1987* (Deventer, The Netherlands: Kluwer Law and Taxation Publishers, 1989).

170. A. Samuel, supra note 14 at 131.

171. A parochial refusal by the courts of one country to enforce an international arbitration agreement would not only frustrate these purposes, but would invite unseemly and mutually destructive jockeying by the parties to secure tactical litigation advantages. . . . The dicey atmosphere of such legal no-man's-land would surely damage the fabric of international commerce and trade, and imperil the willingness and ability of businessmen to enter into international commercial agreements.

Scherk v. *Alberto-Culver Co.* 417 U.S. 506 at 516.

172. *Shearson/American Express Inc.* v. *McMahon* 107 S. Ct. 2332 at 2337. In the *Mitsubishi* case the U.S. Supreme Court stressed that there was "a strong presumption in favor of enforcement of freely negotiated contractual choice-of-forum provisions." Supra note 168 at 3356.

173. See *Corcoran* v. *Ardra Insurance Co Ltd* (1991) 6 Mealey's Int'l Arb. Rep. 12.

174. In the words of the U.S. Supreme Court, "We cannot have trade and commerce in world markets and international waters exclusively on our terms governed by our laws and resolved by our courts." *Scherk* v. *Alberto-Culver Co.*, supra note 171 at 519.

175. The court in *Mitsubishi Motors* noted that "concerns of international comity, respect for the capacity of foreign and transnational tribunals, and sensitivity to the need of the international commercial system for predictability in the resolution of disputes require that we enforce the parties agreement, even assuming a contrary result would be forthcoming in a domestic concern." Supra note 168 at 3355.

176. Supra note 171.
177. Supra note 168.
178. Supra note 79.
179. Supra note 81.
180. W. Burger, "Using Arbitration to Achieve Justice" (1986) 40 *Arb. J.* 4; L. Kanowitz, "Alternative Dispute Resolution and the Public Interest: The Arbitration Experience" (1987) 38 *Hastings L.J.* 239 at 255; J. Allison, "Arbitration of Private Antitrust Claims in International Trade: A Study in the Subordination of National Interests to the Demands of a World Market" (1986) 18 *N.Y.J. Int'l L. & Pol.* 361 at 367.

CHAPTER THREE

Law Governing Arbitration Proceedings

INTRODUCTION

The proposition that municipal courts are bound by the procedural laws of their legal system can not be gainsaid. Municipal courts, created and empowered by the national laws of their *situs*, conduct their proceedings in accordance with rules contained in these national laws. A judge sitting in a municipal court is thus constrained to apply the conflict and procedural rules of his or her *situs*. Even in situations where a dispute implicates matters of international business or involves parties who reside outside jurisdiction, a municipal judge remains obliged to utilize domestic conflict and procedural rules in resolving the dispute, although in some cases the law applicable to the substance of the dispute may be a foreign law.

When a party submits to the jurisdiction of a municipal court, the party concurrently acknowledges that the court will exercise its jurisdiction in conformity with the procedural rules of its *situs*. Indeed, it is never the case that a municipal court sitting in one country conducts its proceedings according to the procedural laws of another country. The only question that sometimes arises in this connection is where to draw the line between procedural and substantive law, because although a judge is constrained by national procedural law, the judge may find that a foreign substantive law is applicable to the merits of the dispute.

Procedural rules reflect the process by which courts exercise the powers conferred on them by their national law, and these rules embody the country's notions of how disputes should be resolved fairly and efficiently. Thus, the rules ensure the impartiality of judges, grant disputants adequate opportunity to prepare their cases, and safeguard the ability of the disputants to present their cases in a fair and equitable manner. Clearly, procedural rules vary among countries, for each country fashions its rules to conform as closely as possible to its notions of fair play, justice, and efficiency.

The position is different in an international commercial arbitration. Unlike judges, arbitrators in an international commercial arbitration do not necessarily derive their adjudicatory competence from the national law of their *situs*. As discussed in Chapter 1, an arbitration is essentially a product of the agreement of the parties involved, and the jurisdiction of international arbitrators is based on the arbitration agreement.[1]

No doubt, some international arbitral tribunals hold hearings in fixed locations just as national courts do, but the practical implications of this fact are different. In the latter case, the connection of the judge with the *situs* is vital because the powers and jurisdiction of the judges are a direct consequence of the national law of the *situs*. Barring the conferment of judicial power on courts by their national law, they would be devoid of any adjudicatory competence. The same proposition does not exactly hold true in the former case, because, at least as a practical matter, the competence of international commercial arbitrators is not exclusively derivable from the national law of its *situs*.[2] Indeed, the *situs* may have been chosen for reasons of convenience, and the arbitration, coupled with the underlying commercial transaction, may more implicate the laws of another jurisdiction than that in which, for reasons of convenience, the arbitration is held. Thus, the argument for the application of the national procedural law of the *situs* to an adjudicatory proceeding is more compelling in judicial proceedings than in private international arbitration.

Yet the *situs* of an arbitration is not entirely insignificant. Notwithstanding the fact that the jurisdiction of the arbitrators is founded on the agreement of the parties, the country where the arbitration is held may perceive itself as having a legitimate interest in ensuring that arbitrations conducted in its territory, which are after all productive of legal consequences, comply with the basic notions of justice and fair play.

The tension between conducting arbitrations in accordance with the will of the parties and the interest of the place of arbitration in regulating arbitrations conducted in its territory is the focus of the questions to be addressed in this chapter. To what extent should party autonomy be respected in conducting arbitration proceedings, and what role, if any, does the law of the place of arbitration (the *lex loci arbitri*) play in conducting arbitration proceedings?

These questions are particularly crucial because the extent of State regulation of arbitration and the degree of autonomy granted to the parties can either stress or mask the difference between domestic and international arbitrations. Unmitigated State control of international arbitration proceedings could also undermine the flexibility and privacy of the arbitral process—two of the major attractions of this type of arbitration.

The chapter commences with an examination of the difference between the law applicable to procedure and the law applicable to the merits of a dispute. It then examines the role of party autonomy in determining arbitral procedure, and the effect of the mandatory laws of the place of arbitration on the conduct of arbitration proceedings. It concludes by considering the extent to which an arbitration proceeding can be detached from the law of its *situs*.

DISTINCTION BETWEEN SUBSTANCE AND PROCEDURE

International commercial arbitrations potentially involve four levels of law: (1) the law applicable to the arbitration agreement,[3] which regulates the obligation of the parties to settle their dispute by arbitration; (2) the law applicable to the reference, which governs the individual reference to arbitration; (3) the law applicable to the arbitration proceedings, which regulates the conduct of the arbitration proceedings; and (4) the law applicable to the substance of the dispute, which determines the rights and obligations of the parties in relation to their substantive contract.[4]

It is conceivable that in an arbitration all four levels may be governed by the same law, although this is not always the case. As a result of the doctrine of the juridical autonomy of arbitration clauses,[5] the arbitration clause is considered separate from the contract in which it is contained, with the result that the law governing the arbitration clause could differ from the law governing the substantive contract. More relevant to the present discussion is the fact that the applicable substantive and procedural laws of an arbitration may derive from different legal systems. Whereas the law applicable to the substance of the dispute governs the substantive rights and obligations of the parties (including, for example, what amounts to performance and circumstances in which nonperformance is excused), the procedural law regulates the conduct of the arbitration and the avenues open for appeal against the award. Thus, the parties may, for example, select the law of France to govern their substantive agreement, while selecting England and English law as the *situs* and applicable procedural law, respectively. Here, the arbitrators would apply French law to the merits of the dispute, and conduct the proceedings in accordance with English law.

The distinction between substantive and procedural law is illustrated by several judicial decisions. In *Compagnie d'Armement Maritime* v. *Compagnie Tunisienne de navigation*,[6] a contract for the carriage of oil was concluded between French and Tunisian companies. The contract that was contained in standard charter-party forms, with additional provisions made by the parties, provided that any ensuing dispute should be resolved by arbitration in London. The arbitrators held that the contract of carriage was governed by French law, whereas the law applicable to the arbitration[7] was English law. On appeal to the House of Lords, the decision of the arbitrators was affirmed. In the law lords' view, although the arbitration was governed by English law, the substance of the dispute was governed by French law as the law most closely connected with the contract.[8]

In *James Miller Ltd.* v. *Whitworth*,[9] the contract between Scottish and English parties contained an arbitration clause, although it did not stipulate the place of arbitration, the law applicable to the arbitration, or the law applicable to the merits of the dispute. A Scottish arbitrator sitting in Scotland conducted an arbitration between the parties under Scottish law. The arbitrator, relying on Scottish law, rejected a request by the English party that he state his award in the form of a "case stated"[10] to the English High Court. On appeal to the House of Lords, it was argued that English law should determine whether or not the arbitrator should state his award to the English High Court. The court held that although the nature of the contract showed that English law was its proper law, the applicable law to the arbitration could differ from the proper law of the contract. In upholding the arbitrator's decision, the court held that the arbitration was governed by Scottish law as the law of the place of arbitration.[11]

French courts also acknowledged this distinction. In *Société O.C.P.C.* v. *la Société Diefenbacher*,[12] the contract between German and Belgian companies provided for arbitration under the rules of the International Chamber of Commerce. It also provided for Belgian law as the law governing the merits of the dispute. In a suit challenging the award in France, the Cour d'appel of Paris held that the choice of Belgian law as the law applicable to the merits of the dispute did not entail that Belgian law equally governed the arbitration. The court found that in the instant case several factors (the choice of ICC rules, an institution based in France; the choice of a French arbitrator, and the choice of France as the seat of arbitration) indicated that French law governed the arbitration proceedings.[13]

This distinction between substance and procedure is widely recognized as a cardinal element of international commercial arbitration.[14] The segregation of the law applicable to the substantive agreement from the law applicable to the arbitration illuminates the fact that the arbitral process is independent of the system of law that regulates the rights and obligations of the parties in relation to their substantive agreement. This segregation also implicitly acknowledges that the determination of each of the two applicable laws is influenced by different considerations. While the parties may prefer a particular national law to govern their arbitration proceedings, they may consider that law unsuitable in resolving disputes that may arise from their substantive agreement.

PARTY AUTONOMY

The principle of party autonomy enables the parties to an arbitration to design their arbitral proceedings to suit their particular needs. With regard to the law governing arbitral procedure, this principle grants the parties the power to select suitable procedural rules.

Parties to an international arbitration expect that by adopting private arbitration they would, at least to a considerable extent, escape the trappings and peculiarities of domestic judicial systems. They seek to resolve their dispute in an informal and flexible arena well suited for the resolution of disputes among business associates, and devoid of the acrimony and aggression often present in judicial proceedings. One way the informality of the arbitral process is guaranteed is for the parties themselves to select the rules of procedure. When parties decide to arbitrate under the auspices of the International Chamber of Commerce, for example, they scarcely expect the arbitration to be burdened by multifarious procedural rules of a national jurisdiction. They see in ICC arbitration a means of escaping from the procedural peculiarities of local courts, of adopting the more flexible ICC procedural rules, and granting to the arbitrators the powers to supplement the ICC rules.[15]

It has long been recognized that party autonomy is an essential element in the promotion of arbitration as a system of private dispute resolution. The Geneva Conventions were the first to acknowledge the role of party autonomy in arbitration, although they sought to dilute it with the "territorial principle."[16] Article 2 of the 1923 Geneva Protocol provides that the constitution of arbitral tribunals and arbitral procedure shall be governed by "the will of the parties *and* by the law of the country in whose territory the arbitration takes place." A similar provision is contained in Article 1 of the Geneva Convention of 1927, which provides, *inter alia*, that one of the prerequisites for recognition and enforcement of awards is that the arbitral tribunal is "constituted in the manner agreed upon by the parties *and* in conformity with the law governing the arbitral procedure." It was generally accepted that by the law governing the arbitral procedure the convention implied the law of the place where the arbitration was held.[17]

The Geneva Conventions, with their blend of party autonomy and the territorial principle, represented the consensus at the time, which insisted that an arbitration was intrinsically connected with the country where it was held and was subject to the control of the national laws of that country. However, judicial and juristic opinion interpreted the Geneva Conventions as placing primacy on party autonomy, with the national law of the place of arbitration playing a supplementary role. National law governed procedural rules only in the absence of an express agreement between the parties. This interpretation of the Geneva Conventions developed into a practice whereby the parties played a primary and active role in fashioning the nature and organization of arbitration, while the law of the place of arbitration played a subsidiary role.[18]

The New York Convention of 1958 embodied the trend toward the acceptance of party autonomy in the determination of arbitral procedure.

The convention provides that recognition and enforcement may be refused where the composition of the arbitral authority or the arbitral procedure does not accord with "the agreement of the parties, *or, failing such agreement*, was not in accordance with the law of the country where the arbitration took place."[19] The convention thus effectively cured the omission in the Geneva Conventions that did not state categorically that the law of the place of arbitration plays a subsidiary role to the law chosen by the parties. The New York Convention, however, applies only to the "recognition and enforcement of awards,"[20] and does not expressly apply at the arbitration stage. This is illustrated by the *Gotaverken case*,[21] where the Court of Appeal of Paris held that the convention is not applicable "where the action in court does not seek the enforcement of an award rendered in an international arbitration."[22] Nonetheless, the important role played by the convention in the enforcement of awards, which is the terminal stage of the arbitral process, underscores the fact that the ramifications of the convention stretch far beyond the enforcement stage. In light of the fact that arbitrators are under a duty to render enforceable awards, it behooves them to bear in mind—during the arbitration proceedings—that disregard of the parties' wishes regarding the choice of procedural law is grounds for setting aside their award. Therefore, the New York Convention invariably influences the conduct of hearings before arbitrators.[23]

The European Convention's provision on applicable procedural rules is similar to that of the New York Convention. It grants primacy to the procedural rules chosen by the parties.[24] However, the Model Law takes a slightly different course. Article 19 provides that, subject to the provisions of the Model Law, the parties are free to decide on the procedure to be followed by the arbitral tribunal. In the absence of such agreement, the tribunal is free, subject to the provisions of the Model Law, to "conduct the arbitration in such manner as it considers appropriate." The article, in addition to other provisions of the Model Law on arbitration procedure, provides a liberal framework that "suits the great variety of needs and circumstances of international cases, unimpeded by local peculiarities and traditional standards which may be found in the existing domestic law of the place [of arbitration]."[25] The subsidiary power granted to the tribunal under the Model Law is questioned by F. A. Mann; he queries how far the freedom goes and whether it extends to the administration of oaths and exclusion of a party from giving evidence, all of which may be in contravention of the law of the place of arbitration.[26] Admittedly, the language of Article 19, if read alone, appears to grant the tribunal a fairly broad discretion when exercising its subsidiary power. However, the scheme of the Model Law reveals that the subsidiary powers of the tribunal are subject to certain mandatory provisions and minimum standards of due process. In fact, Article 19 very clearly states that its provisions are subject to the entire provisions of the Model Law, which include, among other mandatory provisions, that "the parties shall be treated with equality and each party shall be given a full opportunity of presenting his [or her] case."[27] Thus, the autonomy of the parties to determine procedural rules and the subsidiary power of the tribunal to do the same are circumscribed by mandatory provisions.[28]

Mention should also be made of the Convention on the Settlement of Investment Disputes between States and Nationals of Other States. ICSID arbitrations are, to a considerable extent, freed from contact with the municipal judicial system.[29] Under Article 26 of the convention, consent to ICSID arbitration is, unless otherwise stated, exclusive of any other remedy. The practical implication of the article is that the ICSID machinery is self-contained. Once parties consent to an ICSID arbitration they must, unless a contrary intention is evident, content themselves with the remedies and procedures adopted by the convention. Absent a contrary intention, no domestic court of a Contracting State may intervene in the appointment of arbitrators, regulation of the tribunal's jurisdiction or in the setting aside of an ICSID award.[30] The convention contains an in-house procedure for the regulation of arbitral procedure:

> Any arbitration proceeding shall be conducted in accordance with the provisions of this Section and, except as the parties otherwise agree, in accordance with the [ICSID] Arbitration Rules in effect on the date on which the parties consented to arbitration. If any question of procedure arises which is not covered by this Section or the Arbitration Rules or any rules agreed by the parties, the tribunal shall decide the question.[31]

Thus, except for the mandatory provisions of the ICSID Convention contained in the section dealing with "powers and functions of the [arbitral] tribunal," the parties are free to modify the ICSID Arbitration Rules that otherwise supplement the convention provisions. Similar to the Model Law, the ICSID arbitral tribunal has a subsidiary power to determine procedural rules relating to matters not covered by either the Convention or the ICSID arbitration rules.

The above conventions, which have been ratified by a great majority of States, represent a consensus on the conduct and regulation of international arbitrations. Their provisions are thus a vital indicator of the generally accepted trends in international arbitration. Their recognition of the crucial role of party autonomy in the determination of procedural rules is therefore reflective of the broad acceptance of this principle, a trend that is equally embodied in institutional arbitration rules and national laws relating to international arbitration. Institutional arbitration rules typically accord party autonomy a predominant role in the conduct of arbitration proceedings. The Arbitral Rules of the Institute of the Stockholm Chamber of Commerce, for example, stipulate that "the arbitral tribunal shall determine the manner in which the proceedings will be conducted. In so doing, the arbitral tribunal shall comply with the stipulations of the parties in the arbitration agreement and these Rules and shall have regard to the wishes of the parties."[32] A similar provision is contained in the Rules of the London Court of International Arbitration. It states that applicable procedural rules are those chosen by the parties, in the absence of which the tribunal should ensure a "just, expeditious, economical and final determination of the dispute."[33] The ICC Rules equally leave it to the parties and, in the alternative, the arbitrators to determine the manner in which ICC arbitration proceedings should be conducted.[34]

Generally, national laws dealing with international arbitration grant the parties the right to determine the conduct of their arbitration, albeit stipulating minimum standards of fair hearing that the proceedings must meet.[35] Rule 58(2) of *Dicey and Morris*, stating the position in English law, provides that the "law governing arbitration proceedings is the law chosen by the parties, or, in the absence of agreement, the law of the country in which the arbitration is held."[36] English law recognizes that parties to an arbitration may opt for a procedural law different from that of the country where the arbitration is conducted:

> It is a fallacy to suppose that arbitral proceedings must take their authority from the local municipal law of the country within which they take place. . . . The curial law is normally, but not necessarily, the law of the place where the arbitration proceedings are held. . . . Whilst English law, like most foreign legal systems, may seek to exercise some measure of control over arbitration proceedings taking place in this country whatever the curial law, English law does not deny the possibility of a different curial law.[37]

The French Code of Civil Procedure[38] also allows the parties to select applicable procedural rules or to submit the arbitration to the procedural rules of an arbitration institution. It requires the parties to make their choice in their "arbitration agreement"; that is, they must decide on the procedural rules at the outset of the proceedings. In the absence of the parties' choice, the tribunal is empowered to establish rules of procedure "as may be necessary." Similarly, the Swiss Private International Law Act of 1989, which applies to international arbitrations, grants the parties the power to determine arbitral procedure, failing which the tribunal may exercise the power.[39] In either case the tribunal is required to "assure equal treatment of the parties and the rights of the parties to be heard in an adversarial procedure."[40] Even before the promulgation of the Act, Swiss courts respected the will of the parties in the determination of arbitral procedure. In *Muller* v. *Bergesen*,[41] for example, the parties concluded a charter party agreement, which contained an arbitration clause providing for arbitration in New York. It further provided that the arbitration would be subject to New York law and the award would be "final and binding on the parties." When B sought to enforce in Switzerland an award rendered against M, the latter contended that the award had not become binding within the meaning of Article V(1)(e) of the New York Convention.[42] It contended that the award could only become binding and enforceable under the New York Convention after confirmation of the award in the New York courts (an event that had not taken place at the time).[43] B, on the other hand, relied on the arbitration clause that made the arbitral award "final and binding on the parties." Both the Court of First Instance of Zurich and the Court of Appeal of the Canton of Zurich declared the award enforceable. On further appeal to the Swiss Federal Supreme Court, M's argument was rejected on the grounds, *inter alia*, that the parties' agreement by which an award would be final and binding precluded the application of the New York Civil Practice Law and Rules. The New York law, in the court's opinion, was only applicable in the absence of an agreement by the parties:

> The law applicable to the arbitration procedure can, within the framework of the autonomy of the parties, be freely chosen. . . . It follows . . . that the arbitration procedure is in the first instance governed by the agreement of the parties and, failing such agreement, subsidiarily governed by the law of the country where the arbitration takes place.[44]

Parties can express their choice of procedural rules in a variety of ways. They may set out their own detailed rules governing each aspect of the proceedings, or adopt the rules of an established arbitration institution. It should be noted that when parties consent to arbitration under the auspices of an arbitral institution, they are taken to incorporate into their agreement the rules of the institution.[45] The parties may also adopt the procedural rules prevailing in a particular national jurisdiction, or leave it to the discretion of the arbitral tribunal to decide how to conduct the proceedings.

By far the most common method is the adoption of the rules of an arbitral institution. These institutions are dedicated to the organization and management of arbitrations, and a large number of arbitrations are conducted under their auspices each year. Institutional rules thus embody up-to-date rules reflecting the experience of the institutions in the handling of arbitrations, and the rules are designed to contain the problems these institutions come across in their organization of arbitrations.

The preceding discussion has explored the extent of the parties' power to determine the procedural rules of law applicable to their arbitration. It identified a general trend allowing the parties to choose the law governing their arbitration. Party autonomy in the determination of arbitral procedure stems from the recognition that international arbitration is largely transnational in character and that the considerations that recommend strict regulation of domestic arbitration are not always present in international commercial disputes. Does this recognition of the special place of international arbitration necessitate granting the parties an unfettered right to conduct their proceedings as they see fit? Put differently, do the benefits of party autonomy preclude even minimal State supervision of international arbitration proceedings by the courts of the place of arbitration? To what extent should an arbitral tribunal respect the mandatory rules of the place of arbitration?

It seems obvious that a State's recognition of arbitration as a legitimate process of dispute resolution is based on the expectation that the process will be conducted in a manner compatible with basic notions of justice and fairness. At a minimum, a State that accords a high place to arbitration would expect that the arbitral process be chaired by impartial arbiters who give the parties equal and reasonable opportunity to present their cases. Thus, it has always been recognized that party autonomy in the conduct of arbitral proceedings is limited by the requirement of fair hearing. This fact was acknowledged by the UNCITRAL Secretariat during the drafting stages of the Model Law: "it will be one of the more delicate and complex problems of the preparation of a model law to strike a balance between the interests of the parties to freely determine the procedure to be followed and the interest of the legal system expected to give recognition and effect thereto."[46]

The term "mandatory rules" is used in this chapter to denote those rules or provisions from which the parties to an arbitration may not derogate. National laws governing the conduct of domestic and international arbitrations usually contain minimum standards of fair hearing, which are mandatory in all arbitration proceedings. The scope of these mandatory rules varies among countries,[47] and it is not always easy to determine those provisions that are mandatory on arbitrating parties. The position is clear where the legislation delimits the provisions with which parties must comply. In the absence of such a clear designation of mandatory provisions, it would seem that only those provisions that are so basic to the concept of justice as to constitute part of the public policy of every State should be regarded as mandatory.[48]

Mandatory rules, by stipulating provisions with which arbitrating parties must conform, limit the scope of party autonomy in the determination of arbitral procedure. The parties are said to be free to determine arbitral procedure provided they conform with the mandatory rules of the place of arbitration.

Adherents of the jurisdictional theory of arbitration[49] maintain that an arbitration is invalid if it fails to conform with the mandatory laws of the seat of arbitration. This view is reflected in the Model Law under which a court may set aside an award if the award is "in conflict with the public policy of [the forum]."[50] The Model Law contemplates that an award can only be set aside in the country where it was made.[51] Thus, under the Model Law an award rendered in contravention of the mandatory laws of the place of arbitration risks being set aside by the courts of that jurisdiction, an outcome that may significantly impair the international enforceability of the award.[52]

The limits that mandatory rules place on party autonomy are acknowledged in institutional arbitrations. A former secretary-general of the ICC confirmed that the application of ICC rules are subject to "mandatory provisions."[53] In *ICC case 5029*[54] the tribunal stated that the "prevailing interpretation of the Rules of the ICC nowadays is also that the mandatory provisions of the arbitration law of the place of arbitration governs the arbitration."[55] Similarly, Article 1(2) of the UNCITRAL Arbitration Rules stipulates that the "Rules shall govern except that where any of these Rules is in conflict with a provision of the law applicable to the arbitration from which the parties cannot derogate, that provision shall prevail."

However, advocates of delocalized arbitration submit that it is possible to free arbitrations from the mandatory rules of the place of arbitration. They make exception for those mandatory rules that embody accepted international standards. This view is now considered.

DELOCALIZATION OF ARBITRATION

Some commentators suggest that the obligatory force of an award does not necessarily derive from the law of the place of arbitration, and that an arbitration may be conducted independent of the law of the place of arbitration.[56] One implication of this view is that an arbitration proceeding carried out in contravention of the laws of the place of arbitration (including those that are mandatory) may remain enforceable in jurisdictions other than the *situs*. This view was initially voiced by the Asian-African Legal Consultative Committee in its invitation to the United Nations Commission on International Trade Law to consider the possibility of preparing a protocol to be annexed to the New York Convention. This annex was supposed to clarify, among other things, that where parties adopt rules for the conduct of their arbitration, whether an *ad hoc* or institutional arbitration, the arbitration proceedings should be conducted in accordance with those rules "notwithstanding provisions to the contrary in municipal laws and the award rendered should be recognized and enforced by all Contracting States."[57]

Those who subscribe to the jurisdictional theory of arbitration strenuously reject the "heresy"[58] that an arbitration can be completely unbound from the law of the place of arbitration. It is appropriate to closely examine the views of the jurisdictionalists and the contractualists[59] because these contending theories lie at the heart of the debate concerning the role the law of the place of arbitration should play in regulating international arbitration proceedings. These opposing views are analyzed under separate heads, emphasis being placed on their rationale and their implications for the conduct of arbitrations. The enforceability of awards that are the product of unbound (that is, denationalized) arbitrations is also considered.

The Jurisdictional Theory

The jurisdictional theory of arbitration rests on two suppositions: that all arbitrations are ultimately governed by a national law and that the national law of the place of arbitration is the relevant law. An arbitration can only be productive of legal rights and obligations if a particular legal system ascribes to it the power to do so. Barring the ascription of this power, the arbitration process would be devoid of any legal effect whatsoever. Against this background, the protagonists of the jurisdictional theory contend that the legitimacy of an arbitration flows from the laws of the seat of arbitration. Another strand of the theory is that a State facilitates the enforcement of awards by conferring legal effect to arbitrations conducted in its territory; consequently the State should "provide a mechanism for challenging the award's procedural deficiencies."[60]

The foremost advocate of this theory was F. A. Mann, who contended that a State has the right to supervise and regulate every activity occurring within its territory. He believed that the term "international arbitration" is a misnomer because "every system of private international law is a system of national law, every arbitration is a national arbitration, that is to say, subject to a specific system of national law."[61] In his view, the legislative and judicial authorities of the seat of arbitration control the process of arbitration because the legal effect of the process is a product of the sanction given to it by the seat of arbitration.[62] The intentions of the parties as reflected in their agreement can only be binding to the extent that they are sanctioned by the laws of the place where the arbitration is conducted:

> Is not every activity occurring on the territory of a State necessarily subject to its jurisdiction? Is it not for such State to say whether and in what manner arbitrators are assimilated to judges and, like them, subject to the law? Various States may give various answers to the question, but that each of them has the right to, and does, answer it according to its own discretion cannot be doubted.[63]

The practical implications of this strand of the theory is that each State has the unfettered power to regulate all arbitrations conducted in its territory, and any negative pronouncement by the courts of the seat of arbitration on the validity of an arbitration has an undisputed global effect. On this view, international arbitrations would be subject to all provisions relating to arbitration in the same way domestic arbitrations are. International arbitrations would be subject to domestic peculiarities of the arbitration laws of the seat of arbitration, a position that may yield strange results in some situations.[64] For example, a State could set a time limit for the completion of arbitrations or legislate some other rules whose rationales are not immediately obvious to a foreign party; if the jurisdictional theory holds true, every arbitration conducted in that State would be subject to these rules.

To circumvent this possibility, a less-stringent version of the theory, while professing the preeminence of the law of the seat of arbitration, urges that its control should be "limited to ensuring respect for traditional standards of fairness, the limits of the arbitral mission and the right of third parties."[65]

Some judicial decisions and arbitral awards lend support to the jurisdictional theory. In an apparent recognition of the central role of the place of arbitration, the U.S. Supreme Court said that "an agreement to arbitrate before a specified tribunal is, in effect, a specialized kind of forum selection clause that posits not only the *situs* of the suit but also the procedure to be used in resolving the dispute."[66]

The sole arbitrator in the *Sapphire Arbitration*[67] entertained no doubt that the *lex loci arbitri* governed arbitration procedure. In the *BP Arbitration*[68] the sole arbitrator was of the view that the effectiveness of an award lacking nationality, in the sense that its law of arbitration is other than national law, is "smaller than that of an award founded on the procedural law of a specific legal system and partaking of its nationality."[69] He considered it "convenient and constructive" to attach the arbitration to "a developed legal system."[70]

Is the theory correct in assuming that the legal effect of an arbitration is the product of the law of the seat of arbitration? It is hardly true, as Mann would have us believe, that the legal validity of all activities occurring in a State invariably depends on the laws of *that* particular State. Under English conflict rules, for example, the formal validity of a contract could be established not only by the law of the place where it was contracted (the *lex loci contractus*), but also by its proper law (which may differ from the *lex loci contractus*). Thus, a contract that is formally invalid under the law of the place where it was contracted could be validated by its proper law.[71] This demonstrates that the legal effect of an activity is not immutably dependent on the law of the place where the activity occurred. Every State is free to determine for itself the nature of activities that would have legal effect *in its territory*. A State could therefore confer legal effect on an act occurring in another State despite the fact that the latter State denies any legal effect to that act. No doubt, in some cases a State may be constrained to recognize only certain forms of activities, as under the New York Convention, but the fact remains that this limitation arises solely as a result of its consent.[72]

The jurisdictional theory equates international with domestic arbitrations, but there is at least one fundamental difference between the two. In domestic arbitrations the parties are usually from the country where the arbitration is held and the consequences of the arbitration would impact, in most cases, on that country. The fact that cases which arise in domestic arbitrations commonly implicate the policy interests of the seat of arbitration, coupled with the fact that the parties are typically from that country, make it imperative for the country involved to supervise the arbitration. In international arbitrations, however, the parties are in many cases from different countries and the disputes may not necessarily implicate the policy interests of the seat of arbitration, which may have been chosen for reasons of convenience. It follows that the reasons which justify State intervention in domestic arbitrations are not always present in the context of international arbitrations.

The theory seeks to attribute global effect to pronouncements made by the courts of the place of arbitration on the validity of arbitrations conducted in their jurisdiction. This reasoning ignores the fact that other States may recognize the legality and the right-producing effect of an arbitration regardless of the position taken by the country where the arbitration is held. Thus, the validity of an international arbitration may depend not so much on its conferment by the seat of arbitration as on the preparedness of other countries to recognize the arbitration as being productive of legal consequences.

The jurisdictional theory is, however, supported by a practical consideration. It seeks to ensure that the integrity of the arbitral process is protected by the courts of a particular country. The courts of the place of arbitration would supervise the conduct of the arbitration, with a view to ensuring that the proceedings are in conformity with requirements of justice and fairness. If the courts of the seat of arbitration do not play this role, the alternative would be for the losing party to challenge the validity of the award in jurisdictions where its enforcement is sought, a prospect that may be burdensome on that party. Also, the party in whose favor the award is made has the unfair opportunity to forum-shop for jurisdictions with less exacting standards for the recognition of awards. Thus, there is the need for a single jurisdiction to ensure "the administration of justice and thus avoid the risk of arbitrariness";[73] a role the courts of the seat of arbitration are best suited to play. Nonetheless, this practical consideration, while illustrating the need for the validity of an award to be definitively determined in one jurisdiction, does not yield a presumption that arbitrations are invariably governed by the law of the place of arbitration.

The Delocalization Theory

The view that arbitrations should be subjected to the supervisory control of national laws is not shared by those who advocate the delocalization of arbitration. The party autonomy principle, according to this view, enables the parties to tailor the arbitral process to their needs, subject to fundamental public policy.[74] Although advocates of the theory argue that arbitrations may be detached from the laws of the seat of arbitration, they concede that the courts of the seat of arbitration are entitled to ensure that such arbitrations conform to transnational minimum standards of justice. J. Paulsson, one of the better known advocates of the theory, contends that those who favor delocalization do not necessarily insist on a hands-off attitude, but argue that judges of the place of arbitration should ensure that arbitration conform with "transnational minimum standards, such as those embodied in international conventions."[75]

The essence of the delocalization theory is that if transnational minimum standards are complied with, an arbitration proceeding may be conducted independent of the law of the place of arbitration, and that the "obligatory force of an arbitral award need not necessarily be derived from the law of the place where the award happened to be rendered."[76] Delocalization, therefore, has two facets—delocalization of the arbitration proceedings and delocalization of the award. While the former implies excluding the functioning of the arbitral tribunal from the control of domestic laws, the latter entails the removal, or at least the attenuation, of the power of courts of the place of arbitration to make a globally effective declaration on the award's nullity.[77] The two facets are, however, intertwined because they share the characteristic of attempting to free the arbitration from the impact of the domestic arbitration practice of the place of arbitration.

Delocalization, therefore, attempts to free international arbitration from the peculiarities in the arbitration laws of the seat of arbitration in that the control and supervision of local courts, if any, would be limited to upholding international standards.[78] The objective is to liberate international arbitration from the domestically generated mandatory rules of the seat of arbitration that are not in harmony with the spirit of international arbitration conventions and arbitral practice.

A delocalized arbitration is then one that is conducted independent of the *lex loci arbitri*, but subject only to those international minimum standards that are engrafted into the *lex loci arbitri*. A delocalized award would be the end result of a delocalized arbitration.

Some commentators, however, suggest that delocalized arbitrations are still subject to the "procedural public policy of the place of arbitration," even if the parties "expressly exclude it."[79] It is submitted that if an arbitration is subject to those mandatory provisions of the place of arbitration that are not representative of international minimum standards, the arbitration cannot, strictly speaking, be regarded as delocalized because the proceedings remain subject to domestically generated mandatory provisions.[80] The singular factor that distinguishes a delocalized arbitration from other types of arbitrations is its independence from the mandatory provisions of the place of arbitration (with the exception of those that embody international standards). Therefore an arbitration can hardly be considered delocalized if it is subjected to the mandatory provisions of the place of arbitration.

The origins of the delocalization theory are rooted in the sovereign immunity doctrine.[81] It was believed that the sovereign immunity doctrine, under which States are exempted from the jurisdiction of courts in foreign States, precluded arbitrators from applying national arbitration laws to arbitration proceedings involving State parties. In the *Aramco Arbitration*,[82] which involved Saudi Arabia and an American company (the Saudi Arabian Maritime Tanker Ltd.), the arbitrator refused to apply the law of the place of arbitration to the proceedings:

> The jurisdictional immunity of States . . . excludes the possibility, for the judicial authorities of the country of the seat, of exercising the right of supervision and interference in all the arbitral proceedings which they have in certain cases. Considering the jurisdictional immunity of foreign States, recognized by international law in a spirit of respect for the essential dignity of sovereign power, the tribunal is unable to hold that arbitration proceedings to which a sovereign State is a party would be subject to the law of another State. Any interference by the latter State would constitute an infringement of the prerogatives of the State which is a party to the arbitration.[83]

This reasoning was adopted in the *Texaco Arbitration*.[84] In a dispute between Libya, the Texas Overseas Petroleum Company, and the California Asiatic Oil Company, the sole arbitrator, sitting in Geneva, stated that there were potentially two solutions to the question of the law governing arbitration: submitting the arbitration to a given national law, or holding the arbitration to be directly governed by international law. In his view, the parties' provision for the appointment of the sole arbitrator by the president of the International Court of Justice indicated that the "parties intended that any arbitration between them should be governed by international law."[85] This intention of the parties strengthened the "presumption" in favor of the application of international law to the conduct of the proceedings. Although he suspected that awards governed by national law may be more easily enforced than those governed by international law, he stated that "this is a consideration relating to enforcement which is not within the jurisdiction of the Arbitrator."[86]

The reasoning in the above awards is problematic in two respects. First, the contemporary view is that a State waives its sovereign immunity from jurisdiction by consenting to arbitration.[87] A State that consents to arbitration is taken to submit to the jurisdiction of those national courts whose intervention might be necessary for the smooth conduct of the arbitration.[88] The sovereignty argument therefore does not justify the delocalization of arbitrations involving State parties. Second, the internationalization of the arbitration procedure in the above instances poses some practical problems because the parties did not adopt any institutional arbitration rules to govern the arbitration and there are hardly any rules in the international arena that apply to international arbitrations on a general basis.[89] The rules of procedure of the International Court of Justice, which bears the closest resemblance to anything that may be called international law of procedure, is far too formal for the resolution of *ad hoc* arbitrations and it does not cover essential questions such as the appointment and replacement of arbitrators. The UNCITRAL rules, which, as a product of an agency of the United Nations, best approximate an international body of rules, apply only where the parties to an arbitration agree in writing to adopt them.[90] Institutional arbitration rules such as those of ICSID and ICC are institution-specific and do not qualify as a body of customary law of procedure.[91]

The modern protagonists of delocalized arbitration, moving away from its historical origins, now profess that delocalization is available not only in state contract arbitrations but in all international arbitrations. Delocalization is now understood not in terms of subjecting certain arbitrations to international law, but in terms of liberating arbitration proceedings from those laws of the place of arbitration that do not embody transnational standards.

The difficulty with delocalization is that it forecloses the possibility of the national law of the place of arbitration filling the gaps in the procedural law chosen by the parties, and limits the role that the national courts system of the place of arbitration may play in supervising the arbitral process. It restricts the assistance and supervision of national courts to cases where the courts act in accordance with transnational minimum standards. This restriction could potentially affect the effectiveness of the arbitration process because arbitrators lack "sovereign powers equivalent to those of the State with which to enforce their awards; nor do they have adequate powers to ensure the proper conduct of the arbitration proceedings."[92] National court systems usually act as a support mechanism for the conduct of arbitrations, a fact that is recognized by the Model Law, which calls upon each State adopting the Model Law to entrust a particular "court" with the performance of certain functions of arbitration assistance and supervision. These functions relate to the appointment of arbitrators (Art. 11), decisions with respect to the termination of an arbitrator's mandate (Arts. 13 and 14), control of the arbitral tribunal's jurisdiction (Art. 16), and the setting aside of awards (Art. 34).

However, the limitation of judicial assistance to cases where it conforms to transnational minimum standards should not adversely affect the effectiveness of the arbitral process because these standards contain ample grounds on which judicial assistance to arbitration may be based. These standards reflect a broad consensus of the international community on the conduct and regulation of international arbitration and they embody guidelines according to which judicial assistance should be rendered.

Some countries are receptive to the idea of freeing international arbitrations from control of the national arbitration laws of the place of arbitration. In Belgium, for example, Article 1717 of the *Code Judiciare* excludes some international arbitrations conducted in Belgium from the supervisory control of Belgian courts:

> The court of Belgium may be seized of a request for annulment only if at least one of the parties to the dispute decided by the arbitral award is either a physical person having Belgian nationality or residence, or a legal entity created in Belgium or having a branch or any other establishment in Belgium.

The implication of this provision is that Belgian courts lack jurisdiction to review an international arbitration award made in Belgium, thereby leaving the losing party the singular option of challenging the award in the country or countries where recognition and enforcement is sought.

French judicial practice supports the elimination of most national restrictions on the international arbitration process.[93] Its arbitration law allows the parties the freedom to design their own arbitral procedure.[94] In *General National Maritime Transport Company (GMTC)* v. *Gotaverken*[95] the parties held an ICC arbitration in Paris. Their arbitration agreement provided that the proceeding be held in accordance with the ICC arbitration rules in force at the time of the arbitration.[96] The tribunal ruled in favor of Gotaverken and GMTC petitioned the Cour d'appel to set aside the award on the grounds of nullity, grounds that, at the time, were only available in connection with French awards. The court, therefore, had to decide whether or not the award was a French award, the arbitration proceeding having been held in France. Gotaverken contended that the arbitration was international and the award could therefore not be considered an award governed by French Arbitration Law.[97] It submitted that given the fact that neither of the parties had any connection with France, and the choice of Paris was made for reasons of convenience and neutrality, the choice of Paris as the place of arbitration could not be a decisive element for the application of French arbitration law.[98] GMTC replied that French arbitration law governed the arbitration. The Cour d'appel held that the award was not a French award because neither the parties nor the underlying contract had any connection with France, and the award was rendered in accordance with "a procedure other than that of French Law and which is not connected in whatever manner with the French legal system."[99] In light of the ICC rules adopted by the parties, the court found that "the place of arbitration, which is chosen only for the purposes of assuring its neutrality, is of no importance and cannot be considered as an expression of the implicit will of the parties to submit themselves to French procedural law, not even subsidiarily."[100]

Speaking four years later, the French Cour d'appel reiterated its position that an award made according to a procedure that is not governed by French procedural law is not a French award.[101] These decisions would seem to support the view that arbitrations are not imperatively governed by the law of the seat of arbitration, and that the parties are free to immunize their arbitration from the *lex loci arbitri*. The French Arbitration Decree of May 14, 1988,[102] established a separate procedure for the challenge of international arbitration awards[103] rendered in France.[104] The grounds for challenging awards were carefully limited,[105] thereby enabling local courts to "ensure observance of minimum standards for international enforceability of an award without applying additional criteria that may be appropriate only to domestic arbitration."[106]

The practice of delocalization is well demonstrated in the conduct of ICSID arbitrations. Under the ICSID regime, consent to arbitration excludes recourse to the court system. ICSID proceedings are largely unconnected with the national legal system of the place of arbitration. A local court in a country that has ratified the ICSID Convention is obliged to decline jurisdiction if a dispute is brought to it in contravention of an ICSID arbitration clause. This flows from Article 26 of the convention, which provides that "Consent of the parties to arbitration under this Convention shall, unless otherwise stated, be deemed consent to such arbitration to the exclusion of any other remedy."

This provision precludes local courts in ratifying States from assuming jurisdiction over a dispute subject to an ICSID clause, but does not affect the jurisdiction of such courts to recognize, enforce, and levy execution in relation to an ICSID arbitration award. The practical implication of the article is that the ICSID machinery is self-contained. Once parties consent to an ICSID arbitration they must, unless a contrary intention is evident, content themselves with the remedies and procedures adopted under the Convention. Unless the parties express a contrary intention, local courts of contracting States may not intervene in relation to the appointment of arbitrators, regulation of the tribunal's jurisdiction, or in setting aside an ICSID award. The convention contains in-house procedures for the appointment of arbitrators (Arts. 37–40), regulation of the tribunals' jurisdiction (Arts. 36 and 41), and revision and annulment of awards (Arts. 51 and 52). The exclusive nature of ICSID arbitrations ensures that these arbitrations are conducted independent of the laws of the place of arbitration, unless the parties make any indication to the contrary.

One country that has expressed a certain coolness to the idea of delocalized arbitration is Britain. Kerr L.J. in *Helliniki Techniki*[107] summarized the English position when he noted: "Despite suggestions to the contrary by some learned writers under other systems, our jurisprudence does not recognize the concept of arbitral procedure floating in the transnational firmament, unconnected with any municipal legal system."[108]

Given the controversy surrounding the delocalization of arbitration proceedings, it is useful to examine whether delocalized awards are enforceable in law.

Applicability of the New York Convention to Delocalized Arbitration

The enforceability of an award is the ultimate objective of a claimant in an arbitration. If an award is unenforceable, the time and expense expended on the arbitration are wasted. Consequently, if delocalized awards are unenforceable, delocalization would remain little more than a theoretical attraction to academics.

The recognition and enforcement of international awards are governed by international conventions on arbitration. The first of these conventions, the Geneva Convention of 1927, required that before recognition and enforcement of an award could be granted, it was necessary that "the award has been made by the Arbitral Tribunal provided for in the submission to arbitration or constituted in the manner agreed upon by the parties *and* in conformity with the law governing the arbitration."[109] The provision was interpreted as granting the parties an active role in fashioning their arbitral procedure.[110] Some analysts, however, maintained that the provision mandated compliance with the mandatory provision of the seat of arbitration,[111] a view that would make delocalized awards unenforceable under the convention. This writer is not aware of any judicial decision on the effect of the convention with respect to the enforcement of delocalized awards.

The Geneva Convention has been superseded by the New York Convention, which is at present the reference point for the recognition and enforcement of awards.[112] It unifies the law relating to the enforcement of awards and enhances the procedure for enforcement. The convention provides a liberal framework for the enforcement of international commercial awards and limits the grounds on which the recognition and enforcement of such awards could be denied. Its regime represents a considerable improvement on the Geneva Convention.[113]

One of the leading experts on the New York Convention, A. van den Berg, has suggested that delocalized awards are outside the field of application of the New York Convention because delocalization is against the "system and text" of the convention, runs contrary to the Convention's presumption that an award is governed by national law, and is inconsistent with the Convention's legislative history.[114] Let us examine each of these reasons in turn, for they constitute the grounds that are often canvased as making delocalized awards unenforceable under the New York Convention.

According to van den Berg, the system and text of the convention argue against its application to delocalized arbitrations because the convention governs "the recognition and enforcement of arbitral awards made in the territory" of a State other than that in which enforcement is sought.[115] In his view, delocalized awards do not come within the ambit of the convention because advocates of delocalization hold that delocalized awards are not made in any particular country. This view is, however, erroneous. First, it is incorrect that the protagonists of delocalization assert that delocalized awards are not made in any particular country. On the contrary, they submit that a delocalized award is one that is independent of the law of the country where it was made.[116] Second, there is nothing in the provision of the convention to suggest anything other than a requirement that an award should be rendered in a jurisdiction different from that in which enforcement is sought. It would be a considerable strain on the language of the provision to read into it a precondition that the award be made according to the national arbitration law of the place of arbitration or indeed any other national law.[117] This argument also applies to the reciprocity provision under which contracting States may limit their application of the convention to "the recognition and enforcement of awards made in the territory" of another Contracting State.[118] It is submitted that in either case the convention should be read as requiring a geographical connection between the award and a particular jurisdiction, without demanding that such awards be governed by the national law of that jurisdiction. Third, if a recent decision of the House of Lords is accepted,[119] an award need not necessarily be "made" at the seat of arbitration. According to the House of Lords, the place of signature, not the seat of arbitration, is the relevant test in determining where an award is made. If this interpretation is accepted, a delocalized award would be deemed to be "made" in the place of signature. Thus, if the country where the award was signed is a party to the New York Convention, the requirement of Article I(3) would have been met.[120]

Relying on two of the convention's provisions,[121] van den Berg further contends that the Convention rests on the presumption that arbitrations are governed by national law.[122] This interpretation is flawed. According to Article VI(a), the law of the place where the award was made applies only subsidiarily in determining the validity of arbitration agreements. It accords undisputed primacy to the will of the parties and invites the application of national law solely in cases where the parties fail to indicate their choice. It is difficult to see how the subsidiary role granted to national law by this provision could be regarded as indicative of the preeminence of national law. Additionally, van den Berg's contention that the convention rests upon the presumption that arbitrations are governed by national law does not follow inexorably from the provisions of Article V(1)(e). The article provides that recognition and enforcement "*may* be refused" where the award has been set aside in the place where it is made.[123] The language of the section ("may be refused") makes it clear that its provisions are not mandatory in that the court where enforcement is sought evidently has a discretion whether or not to allow recognition in such situations.[124] Furthermore, the provision of Article V(1)(e) should be read in conjunction with Article VI. Article VI specifies that the convention provisions "shall not . . . deprive any interested party of any right he may have to avail himself of an arbitral award in the manner and to the extent" allowed in the country where enforcement is sought. This provision was interpreted by the French Cour de Cassation in *Pabalk Ticaret* v. *Norsolor* as implying that "a judge cannot refuse enforcement when his own national legal system permits it," regardless of the fact that the award has been set aside in the place where it was made.[125] The court considered it the "duty" of the enforcing court to determine whether the laws of its jurisdiction allowed enforcement in such instances.[126] Following this analysis, a cumulative reading of Articles V(1)(e) and VI reveals that the enforcement jurisdiction has a discretion to recognize and enforce awards annulled in the place where they were made, and that an annulled award can benefit from more favorable recognition laws in the enforcing jurisdiction. If any deduction could be made from these provisions, it is certainly not that made by van den Berg; on the contrary, the provisions yield the conclusion that an enforcing jurisdiction is free to adopt a liberal regime that recognizes and enforces delocalized awards.

Finally, van den Berg asserts that the legislative history of the convention indicates that it was not meant to apply to delocalized awards.[127] However, legislative history is just one of the tools in interpreting a convention.[128] Moreover, as van den Berg himself admits, the debates at the New York Conference that resulted in the New York Convention did not clearly reject delocalization.[129]

It is submitted that there is nothing in the provisions of the New York Convention that obligates contracting States to deny recognition and enforcement to delocalized awards. Nonetheless, an enforcing court may find it contrary to the public policy of its forum to enforce delocalized awards. It could then rely on the public policy exception[130] as grounds for refusal to enforce such awards. Other than this omnibus public policy ground, there appears no other obvious ground for the denial of recognition and enforcement of delocalized awards under the New York Convention.[131]

Although English courts remain unreceptive to the notion of delocalized arbitrations,[132] other jurisdictions acknowledge the enforceability of delocalized awards.[133] In *Gould* v. *Iran*[134] the U.S. District Court acknowledged the enforceability of delocalized awards under the convention. The case involved proceedings to enforce an award rendered by the Iran-U.S. Claims Tribunal.[135] D argued that the award did not comply with the New York Convention's supposed requirement that the proceeding be subject to a national arbitration law. Insisting that the tribunal's awards are delocalized, D stated that recognition of such awards would render the provisions of Article V(1)(e) of the New York Convention devoid of any practical meaning. The District Court rejected the argument. In upholding the lower court's decision, the U.S. Court of Appeals held that "an award need not be made 'under a national law' for a court to entertain jurisdiction over its enforcement pursuant to the Convention."[136] In the court's view, if the parties decide to delocalize their arbitration, the defenses under Article V(1)(e) would not be available to the losing party.[137] Responding to the argument that delocalization leaves little mechanism for ensuring the fairness of arbitrations, the court noted that

> allowing the parties to untether themselves from pre-existing "national law" still leaves certain safeguards in place to guard against enforcement of an otherwise unfair award. The Convention contains several due process protections requiring notice and the opportunity to be heard as well as a defense to guard against the enforceability of awards contrary to public policy.[138]

In summary, the New York Convention does not obligate contracting parties to deny recognition and enforcement to delocalized awards, although the public policy exception may potentially be invoked against such an award in those enforcing jurisdictions that reject delocalization. Further, the courts of the seat of arbitration may rely on the public policy exception under the Model Law to set aside a delocalized award, and this may impair the international enforceability of such an award under the New York Convention. Thus, to guarantee the smooth enforcement of their awards, arbitrators should as a practical matter endeavor to respect the mandatory rules of the seat of arbitration.

CONCLUSION

The nature of the debate about the possibility of delocalizing arbitration procedure and awards often conceals the real concerns that underlie the debate. The cardinal issue is not whether or not arbitrations are jurisdictional or contractual in nature, but to what extent and according to what standards international arbitrations should be regulated and administered. As we have seen, most legal systems accord parties considerable freedom in determining arbitral procedure, while reserving the right to ensure the fairness and integrity of the process. The controversy regarding the independence of arbitration from national law actually addresses concerns regarding the standards by which the fairness and integrity of the process should be governed: domestic or international standards?

To be sure, there is much to be said for setting an international standard by which international arbitrations should be superintended, as opposed to leaving each State to enact its own individual standard, which may run contrary to the aspirations of foreign arbitrating parties. International conventions on arbitration are designed to provide an effective international regime for the conduct of arbitrations. These conventions are aimed at conflating and modernizing national arbitration practices relating to international arbitration, thus obviating the need for States to establish their own domestically influenced regimes. The most notable international convention on arbitration, the New York Convention, governs only the recognition and enforcement stage of the arbitral process, and does not extend to the arbitration stage. Nevertheless, it lays down minimum standards that must be met before an award can be enforced.[139] These prerequisites for enforcement provide an indirect guideline for the conduct of arbitrations since only awards that conform to them can be enforced under the convention.

However, the limited scope of the convention prevented it from stipulating detailed provisions for the conduct of arbitration proceedings. It is in this area that most States have introduced domestic standards to cover the lacunae left by the convention. Some of these domestic standards embody inflexible rules that are not amenable to the needs of international commerce, and that may, where they are mandatory, frustrate the objectives of the parties.[140] To ameliorate this problem, the Model Law was designed to establish a uniform legal framework for the fair and efficient conduct of arbitration proceedings. Elaborated by arbitration experts and representatives from various countries and international agencies, the Model Law seeks to refurbish and unify national laws dealing with international commercial arbitration. "In view of the desirability of uniformity of the law of arbitral procedures and the specific needs of international commercial arbitration," the United Nations General Assembly recommended member States to adopt the Model Law.[141] If well received by member States, it would unify national laws on international arbitration, thereby precluding international arbitrations from being subject to the domestic peculiarities of the place of arbitration.

Thus, the present trend inclines toward the harmonization of international arbitral practices through the provision of internationally accepted standards for the conduct, regulation, and enforcement of arbitration proceedings and awards. Significantly, both the New York Convention and the Model Law, which are the two major international projects on arbitration, recognize the doctrine of party autonomy and provide liberal arbitration regimes that respect the will of the parties, while at the same time demanding that arbitrations conform with the international minimum standards they embody. As this trend toward the harmonization of arbitration practice continues, there would be little need for delocalization.

NOTES

1. This is why an award may be set aside or recognition denied if the arbitrators exceed the powers granted them by the parties. See Article 52(1)(b) of the Washington Convention, Articles 34(2)(a)(iii) and 36(1)(a)(iii) of the Model Law, and Article V(1)(c) of the New York Convention. For a somewhat extreme version of the basis of arbitral authority, see the preliminary award in *ICC Case 2321 of 1974*, where the arbitrator said:

> I myself do not see the need for referring to any particular set of national law rules or the court practice of any particular country. . . .

As arbitrator, I am myself no representative organ of any State. My authority as arbitrator rests upon an agreement between the parties to the dispute and by my activities I do not, as State judges . . . engage the responsibility of [a State]. Furthermore, the courts and other authorities of [a State] can in no way interfere with my activities as arbitrator, neither direct me to do anything which I think I should not do nor direct me to abstain from doing anything which I think I should do.

[1976] *Y. Comm. Arb.* 133 at 134.

2. See A. von Mehren, "Arbitration between States and Foreign Enterprises: The Significance of the Institute of International Law's Santiago de Compostela Resolution" (1990) 5 *ICSID Review* 54 at 57; P. Fouchard, *L'arbitrage Commercial International* (Paris: Dalloz, 1965) at 356–357.

3. This has been discussed in Chapter 2.

4. See Kerr L.J. in *Naviera Amazonica Peruana S.A.* v. *Compania Internacional del Peru* [1988] 1 Lloyd's L.R. 116 at 119, and Lord Mustill in *Channel Tunnel Group Ltd* v. *Balfour Beatty Construction Ltd* [1993] 1 All E.R. 664 at 682. See also M. Mustill and S. Boyd, *The Law and Practice of Commercial Arbitration in England,* 2d ed. (London: Butterworths, 1989) at 61; M. Hunter, J. Paulsson, N. Rawding, and A. Redfern, *The Freshfield Guide to Arbitration and ADR: Clauses in International Contracts* (Deventer, The Netherlands: Kluwer Law and Taxation Publishers, 1993) at 31.

5. See Chapter 2.

6. [1971] A.C. 572.

7. The law applicable to the arbitration is sometimes referred to as the curial law in English jurisprudence.

8. Id. at 604.

9. [1970] A.C. 583.

10. The English Arbitration Act, 1950, contained provisions under which English courts could decide issues of law involved in an arbitration by way of "case stated." This procedure was abolished by the English Arbitration Act of 1979.

11. [1970] A.C. at 607, 612, and 616. See also *Bank Mellat* v. *Helleniki Techniki* [1983] 3 W.L.R. 783 at 789.

12. Cour d'appel of Paris, June 18, 1974, [1975] *Revue D'Arbitrage* 179.

13. Id.

14. See M. Rubino-Sammartano, *International Arbitration Law* (Deventer, The Netherlands: Kluwer Law and Taxation Publishers, 1990) at 281; W. Park, "The Lex Loci Arbitri and International Commercial Arbitration" (1983) 32 *I.C.L.Q.* 21.

15. See W. Craig, W. Park, and J. Paulsson, *International Chamber of Commerce Arbitration*, 2d ed. (Dobbs Ferry, NY: Oceana Publications, 1990) at 271.

16. The territorial principle holds that arbitrations are subject to the law of the country where the arbitration is conducted.

17. See M. Ferrante, "About the Nature (National or A-National, Contractual or Jurisdictional) of ICC Awards under the New York Convention" in J. Schultsz and A. van den Berg (eds.) *The Art of Arbitration: Essays on International Arbitration, Liber Amicorum Pieter Sanders* (Deventer, The Netherlands: Kluwer Law and Taxation Publishers, 1982) 129 at 133.

18. J. Robert and T. Carbonneau, *The French Law of Arbitration* (New York: Matthew Bender, 1983) at 2–11.

19. Article V(1)(d). Emphasis added.

20. Article 1.

21. (1981) VI *Y. Comm. Arb.* 221.

22. Id. at 224.

23. See A. van den Berg, "Should an International Arbitrator Apply the New York Convention of 1958?" in J. Schultsz and A. van den Berg, supra note 17, 39 at 42 and 49.

24. Article IX(1)(d).

25.The UNCITRAL Secretariat Analytical Commentary on the Draft Text of the Model Law, extracted in H. Holtzmann and J. Neuhaus, *A Guide to the UNCITRAL Model Law on International Commercial Arbitration: Legislative History and Commentary* (Deventer, The Netherlands: Kluwer Law and Taxation Publishers, 1989) at 583.

26. F. A. Mann, "Private Arbitration and Public Policy" (1985) 4 *Civil Justice Q.* 256 at 266.

27. Article 18. See also Articles 24(3) and 27.

28. The effect of mandatory provisions on the conduct of arbitration proceedings is discussed below.

29. See generally O. Chukwumerije, "ICSID Arbitration and Sovereign Immunity" (1990) 19 *Anglo-American L.R.* 166.

30. Id. at 174.

31. Article 44.

32. Article 16.

33. Article 5.

34. Article 11. See W. Craig et al., supra note 15, at 269 *et seq*.

35. It has been suggested that application of Islamic procedural law is mandatory for arbitrations that take place in most Moslem countries. See Rubino-Sammartano, supra note 14, at 285.

36. L. Collins (ed.) *Dicey and Morris on Conflict of Laws*, 11th ed. (London: Stevens and Sons, 1987) at 534. See also M. Mustill and S. Boyd, supra note 4, at 64. This statement of law was approved by the House of Lords in *James Miller* v. *Whitworth* [1970] A.C. 583. See also *Channel Tunnel Group Ltd* v. *Balfour Beatty Construction Ltd* [1993] 1 All E.R. 664 at 682 (per Lord Mustill).

37. Per Hobhouse J. in *Dallal* v. *Bank Mellat* [1986] 1 All E.R. 239 at 252.

38. Article 1494.

39. Article 182. See P. Lalive, "The New Swiss Law on International Arbitration" (1988) 4 *Arb. Int'l* 2 at 12.

40. Id.

41. (1984) IX *Y. Comm. Arb.* 437.

42. Under the provision, the recognition or enforcement of an award may be denied if the award "has not yet become binding on the parties."

43. It relied on Section 7510 of the New York Civil Practice Law and Rules, which provided that "The court shall confirm an award upon application of a party made within one year after its delivery to him, unless the award is vacated or modified upon a ground specified in Section 7511." The U.S. District Court and

the Court of Appeals later granted enforcement of the award. See (1984) IX *Y. Comm. Arb.* 487.

44. (1984) IX *Y. Comm. Arb.* at 439. Arbitral tribunals also acknowledge the vitality of party autonomy. In the well-known *Aminoil Arbitration* [(1982) 21 *I.L.M.* 976] the arbitrators followed the parties' choice of procedural rules. See also the Interim Award in ICC case no. 1695 (1986) XI *Y. Comm. Arb.* 149; *Sapphire International Petroleum Ltd.* v. *National Iranian Oil Company* (1967) 35 I.L.R. 136 at 169.

45. See Kerr J. in *Naviera Amazonica Peruana* [1988] 1 Lloyd's L.R. 116 at 120. In the context of ICC arbitration, Article 8(1) of the ICC rules provides that "Where the parties have agreed to submit to arbitration by the International Chamber of Commerce, they shall be deemed to have submitted *ipso facto* to the present Rules."

46. UN doc. A/CN.9/207, para. 21.

47. R. David refers to a Lausanne court decision that set aside an award because it was not made by an odd number of arbitrators. Apparently the requirement of an odd number of arbitrators was (at the time) part of the mandatory rules of Lausanne. See R. David, *Arbitration in International Trade* (Deventer, The Netherlands: Kluwer Law and Taxation Publishers, 1985) at 307.

48. One may say generally that certain fundamental principles of justice and arbitral procedure more or less appear to be mandatory in all national laws. Their aim is to assure the need for a valid arbitration agreement, the parties' independence, equal chances to both parties, the parties' right to be heard and be represented or assisted, and finally the competence of national courts to scrutinize certain fundamental aspects of arbitral procedure.

K. Bockstiegel, "The Relevance of National Arbitration Laws for Arbitration under the UNCITRAL Rules" (1984) 1 *J. Int'l Arb.* 221 at 233. B. Goldman has suggested that with respect to arbitration hearing and related procedure, mandatory rules are those that "lay down that each party's right to present its case and to discuss the position of the other party must be respected." See "The Complementary Roles of Judges and Arbitrators in Ensuring that International Commercial Arbitration is Effective" in *International Commercial Arbitration: 60 Years of ICC Arbitration, A Look at the Future* (Paris: ICC Publishing, 1984) at 267.

49. See discussion in the section on "Delocalization of Arbitration."

50. Article 34(2)(b)(ii).

51. See comment by Mr. Broches during the negotiation of the Model Law, reported in H. Holtzmann and J. Neuhaus, supra note 25 at 974.

52. Under Article V(1)(e) of the New York Convention, the recognition and enforcement of an award *may* be refused if the award "has been set aside or suspended by a competent authority of the country in which, or under the law of which, that award was made." The implications of this provision are considered below.

53. F. Eisemann, "The Revised Rules of Arbitration of the International Chamber of Commerce" (1976) 1 *Y. Comm. Arb.* 167 at 169.

54. (1987) XII *Y. Comm. Arb.* 113.

55. Id. at 115. It cited with approval the view expressed in *Guide to Arbitration* that "To make sure that the award will be enforced, the mandatory rules of national law applicable to international arbitrations in the country where the arbitration takes place must anyway be observed, even if other rules of procedure are chosen by the parties or the arbitrators." ICC Publication No. 382 at 39.

56. See, for example, J. Paulsson, "Delocalisation of International Commercial Arbitration: When and Why it Matters" (1983) 32 *I.C.L.Q.* 53 at 57.

57. Reproduced in H. Holtzmann and J. Neuhaus, supra note 25 at 1162. The committee, however, entered the caveat that where an award is rendered under "procedures which operate unfairly against either party, the recognition and enforcement of the award should be refused." UNCITRAL interpreted the suggestion as implying that party autonomy in the determination of arbitral procedure should be respected, provided the procedural rules are fair to both parties, "even if they are in conflict with the mandatory provisions of the law applicable at the place of arbitration or at the place where recognition and enforcement of the arbitration award is sought." Id. at 1163. The AALCC's initiative was one of the catalysts that led to the formulation of the Model Law, although the particular suggestion above did not meet with UNCITRAL's approval because, in the latter's view, the general rule is that "the parties cannot deviate by agreement from the mandatory provisions of the law applicable at the place of arbitration." Id. at 1164.

58. W. Park, supra note 14 at 25.

59. I classify those who argue for the enforceability of unbound arbitration as contractualists because they essentially argue the case for fidelity to the parties professed manner of settling their dispute.

60. W. Park, supra note 14 at 30.

61. F. A. Mann, "Lex Facit Arbitrum," in P. Sanders (ed.) *International Arbitration: Liber Amicorum for Martin Domke* (The Hague: Martinus Nijhoff, 1967) 133 at 159.

62. Id. at 161.

63. Id. at 162.

64. Recall the Lausanne decision, which set aside an award on the ground that it infringed the domestic requirements that awards be rendered by an odd number of arbitrators. Id. at note 47.

65. W. Park, supra note 14 at 51.

66. *Scherk* v. *Alberto-Culver Co.* (1974) 417 US 506 at 519. Compare the decision of the same court in *Gould* v. *Iran* (1989) *Y. Comm. Arb.* 763. See also the decision of the Supreme Court of Italy in *Damiano* v. *Tropfor* (1984) IX *Y. Comm. Arb.* 418.

67. (1967) 35 I.L.R. 136 at 164, 169.

68. (1980) V *Y. Comm. Arb.* 143.

69. Id. at 147.

70. Id. Impressed by the "wide scope of freedom and independence enjoyed by arbitral tribunals under Danish Law," which was the law of the seat of arbitration, he chose to apply that law. However, he seemed to have opened the possibility for the application of a foreign national law in the event that an arbitration is held in a country without a "developed legal system," a term that is undefined in the award. The possibility of an arbitration law different from the *lex loci arbitri* is acknowledged by some jurisdictions. In *Naviera Amazonica*, supra note 4 at 120, Kerr L.J. stated that there was no "reason in theory which precludes parties to agree that an arbitration shall be held at a place in country X but subject to the procedural laws of Y," although he recognized the "complexities and inconveniences" this might cause. Among these complexities is the question, which court would supervise the arbitration—that of the seat of arbitration or that of the *lex arbitri*? If that of the seat of arbitration, "how is it to regulate an arbitral procedure

which is unfamiliar to it and possibly based on quite different procedural concepts." M. Mustill and S. Boyd, supra note 4 at 64.

71. See L. Collins, supra note 36 at 1207; J. Castel, *Canadian Conflict of Laws*, 2d ed. (Toronto: Butterworths, 1986) at 549.

72. See *Clair* v. *Berardi* (1982) VII *Y. Comm. Arb.* 319 at 321. The issue whether the New York Convention denies recognition to delocalized awards is discussed below.

73. F. A. Mann, supra note 26 at 267. See also Mann, "England Rejects 'Delocalised' Contracts and Arbitration" (1984) 33 *I.C.L.Q.* 193 at 196–197.

74. T. Carbonneau, "Arbitration Adjudication: A Comparative Assessment of Its Remedial and Substantive Status in Transnational Commerce" (1984) 19 *Texas Int'l L.J.* 33 at 36.

75. J. Paulsson, "Arbitration Unbound: Award Detached from the Law of Its Country of Origin" (1981) 30 *I.C.L.Q.* 358 at 370. He concedes that were the exponents of delocalization to insist on a hands-off attitude, the theory would be "justly criticised on the ground that it leaves no forum where a manifestly deficient award may be set aside." Id. at 371.

76. J. Paulsson, supra note 56 at 53.

77. J. Paulsson, "The Extent of Independence of International Arbitration from the Law of the Situs" in J. Lew (ed.) *Contemporary Problems in International Arbitration* (London: Centre for Commercial Law Studies, 1986) 141.

78. These are the standards embodied in international conventions and other international agreements on arbitration. See J. Paulsson, supra note 75 at 370.

79. According to Rubino-Sammartano,

> [t]he fact that arbitral proceedings are not subject to a national procedural law does not . . . relieve them from the duty to respect the procedural public policy in force at the place of arbitration. This public policy may in no case be disregarded; if it is, the arbitral proceedings are null and void.

Supra note 14 at 289, 297.

80. Such an arbitration would fall within the category of ordinary international arbitrations. See A. van den Berg, *The New York Convention of 1958: Towards a Uniform Judicial Interpretation* (Deventer, The Netherlands: Kluwer Law and Taxation Publishers, 1981) at 31.

81. On the impact of the doctrine on ICSID arbitrations, see O. Chukwumerije, supra note 29.

82. (1978) 17 I.L.M. 3.

83. Id. at 155–156. The arbitrator in *BP Arbitration* rejected this line of argument because, according to him, the sovereign immunity of states is "within the limits of international law," subject to the limitations imposed by each jurisdiction. Supra note 68 at 147.

84. (1978) 17 I.L.M. 3.

85. Id. at 8.

86. Id. at 8.

87. *SPP (Middle East) Ltd.* v. *Egypt* (1983) 22 I.L.M. 752 at 722; *LIAMCO* v. *Libya* (1981) VI *Y. Comm. Arb.* 89 at 96; *ICC Case 2321* (1976) I *Y. Comm. Arb.* 133 at 134; *ICC Case 1803* (1980) V *Y. Comm. Arb.* 179 at 186.

88. This presumption does not hold in connection with ICSID arbitrations. See discussion following note 106, infra.

89. In questioning the utility of adopting international law in the conduct of arbitration proceedings, R. Redfern and M. Hunter query:

> What provisions are there in international law, for instance, for the appointment of arbitrators, if the parties cannot agree and there is no other provision in the arbitration agreement? What provisions are there in international law about filling a vacancy on the arbitral tribunal, if one should arise, or for removing an arbitrator, if he fails in his duty of impartiality?

A. Redfern and M. Hunter, *Law and Practice of International Commercial Arbitration*, 2d ed. (London: Sweet and Maxwell, 1991) at 86.

90. Article 1.

91. See S. Toope, *Mixed International Arbitration: Studies in Arbitration between States and Private Persons* (Cambridge: Grotius, 1990) at 41.

92. R. Redfern and M. Hunter, supra note 89 at 306.

93. See T. Carbonneau, Book Review (1984) 24 *Virg. J.* 527 at 530.

94. See Article 1494 of the French Code of Civil Procedure.

95. (1981) VI *Y. Comm. Arb.* 221.

96. The rules in force at the time of the arbitration were those that came into effect in 1975. Art. 11 of the rules provides:

> The rules governing the proceedings before the arbitrator shall be those resulting from these rules and, where these rules are silent, any rules which the parties (or, failing them, the arbitrator) may settle, and whether or not reference is thereby made to a municipal procedural law to be applied to the arbitration.

97. Interestingly, in another proceeding related to the award, Gotaverken implied that the arbitration was in accordance with French procedure, a view that the then secretary of the ICC, in a letter to Gotaverken, seemed to have shared. See (1981) VI *Y. Comm. Arb.* at 222. The Cour d'appel, however, held that these opinions were of "little importance" in the determination of the instant case. Id. at 223.

98. Id. at 222.

99. Id. at 223.

100. Id. at 224.

101. *Iran* v. *Bendone Derossi International* (1987) XII *Y. Comm. Arb.* 482 at 483.

102. Reprinted in (1981) 20 *I.L.M.* 917.

103. Article 1492 liberally defines an international arbitration as that which "implicates international commercial interests."

104. See Article 1504.

105. They are: (a) if the arbitrator decided in the absence of an arbitration agreement or on the basis of a void or expired agreement; (b) if the arbitral tribunal was irregularly composed or the sole arbitrator irregularly appointed; (c) if the arbitrator decided in a manner incompatible with the mission conferred upon him; (d) if due process was not respected; and (e) if recognition or enforcement would be contrary to international public policy. See Article 1502.

106. W. Craig et al., supra note 15 at 493.

107. Supra note 11.

108. See also *Naviera Amazonica Peruana*, supra note 4 at 119; A. Schindler, "Arbitration Still Bound" (1986) 102 *L.Q.R.* 500; G. Morse, "England" in M. Rubino-Sammartano and G. Morse, *Public Policy in Transnational Relationships* (De-

venter, The Netherlands: Kluwer Law and Taxation Publishers, 1991) at England-175.

109. Article 1. Emphasis added.

110. See text accompanying note 18 supra.

111. See A. van den Berg, supra note 80 at 34. The ICC was of the impression that one of the main defects of the convention was its provision for "the enforcement of only those awards that are strictly in accordance with the rules of procedure laid down in the law of the country where the arbitration took place." Id. at 35.

112. The 1927 Geneva Convention ceases to have effect and is superseded by the New York Convention to the extent that the latter is ratified by contracting states. See Article VII(2) of the New York Convention.

113. For a discussion on the improvements made by the New York Convention, see T. Carbonneau, *Alternative Dispute Resolution: Melting the Lances and Dismounting the Steeds* (Urbana: University of Illinois Press, 1989) at 65–67.

114. A. van den Berg, supra note 80 at 34–40. See also G. Delaume, "State Contracts and Transnational Arbitration" (1981) 75 *A.J.I.L.* 784 at 813; "Foreign Sovereign Immunity: Impact on Arbitration" (1983) 38:2 *Arb. J.* 34 at 36.

115. Article 1(3).

116. J. Paulsson, supra note 56 at 57.

117. Concurring in this opinion, A. Avenessan states that

> in the enforcement proceedings brought before a national court of a state party to the Convention, all the court should do is to ascertain that the Award was issued in another Contracting State, and, if so, it should grant enforcement whatever the procedural law applied to the arbitration process, subject, of course, to defences for resisting enforcement as provided in the Convention.

A. Avenessan, "The New York Convention and Denationalized Arbitral Awards: With Emphasis on the Iran-United States Claims Tribunal" (1991) 8 *J. Int'l Arb.* 5 at 26.

118. Article 1(3).

119. *Hiscox* v. *Outhwaite* [1991] 3 W.L.R. 297.

120. This conclusion follows logically from the decision in *Hiscox*, id, although one doubts that the House of Lords foresaw it. For a critique of *Hiscox*, see O. Chukwumerije, "Is an Arbitration Award 'Made' Where It Is Signed?" (1992) 20 *Canadian Bus. L.J.* 305.

121. These are Article V(1), which provides that recognition and enforcement may be refused (a) where the arbitral agreement is invalid under the law to which the parties have subjected it or, failing any indications thereof, under the law of the country where the award is made, and (e) where an award has been set aside by the courts of the state in which, or under the law of which the award was made.

122. A. van den Berg, supra note 80 at 37.

123. Emphasis added. This provision is noteworthy because under Article 34(2)(b)(ii) of the Model Law the court of the place where an award is made may set aside the award if the award is "in conflict with the public policy" of the forum. See note 50, supra. Such a court may therefore set aside a delocalized award if it considers such awards contrary to the public policy of its forum.

124. Compare *Pabalk Ticaret Ltd.* v. *Norsolor* (1985) 24 *I.L.M.* 363 with *Clair* v. *Berardi* (1982) VII *Y. Comm. Arb.* 219. The French text of the convention is less clear

on the point. It provides that recognition and enforcement of an award "will not be refused unless . . . the award has been annulled."

125. Id.

126. Id. at 364.

127. A. van den Berg, supra note 80 at 34.

128. M. McDougal, H. Lasswell, and J. Miller, *The Interpretation of Agreements and World Public Order: Principles of Content and Procedure* (New Haven: Yale University Press, 1967) at 39 *et seq*. See also L. Chen, *An Introduction to Contemporary International Law: A Policy-Oriented Perspective* (New Haven: Yale University Press, 1989) at 278.

129. Supra note 80 at 34.

130. Article V(2)(b) of the New York Convention.

131. As indicated above, the courts of the seat of arbitration may rely on the public policy grounds in Article 34(2)(b)(ii) of the Model Law to set aside a delocalized award. Even then, an enforcing court under the New York Convention has a discretion whether or not to recognize and enforce the award.

132. See *Bank Mellat* v. *Helliniki Techniki*, supra note 11 at 43; *Dallal* v. *Bank Mellat*, supra note 37 at 756–759. See also J. Lew, "The Place of Arbitration and the Applicable Procedural Law in English Common Law" in M. Storme and F. Ly (eds.) *The Place of Arbitration* (Ghent: Mys and Breesch, 1992) at 77.

133. See, for example, *SEE* v. *Yugoslavia* (1985) 24 *I.L.M.* 345. G. Delaume—in his Introductory Note to the case decided by the Court of Appeal of Rouen, France—submits that it adopted "the position that the New York Convention applies to 'anational' awards 'made' (in the purely geographical meaning of the term) in another Contracting State." Id. See also W. Atterbury, "Enforcement of A-National Arbitral Awards under the New York Convention of 1958" (1992) 32 *Virginia J. Int'l L.* 471; B. Demeulenaere, "The Place of Arbitration and the Applicable Procedural Law: The Case of Belgium" in M. Storme and F. Ly, id. at 67.

134. (1989) 14 *Y. Comm. Arb.* 763.

135. The tribunal was created by an international agreement between the governments of the United States and Iran. It was established to determine claims by nationals of one government against the government or national agencies of the other. The tribunal sits at The Hague.

136. (1990) XV *Y. Comm. Arb.* 605 at 610. The U.S. Supreme Court denied without comment Gould's petition for a writ of certiorari. (1991) XVI *Y. Comm. Arb.* 621.

137. Id.

138. Id.

139. Article V.

140. See note 47, supra.

141. General Assembly Resolution 40/72, 40 GAOR Supp. No. 53, A/40/53 at 308. Reproduced in H. Holtzmann and J. Neuhaus, supra note 25 at 1.

CHAPTER FOUR

Law Governing Substantive Issues

INTRODUCTION

An arbitral tribunal accomplishes its central mission, the resolution of the parties' dispute, by determining the contractual obligations of the parties and using the balance of obligations as a guide in resolving the dispute. As contractual documents are generally designed to allocate contractual duties and obligations, an arbitral tribunal called upon to resolve a contractual dispute would logically be drawn, as a first step, to an examination of the parties' contractual provisions. But on what grounds are contractual provisions binding on parties, and why is the choice of law of the parties, as expressed in their contract, effective in law? Are parties bound to choose only national laws to govern their agreements or can they submit their agreements to non-national standards, such as the *lex mercatoria*? What happens in cases where the parties do not make a choice of law? These are the issues that will be considered in this chapter.

This chapter commences with a brief synopsis of the doctrine of party autonomy as it relates to the choice of substantive law. It examines the practical implications of a choice of the *lex mercatoria* or amiable composition by arbitrating parties. It then considers the theory of implied choice of law, and concludes with an examination of how substantive law is determined in the absence of an express choice by the parties.

PARTY AUTONOMY

One of the few principles of law that is commonly recognized and accepted in almost all national jurisdictions is that of party autonomy. In the context of applicable substantive law, this principle enables the parties to a contract to determine the law to govern the substance of their contract. The principle has its origins in the adherence of Victorian judges to the

"Benthamite dogma of *laissez-faire*."[1] These judges respected the intentions of the parties and allowed parties a broad discretion in regulating their contractual arrangement. The principle has since become generally accepted[2] and, according to one commentator, is now "a general principle of law recognized by civilized nations."[3] Both civil and common law jurisdictions endorse the principle:

> [D]espite their differences, common law, civil law and socialist countries have all equally been affected by the movement towards the rule allowing parties to choose the law to govern their contractual relations. This development has come about independently in every country and without any concerted effort by the nations of the world; it is the result of separate, contemporaneous and pragmatic evolution within the various national systems of conflict of laws.[4]

The main advantage of party autonomy is that it allows parties to select the law that is well known to them and whose allocation of contractual risks and obligations is suitable for their purposes. It also makes for certainty and predictability because the parties know precisely what they can legitimately expect from each other. In this era of free market theory and privatization, the doctrine of party autonomy meshes neatly with the attempt to reduce the role of government in the marketplace and the emphasis on individual choices and personal freedom.

Party autonomy is engrafted in virtually all international conventions dealing with arbitration and contract law. For example, Article 28(1) of the Model Law provides: "The arbitral tribunal shall decide the dispute in accordance with such rules of law as are chosen by the parties as applicable to the substance of the dispute." Also, Article 7(1) of the European Convention on Commercial Arbitration stipulates that "[t]he parties shall be free to determine by agreement the law to be applied by the arbitrators to the substance of the dispute." Similarly, Article 3 of the European Convention on the Law Applicable to Contractual Obligation provides that a "contract shall be governed by the law chosen by the parties."

Party autonomy is also a consistent and pervasive feature of international arbitral practice. Some arbitrators base their respect for the will of the parties on some national law (for example the law of the arbitral seat), whereas the more common practice is for arbitrators to apply the doctrine without reference to national law.[5] Tribunals that apply the doctrine without reference to national law do so on the basis that the doctrine is so generally accepted as to deserve arbitral notice. According to the tribunal in *ICC Case No. 1512 of 1971*:

> [I]t is possible to speak, to a large extent, of a common or universal private international law, at least whenever the question is that of the law governing the contract when there is an expressed choice by the parties. There are a few principles more universally admitted in private international law than that referred to by the

standard terms of the "proper law of the contract," according to which the law governing the contract is that which has been chosen by the parties, whether expressly or (with certain differences or variations according to the various systems) tacitly.[6]

Party autonomy is, however, not without its limitations in national law. Under English law and its progeny, a choice of law may be disregarded if the choice is not *bona fide* or there is otherwise a public policy ground for avoiding it.[7] The scope of these limitations is not particularly clear; these limitations are evidently aimed at situations where the choice of law is unfairly designed to avoid the application of mandatory rules of an otherwise applicable national law.[8] These limitations, sometimes called *fraude a la loi*, are also applied in other jurisdictions.[9] The practical effect of these limitations is, in appropriate cases, to delegitimize the parties' express choice of law, thereby reverting the determination of the applicable substantive law to traditional conflicts principles.

Some writers suggest that these limitations also apply to international commercial arbitrations.[10] On this view, an arbitrator would disregard the choice of law of the parties if the choice is not *bona fides*, that is, if the choice is aimed at avoiding the application of an otherwise applicable mandatory rule of law. This writer disagrees with this view. International commercial arbitrators can and in fact do apply the mandatory rules of national laws that are substantially connected to the contract, regardless of the law chosen by the parties. That is, the parties' choice of law in no way precludes a tribunal from determining that their contract is so closely connected with a jurisdiction that the mandatory rules of that jurisdiction must be applied to the contract, regardless of the fact that the national law of that jurisdiction is not the law applicable to the contract. There is thus no reason for an arbitral tribunal to entirely disregard a choice of law on the grounds of lack of *bona fides*. The tribunal nonetheless ensures that those mandatory rules that the parties sought to circumvent, and that are substantially connected to the contract, are enforced. Once it is recognized that a choice of law cannot preclude the application of relevant "foreign" mandatory rules of national law, there is little need to erect the limitation of *bona fides* or public policy. This is the approach adopted by the European Convention on the Law Applicable to Contractual Obligations. Article 3(3) of the convention provides as that "[t]he fact that the parties have chosen a foreign law, whether or not accompanied by the choice of a foreign tribunal, shall not, where all the other elements are connected with one country only, prejudice the application of rules of the law of that country which cannot be derogated from by contract [mandatory rules]."

It is generally believed that parties can exercise their autonomy in two ways. First, they may expressly designate their choice of law. Second, they could, by their words or actions, manifest their expectation to have their agreement regulated by a particular national law.[11] We shall first examine situations where the parties make an express choice of law to govern their agreement.

The most common choice of law made by arbitrating parties is national law. Parties usually search for a well-developed and sophisticated national law that is suitable to their needs. Often this law is that of a leading financial or commercial center, or in other instances, that of one of the parties to the transaction. In some cases, however, arbitrating parties choose nonnational standards such as the *lex mercatoria* or amiable composition. These latter choices are somewhat controversial in that their legal status is not yet fully determined in some jurisdictions, and their scope and scheme of application are not entirely settled. It is therefore necessary to examine them in some detail.

LEX MERCATORIA

Parties to arbitration sometimes choose to apply the *lex mercatoria* to their transaction.[12] In choosing the *lex mercatoria,* parties seek to regulate their transaction by a system of rules that is amenable to the realities of international commerce and that avoids the vagaries of national laws. As one commentator notes, by utilizing the *lex mercatoria* the parties oust the technicalities of national legal systems and avoid the application of rules that may be unfit for international commerce.[13] Thus, the *lex mercatoria* is essentially a means of escaping the application of conflicting national laws whose disparity, Redfern and Hunter note in evocative words, "resembles a modern Tower of Babel from which some escape is sought."[14] As a transnational body of rules, the *lex mercatoria* would render it unnecessary to localize commercial transactions in any jurisdiction, with the result that, in appropriate cases, the *lex mercatoria* becomes immediately applicable.[15]

What then is the *lex mercatoria*? A brief historical introduction is appropriate. It has long been recognized by commercial people and jurists that the fulcrum of commerce lies in customs, not law.[16] Thus, in the Middle Ages, international merchants who engaged in European and Eastern trade developed customs and usages to regulate their trade. These customs and usages, the *lex mercatoria,* were handed down orally by merchants and their binding effect was presumed by these merchants. With time, the law merchant was developed in different areas of trade and was accepted in various marketplaces as binding rules of an international character.[17] The emergence of the concept of nation-states around the sixteenth century led to the incorporation of this medieval *lex mercatoria* into national laws by codification (in the civil law systems), and by incorporation into the common law and statutes (in the common law systems). The medieval law merchant did not, however, completely lose its character, as it was still possible in most jurisdictions to incorporate new customs and usages into contract law.[18]

The contention of those who support the application of the *lex mercatoria* to international commercial relations is that a new *lex mercatoria* has since evolved, an autonomous brand different from the old *lex mercatoria* that was incorporated into national laws. The root of this new *lex mercatoria* is said to lie not in national laws, but in crystallized and evolving practices and usages of international commercial relations. As one commentator points out, the new *lex mercatoria* is "a set of general principles and customary rules spontaneously referred to or elaborated in the framework of international trade, without reference to a particular national system of law."[19] O. Lando explains the concept of the new *lex mercatoria* as follows:

> [Parties to an international contract may submit their disputes] to customs and usages of international trade, to the rules of law which are common to all or most of the States engaged in international trade or to those States which are connected with the dispute. Where such common rules are not ascertainable, the arbitrator applies the rules or chooses the solution which appears to him to be the most appropriate or equitable. In doing so he considers the law of several legal systems. This judicial process which is partly an application of legal rules and partly a selective and creative process, is here called application of the *lex mercatoria*.[20]

It may be deduced from the above two views that the new *lex mercatoria* is essentially the embodiment of emerging customs and usages of international trade, supplemented in appropriate cases by resort to commonsense notions of justice and fairness.

In order to determine the existence of such a new and autonomous *lex mercatoria* and its suitability for the resolution of international trade disputes, it is necessary to closely examine its professed sources. One quickly learns when searching for the sources of the *lex mercatoria* that even its most ardent protagonists are not completely agreed on its sources. O. Lando, for example, lists the relevant sources as: public international law, general principles of law, uniform laws, rules of international organizations, customs and usages, standard form contracts, and the jurisprudence of arbitral awards.[21] According to J. Lew, the sources are the substantive rules of international trade, the code of practice of international trade, and the customs and usages of international trade. C. Schmitthoff, on the other hand, gives the sources as international legislation (by which he means "normative regulations devised internationally and then introduced into national law by national legislation") and international commercial customs (by which he means practices and usages formulated by international agencies or international trade associations).[22] Although the sources put forward by the above writers are not identical, the sources that are commonly agreed on by advocates of the *lex mercatoria* are as follows: general principles of law; customs, usages, and uniform laws of international trade; and arbitral jurisprudence. Let us consider these sources in turn.

General Principles of Law

The distillation of general principles of law involves a comparative survey of a representative selection of national laws with a view to determining those principles of law that are common to all of them or, at least, an overwhelming majority of them. General principles are said to be part of the *lex mercatoria* because they are generally accepted and thus form a sort of universal practice that parties to an international commercial transaction implicitly accept as part of the regulatory framework of their transaction.

Which rules or principles are common to a generality of nations? If the search for common principles were restricted to nations with the same type of legal systems, perhaps principles could be found that are shared by these nations. However, the diversity of national legal systems (civil law, common law, Islamic law, and customary law) and the sheer number of States, lead one reluctantly to the conclusion that legal principles that are *truly* common to a representative selection of legal systems would invariably be few and often too general and too broad to be helpful in the regulation of complex and particular commercial relations.

The general principles usually proffered by writers include the principles of good faith, *pacta sunt servanda* and estoppel. However, in most national legal systems these enumerated principles are elaborated and defined by supplementary rules that condition them for application in substantive cases. The principle of good faith, for example, sounds very abstract except where there are supplementary rules that define the meaning and requirements of good faith and state when the principle is inapplicable. It is difficult to imagine that these supplementary rules would be similar in a representative selection of countries. This difficulty has not prevented some arbitrators from professing the universality of certain rules, a claim that is rarely supported by a citation of sources.[23]

The point being made here is not that there are no truly general principles of law. General principles exist, and reference was made earlier to the general acceptance of the principle of party autonomy. The argument here is that truly general principles of law are few, and even when they exist, they are by definition abstract. Within the context of national law, these principles are supplemented by explanatory rules that are themselves rarely general.

Customs, Usages, and Uniform Laws of International Trade

The uniform laws of international trade are to be found in multilateral conventions and model laws that are adopted by States. These laws, elaborated by jurists from different parts of the world, are said to represent a consensus (more often, a compromise) on the legal principles governing certain aspects of international trade. Examples of these uniform laws are the Uniform Law for Bill of Exchange and Promissory Notes and the Model Law on International Commercial Arbitration. These uniform laws are drafted by institutions such as the International Institute for the Unification of International Private Law (UNIDROIT) and the United Nations Commission on International Trade Law (UNCITRAL),[24] whose primary objective is the harmonization of international trade laws.

However, these uniform or model laws are authoritative only when they are adopted by a majority of States. Where they are so adopted (for example the New York Convention on the Enforcement of Foreign Arbitral Awards), it would be legitimate to assume that such laws or conventions embody principles of general application and are therefore representative of international practice. On the other hand, where the law is not adopted in a majority of States, it is difficult to see how it could in any reasonable sense be said to constitute part of a new *lex mercatoria*. It would seem that if a *lex mercatoria* exists, only those uniform laws that receive general acceptance can constitute part of it.

Customs and usages are another source of the new *lex mercatoria*. Customs and usages are said to be found in international rules and standard form contracts. Some international organizations, like the International Chamber of Commerce, develop rules and regulations that are designed for application in certain areas of international trade. These rules, commonly drafted by experts in the particular area of trade, embody the experience and practices in that area of trade. Examples of such rules are the ICC Incoterms and the ICC Uniform Customs and Practice for Documentary Credits.[25] If these rules are generally accepted and considered binding by commercial people, they become directly relevant in the resolution of international commercial disputes. As Mustill rightly points out, customs and usages of this sort are commonly applied by courts and tribunals and there is nothing peculiar about the *lex mercatoria* in this respect.[26]

It is also suggested that standard form contracts are another source of the new *lex mercatoria*. These form contracts are said to be a "dynamic process through which rules of law are elaborated in fairly spontaneous fashion."[27] One wonders how these contracts can create rules of law. Standard form contracts are usually formulated by trade groups or associations as models or prototypes on which parties may base their contractual arrangements. Most seasoned lawyers use these standard contracts only as a starting point for negotiation. Aware of how the standard contracts deal with risk allocation, lawyers in appropriate cases seek to amend them to reflect their clients' particular interests in business arrangements. As mere prototypes, it is unclear how these standard form contracts could be seen as customary practices that constitute part of a new *lex mercatoria*. The unlikelihood of standard form contracts being embodiments of customary practices is heightened by the fact that they often vary from one trade association to the other, and from one country to the next. For example, the trade rules of the Canadian grain association may not be the same as those of their Russian counterparts. Indeed, some institutions issue a repertoire of standard form contracts from which the parties choose the one most suitable to their needs.[28] In such cases where there is no homogeneity in the provisions of standard form contracts, which of them could be said to constitute part of the new *lex mercatoria*? In sum, standard form contracts are by definition prototypes that do not necessarily evince binding customary practices.

Arbitral Jurisprudence

Some proponents of the new *lex mercatoria* view arbitral tribunals as vehicles for the articulation and elaboration of the principles of the law merchant. They argue for the formulation and publication of reasoned awards in the hope that this will lead to the development of generally accepted principles that may be applied without reference to specific national laws.[29] The systematic examination of arbitral awards may, they suggest, reveal certain principles that are accepted by the international commercial community, and that are applied not because they are mandated by some national law, but because they conform to the legitimate expectations of the parties.[30] The authors of the *International Chamber of Commerce Arbitration* list some of these principles that have been applied by ICC tribunals without reference to national law. These include the freedom of parties to establish procedural and substantive rules, *pacta sunt servanda*, performance and renegotiation in good faith, rules of *force majeure*, mitigation of damages, estoppel, and unenforceability of contracts contrary to international morality.[31]

This process of articulating the new *lex mercatoria* also has its own problem. Rules that are distilled from arbitral jurisprudence are often expressed in very general terms, as the above list reveals. They are hardly detailed enough to govern all aspects of complex contractual relations. For example, assuming that, as the above list suggests, performance and renegotiation of contractual obligations in good faith are part of the new *lex mercatoria*, what precisely are performance and renegotiation, and under what conditions is renegotiation mandated? What constitutes renegotiation in good faith? True, with time arbitral jurisprudence may develop to include subsidiary rules that graft flesh onto skeletal principles, but this possibility offers little succor to parties searching for definite principles to govern their relationship. Thus while it is possible to distill general principles from arbitral practice,[32] these principles are often not comprehensive enough to govern complex commercial relations.

One fact that clearly emerges in this examination of the sources of the new *lex mercatoria* is that none of these sources (or even a cumulative application of all of them) affords rules that are comprehensive enough to regulate international commercial transactions.[33] It is true that there are customs and usages in international trade. It is equally true that international rules and conventions are formulated on an increasingly frequent basis to govern aspects of international trade. Nonetheless, one doubts that there would be a time when these customs, conventions, or codes would in themselves constitute an autonomous and comprehensive regime to govern all international trade transactions. Most supporters of the *lex mercatoria* recognize this fact. One protagonist of the *lex mercatoria* notes that it is a "diffuse and fragmented body of law" that will grow "with the growth of uniform laws, international trade customs and usages," although he accepts that it would never achieve "the level of the copious and well-organised national legal systems."[34] H. Berman and F. Dasser on their part accept that:

> The customary law merchant is not a complete legal system—it was never meant to be complete. The merchants themselves count on the help of a national legal system in case of dispute. They know very well that custom and contractual agreement cannot regulate all questions to which a commercial transaction may give rise and they welcome the backing of a national law when the law merchant fails to give [a] clear and satisfactory answer.[35]

Curiously enough, the authors do not state which national law the arbitrators should use in supplementing the *lex mercatoria.* Is it the otherwise applicable law, is it the law of the arbitral *situs*, or is it any national law that the arbitrators deem suitable to the needs of international commerce? In response, Lando suggests that in the event that the new *lex mercatoria* does not address a certain issue, an arbitrator should make a comparative survey of national laws, and where there is no commonality of practice, the arbitrator "must make a choice or find a new solution."[36] In this sense the arbitrator becomes, in his words, a "social engineer" and the *lex mercatoria* "a creative process." Considering that in most cases the content of the *lex mercatoria* is imprecise, and in many other cases the so-called *lex mercatoria* does not contain relevant principles to govern particular disputes, the arbitrators would very frequently act as "social engineers."

One doubts that parties to an arbitration who choose the *lex mercatoria* as the governing law of their transaction are actually aware that their arbitrators would frequently apply their own standards of justice. If indeed the mission of an arbitrator applying the *lex mercatoria* is to engineer an equitable solution in the event of a lack of appropriate principles of the law merchant, the process may well become a means of substituting the will of the arbitrators for otherwise applicable legal principles. As Reisman notes, the imprecision and high level of abstraction of the *lex mercatoria* make its application "perilously close to a craps shoot."[37] Similarly, F. A. Mann opines that the "undefined and undefinable" standards of the *lex mercatoria* makes the outcomes of proceedings where it is applied somewhat of a "lottery."[38]

Another problem with the *lex mercatoria* is that of the hierarchy of norms. Which of the various sources of the law merchant has the highest normative value? Assuming there is a conflict between an international rule and a principle of arbitral jurisprudence, which of them takes precedence? Moreover, there may be conflicting rules in one of the sources. For example, there may be in arbitral jurisprudence two contending views on a particular area of law. How do the arbitrators decide which one to adopt? Is it for them to use their own sense of justice, or should they speculate on which norm or practice is more amenable to the needs of international commerce?

What all this comes down to is that there is no comprehensive and accessible body of rules of the law merchant that can, as an autonomous system, govern modern-day commercial disputes. This is not to say that there are not in existence customs, practices, uniform laws, and arbitral jurisprudence that may be helpful in the resolution of international disputes. All of these exist, and all, in one form or another, crystallize into customary practices of international trade. However, they are not a comprehensive set of principles, and parties seeking determinacy and certainty in their contractual relations are better advised to select national law to govern their dispute. If the intention of the parties is to grant the arbitrators the power to act as "social engineers," they may well invest them with the power to act as *amiable compositeurs*.[39]

It is the writer's view that the role the *lex mercatoria* can play in the arbitration of international disputes is to supply customary practices that would be used as a guiding light in interpreting and enforcing contractual obligations, a role similar to that played by customary practices in domestic laws.[40] This role is given to the *lex mercatoria* by Article 28(4) of the Model Law, which provides that "[i]n all cases, the arbitral tribunal shall decide in accordance with the terms of the contract and shall take into account usages of the trade applicable to the transaction."[41] Viewed in this respect, the *lex mercatoria* would be seen as constituting customary practices and usages of international trade, and its role would be twofold.[42] First, its principles would be immediately applicable without the need to locate their source in national law, so long as they do not contravene the provisions of the governing law of the contract. For example, if the governing law of a contract is New York law, the arbitrators may nevertheless apply customary practices of international trade as long as there is no contrary indication in New York law. Second, the arbitrators may use customary practices to avoid the application of the otherwise applicable nonmandatory national rules that are contrary to the intention or legitimate expectations of the parties.[43]

It should be pointed out that although the new *lex mercatoria* is recognized in some conventions[44] and by some national legal systems, notably the French,[45] its validity as a governing legal standard is disputed in some countries, notably England.[46] It is therefore important that parties who take the unwise step of granting arbitrators the power to apply the *lex mercatoria* as the governing standard of their transaction ensure that the choice would not lead to the setting aside of their award or a refusal to recognize and enforce the award in jurisdictions that do not recognize the *lex mercatoria* as a governing legal standard.[47]

It is instructive to note that arbitrators remain bound by the relevant mandatory rules even while applying the *lex mercatoria.* As one supporter of the new law merchant rightly notes, the law merchant is applied "in every national jurisdiction by tolerance of the national sovereignty whose public policy may override or qualify a particular rule of that law."[48]

In conclusion, arbitrating parties are better advised not to choose the *lex mercatoria* as their governing law, unless they are prepared to have their arbitrators play the role of innovators. In assessing the position of the new *lex mercatoria* after its first 20 years, Lord Mustill was able to garner only a "modest haul" of 20 principles,[49] most of which are too broad and too general to be helpful in resolving complex commercial disputes. This means that in most instances arbitrators applying the *lex mercatoria* would have to innovate or, as it is sometimes put, act as "social engineers." Perhaps parties who are tempted by the lures of the concept of the new *lex mercatoria* should read the words of one of its ardent advocates, O. Lando:

> If the parties direct the arbitrator to apply the *lex mercatoria* they will know its merits and demerits, one of which is scarcity of "authority" on which the arbitrator can base his [or her] decision. They will know that the arbitrator cannot make scientific investigations to ascertain the "common core" of many legal systems and that he [or she] will have often to use his [or her] *bono sens.*[50]

AMIABLE COMPOSITION

International commercial arbitration laws in some countries allow arbitrating parties to grant their arbitrators the power to resolve their dispute without being bound "hand and foot" to the law. This is done by granting the arbitrators the power to act as *amiable compositeurs.* This power enables arbitrators to rely on notions of justice and fairness in resolving disputes. *Amiable compositeurs* are freed from the strict responsibility of applying systemized principles of law and are invested with the authority to have recourse to notions of equity and justice with the objective of avoiding the inequitable results that might arise from a strict reliance on legal rules.[51] As one tribunal puts it, arbitrators called upon to act as *amiable compositeurs* "may decide a case according to the principles of fairness and equity."[52] Thus, they could decide to give effect to a technically invalid agreement when it is clear that the parties intended to be honor bound by such agreements or to ignore technical defenses that are unworthy and shame-faced.[53]

Does this mean that amiable composition shares the same characteristics with conciliation and mediation—namely, a nonbinding dispute resolution process? The answer is no, for while *amiable compositeurs* may not base their awards entirely on legal rules, their awards are nonetheless binding on the parties. They perform the judicial function of rendering legally enforceable awards, although they are not bound to apply strict legal principles.

Does the power of amiable composition oblige arbitrators to disregard legal rules entirely? It is often thought that the power of amiable composition obliges the arbitrators to rule in equity on each issue that arises in the arbitration. This assumption may have led one commentator to ask what is so wrong with rules of law that arbitrators "can carry out their work not only without law, but can indeed regard themselves as better off without the assistance which law might afford them." He further queries: "how is it possible that eminent lawyers can support them in this belief?"[54] This writer is quite happy to allow eminent lawyers to come to their own defense. Nonetheless, it is instructive to indicate that the power of amiable composition does not oblige a disregard of law. It merely allows arbitrators to temper strict legal provisions with considerations of equity, a role akin to that played in the past by Courts of Equity. The mission of *amiable compositeurs* is not to banish legal rules, neither is the power of amiable composition designed to deprive arbitrators of the assistance of legal rules. On the contrary, their mission, as a practical matter, is to draw from the experience of legal provisions—to follow these provisions when experience reveals their consistency with commonsense justice, and to depart from them when their application, although generally fair, would lead to inequitable results in the particular case at hand.[55] In essence, *amiable compositeurs* often apply legal rules, while reserving "the right to deviate in the event that they deem that [the] applicable law would lead to an unfair solution."[56] As R. David puts it:

> In the vast majority of cases *amiable compositeurs* do not intend to work out a compromise, but they feel bound to decide as is prescribed by the law; they see in the law a kind of *ratio scripta* and do not find any good reason for departing from its application in particular cases. The *amiable compositeur* is in fact a judge, but one who enjoys greater flexibility in adopting the solution which he regards as best, even though from a strictly legal point of view it may not be absolutely correct.[57]

The provision for amiable composition is very useful in cases where the parties appoint as arbitrators technical experts who, although not lawyers, are knowledgeable in the subject matter of the dispute. For example, in a dispute involving complex engineering and design agreements, the parties may consider engineering experts more suitable than lawyers. If these experts are granted the power of amiable composition, they would not be disabled by their lack of legal training. Relying on their professional experience and their familiarity with the customs of the field, they would render an award based on the common experience of engineering practice, rather than on formalized rules of law. Additionally, amiable composition could be useful in long-term contracts where the assumptions on which contractual arrangements are entered into are sometimes radically altered by changing business and economic climates.[58] In these cases, *amiable compositeurs* would be able to take these changes into consideration in rendering their award, considerations that are sometimes viewed as irrelevant in some legal systems.

It should be noted that the concept of amiable composition has very little substantive content other than the discretion it invests in the arbitrators to go beyond the realms of legal principles in rendering their awards. Thus, if the parties wish to further define the scope of the arbitrators' discretion, they should do this in their arbitration agreement. This is the attitude adopted by the drafters of the Model Law:

> No attempt is made in the Model Law to define this type of arbitration [amiable composition] which comes in various and often vague forms. It is submitted, however, that the parties may in their authorization provide some certainty, to the extent desired by them, either by referring to the kind of amiable composition developed in a particular legal system or by laying down rules or guidelines and, for example, request a fair and equitable solution within the limits of the international public policy of their two States.[59]

What are the limits to the powers of *amiable compositeurs*? Can they disregard each and every provision of law? These are very important questions because their answers would determine the extent to which the practice of amiable composition could be tolerated by national legal systems. States would be reluctant to sanction a dispute resolution system that refuses to acknowledge relevant fundamental public policy. Thus, it has long been recognized that while *amiable compositeurs* have the power to disregard strict legal rules, they are nevertheless bound to apply relevant mandatory rules. The power to act as *amiable compositeurs* does not relieve arbitrators from their responsibility to respect and apply the relevant mandatory provisions of law.[60] Since the powers of arbitrators cannot be greater than the powers of the parties who appointed them, and since arbitrating parties are, as we shall see in Chapter 6, incapable of excluding the application of relevant mandatory rules (such as foreign exchange regulations), arbitrators chosen by them or on their behalf can not derogate from mandatory rules, even when they are acting as *amiable compositeurs*. Thus, one tribunal notes that *amiable compositeurs* are "not authorized to make a decision contrary to an absolutely constraining law, particularly the rules concerning public order or morals."[61] An *amiable compositeur* therefore can not, for instance, decide to enforce a contract that is clearly contrary to public morals.

Are *amiable compositeurs* free in the name of equity and justice to disregard contractual provisions and in effect rewrite the contractual obligations of the parties? Since *amiable compositeurs* are invested with the power to rule in equity and fairness, it could be argued that they implicitly have the power to disregard those contractual provisions they deem inconsistent with equitable results. However, it should be remembered that contractual provisions are as much a part of the parties' agreement as the arbitration agreement that invests the arbitrators with adjudicatory competence. It is thus reasonable to presume that arbitrators should not be able to rewrite the parties' express agreement, unless they are expressly granted such powers by the parties. The grant of the power of amiable composition is certainly not akin to a license for arbitrators to rewrite contractual provisions; their power of amiable composition extends only to placing, where appropriate, a broad and liberal interpretation on these contractual provisions in such a manner as to moderate their effect on the parties. Thus, while *amiable compositeurs* may disregard non-mandatory legal rules, they cannot in the same vein disregard clear contractual provisions. This principle was acknowledged by the arbitral tribunal in *ICC Case No. 3267*:[62]

> Although some legal writers have expressed the opinion that arbitrators sitting as "amiable compositeurs" may disregard the provisions of the agreement between the parties, this view has not been accepted in international arbitration. On the contrary, it is a generally accepted principle in international arbitration that the paramount duty of the arbitrator, even as "amiable compositeur" is to apply the contract of the parties, unless it is shown that the provisions relied on are clearly against the true intent of the parties, or violate a basic commonly accepted principle of public policy. . . . In the view of the Arbitral Tribunal this principle is a basic requirement for the security of international trade.[63]

This principle is contained in Article 28(4) of the Model Law, which provides, *inter alia*, that in all cases "the arbitral tribunal shall decide in accordance with the terms of the contract." Article 13(5) of the ICC Rules of Arbitration also provides that arbitrators have a duty to apply contractual provisions. Similar provisions are found in several national legislations. Art 944.10 of the Quebec Code of Civil Procedure, for example, provides that arbitrators "shall in all cases decide according to the stipulations of the contract." Nonetheless, it would seem to follow from the nature of the power of amiable composition that *amiable compositeurs* could use the civil law concept of abuse of rights to ensure that the underlying purpose of the contract is not unduly frustrated by a party's strict reliance on contractual stipulations.

The concept of amiable composition is accepted in many jurisdictions. Its application in international commercial arbitration was an innovation of French jurisprudence;[64] it was then borrowed by those jurisdictions whose legal systems were modeled on the French.[65] At present, the concept is accepted in all the countries of the European Community, with the exception of England.[66] It is also accepted in those jurisdictions that have adopted the Model Law.[67]

The traditional English position is that arbitrators must in general "apply a fixed and recognizable system of law" and that "they cannot be allowed to apply some different criterion such as the view of the individual arbitrator or umpire on abstract justice or equitable principles."[68] The policy behind this attitude was explained by Bankes L.J. as follows:

> Among commercial men what are commonly called commercial arbitrations are undoubtedly and deservedly popular. That they will continue their present popularity I entertain no doubt, so long as the law retains sufficient hold over them to prevent and redress any injustice on the part of the arbitrator and to secure that the law that is administered by the arbitrator is in substance the law of the land, and not some home-made law of the particular arbitrator or the particular association. To release real and effective control over commercial arbitration is to allow the arbitrator or the arbitration tribunal to be law unto himself or themselves, to give him or them a free hand to decide according to law, or not according to law as he or they think fit; in other words, to be outside the law.[69]

However, in *Eagle Star Insurance*[70] the English Court of Appeal approved an arbitration clause that provided that the arbitrators shall not be bound by strict legal principles but "shall settle any differences referred to them according to an equitable rather than a strictly legal interpretation of the provisions of this agreement." Lord Denning found the provision reasonable in that it "only ousts technicalities and strict constructions." In his view, "That is what equity did in the old days. And it is what arbitrators may properly do today under such a clause as this."[71] This interpretation of the equity clause is somewhat narrower than the ambit granted such clauses in continental jurisprudence,[72] because it precludes the arbitrators from dispensing with the application of legal principles if they deem their result inequitable. English courts have consistently put this narrow interpretation on equity clauses. In *Home and Overseas Insurance*,[73] Parker L.J. affirmed Denning's interpretation that equity clauses merely enable arbitrators to depart from the ordinary and literal meanings of the words used in contractual documents. According to him, "a clause which purported to free arbitrators to decide without regard to the law and according, for example, to their own notions of what would be fair would not be a valid arbitration clause."[74]

Although English law has traditionally been hostile to the idea of arbitrators entirely disregarding legal rules,[75] the termination of the case stated procedure,[76] and the right to exclude appeals to English courts in international commercial arbitrations,[77] decrease the opportunity for English courts to enforce the perceived obligation of arbitrators to apply legal principles. Nonetheless, parties who arbitrate in England ought to take into account the current judicial attitude in there toward amiable composition.

Opposition to the concept of amiable composition is also found in academic circles. One common denominator in reasons advanced against amiable composition is that law, no matter how imperfect, is preferable to arbitrators' personal notions of justice and fairness. According to Mann, "it is infinitely more dangerous to allow discretion to arbitrators than to compel parties to accept the law, its relative certainty, its authority and, above all, its non-discriminatory character. The law is rarely an instrument of oppression."[78]

This attitude is very paternalistic in assuming that the benefits of law are such that the parties may not, if they deem fit, decide to trust their arbitrators' notions of justice more than the letters of the law. It is true, law is relatively definite, often readily identifiable, and, in many cases, a product of reasoned analysis of policy and experience. However, none of these considerations afford a cogent reason for depriving parties the right to decline to apply nonmandatory rules of law, if they so wish. In most cases parties to international commercial arbitration are sophisticated enough to appreciate the implications of choosing amiable composition. To deny these parties the right to have their dispute resolved without the rigors of strict legal rules is to forget what D. Thomas tells us: "Justice according to law is but one manifestation of justice; justice according to an arbitral scheme established by parties in dispute is another."[79]

IMPLIED CHOICE OF LAW

Parties to a commercial agreement do not always exercise their right to expressly determine their own choice of law. This factor led to the development of the theory of implied choice of law whereby certain actions of the parties are deemed to manifest an intention to have their agreement regulated by a particular national law. According to this theory, the parties' intention regarding their choice of law could, in some instances, be reasonably inferred from their contractual document.

The most common manifestation of this doctrine is the principle that a choice of arbitral seat implies a choice of the law of the seat as the governing law of the contractual agreement.[80] This principle, once hallowed in English contract doctrine, was viewed as a conclusive presumption. For example, in *Tzortzis* v. *Monark Line A/B*[81] the contract in issue, except for its provision for arbitration in England, had its most real and substantial connection with Sweden. Nonetheless, the English Court of Appeal considered that the choice of England as the seat of arbitration implied a choice of English law as the governing law of the contract. The court held that the choice of the arbitral seat "raises an irresistible inference that overrides all the other factors."[82] French and German courts have also applied this principle.[83]

This principle is viewed as applicable to arbitration;[84] and indeed some arbitral awards have applied it. In *Societe M.N.* v. *Koospol S.A.*,[85] which involved a German and a citizen of the then Czechoslovakia, the arbitrators sitting in Czechoslovakia held that Czechoslovakian law governed the parties' contract. Explaining their decision the arbitrators stated:

> [We] were of the opinion that the parties have, by reserving the matter for Czechoslovak Arbitration Court, tacitly subjected their relations to Czechoslovak law. This signification of the arbitration clause should be clear even to the plaintiff, an experienced businessman, for similar clauses are interpreted in the same way both by international doctrine and legal decisions.[86]

This method of equating a choice of forum to a choice of law is objectionable on several grounds. First, most parties to an arbitration choose a seat of arbitration because of the convenience of the location or the amenability of its arbitral laws to their needs. It rarely occurs to them that such a choice would amount to a choice of governing law. To illustrate, Canadian and German contracting parties may choose London as their seat of arbitration because of the convenience of the location (perhaps because the arbitrators reside in London). In such a case, which is typical of reasons for choosing an arbitral seat, it seems odd that the choice of London as the seat of arbitration should be interpreted as implying that the parties implicitly chose English law as the governing law. The fallacy of this presumption is further buttressed by the fact that the seat of arbitration may have been chosen by an arbitral institution on behalf of the parties, and usually after the dispute has arisen. One finds it difficult to imagine why the choice of an arbitral seat made by a third party institution after the dispute has arisen would be dispositive of the issue of applicable law.

A further problem with the doctrine of implied choice is that an arbitration proceeding may be carried out in several countries. An arbitral tribunal may, for example, hold hearings in London, Toronto, Hong Kong, and New York. Using the doctrine of implied choice, which law would govern the contract? Does the governing law change each time the venue of the arbitral proceedings is shifted to a different country? One might answer that in such cases the relevant law is that of the seat of arbitration that is designated in the parties' agreement or by the relevant arbitral institution.[87] If anything, such a response highlights the artificiality of this method of determining the choice of law.

There has been a shift from the orthodox view equating choice of arbitral seat with a choice of law. In England the principle is now considered rebuttable,[88] although "the inference raised by an arbitration clause is one that is not easy to rebut."[89] International arbitrators are also moving away from the orthodox view; arbitrators now rarely equate a choice of arbitral forum with a choice of law:

> In the event of an arbitral clause, international arbitrators are nowadays usually reluctant to attribute any role, other than providing the mandatory framework for the proceedings, to the *lex fori*. The fact that the venue of an arbitration is in the Netherlands will not be regarded as decisive for the substantive law, i.e. it will not be interpreted as an implied choice of Dutch law.[90]

Attempts to construct the implied will of parties to a contract are generally artificial endeavours, especially when the construction is based on such tenuous grounds as the parties' choice of arbitral seat. It would seem that the construction of an implied choice of law should be restricted to instances where the parties' contractual provisions clearly and unequivocally manifest a preference for a particular law. For example, the contract may be contained in a standard form that is generally known to be governed by a particular system of law, such as Lloyd's policy of marine insurance.

CHOICE BY ARBITRATORS

Quite often parties to an arbitration fail to exercise their right to select the applicable law to govern the substance of their contract. The pages of arbitral reports are replete with cases where arbitrators had to deal with the problem of applicable law because the parties failed to make a choice of law. There are a variety of reasons why some parties do not include a choice of law in their agreement. The first is that the parties may simply have failed to reach an agreement on which law to select, perhaps as a result of each party insisting on its own national law. Another reason is that the parties may have been much more interested in making a deal than in addressing the issue of applicable law. In one case, the witnesses before a tribunal explained that the parties did not want to risk a rupture of their negotiation process by drafting a clause on applicable law.[91] Still, it could be that the parties simply had incompetent lawyers who forgot to engraft a choice of law clause into their contract. Whatever the reason for the absence of a choice of law clause in a contract, the fact is that it places arbitrators in a legal quandary.

Arbitrators are in a somewhat unique position in this regard. National judges faced with a similar problem would be obliged to refer to their national conflict of law rules. However, arbitrators, unlike judges, do not have national conflict rules to which they could seek recourse in these cases. As one tribunal put it, "The international arbitrator has no *lex fori* from which he can borrow rules of conflict of laws."[92] Yes, arbitrators sit in national jurisdictions, but they are not bound by the conflict of law rules of these jurisdictions because they are not instruments of a State's judicial process in the same way that national courts are.[93] Moreover, national conflict of law rules are designed for national courts, not for international commercial arbitrators.

The general trend in international conventions on arbitration and in institutional arbitration rules is to confer on arbitrators the responsibility to determine applicable law in the absence of an express choice by the parties. A few examples will suffice to illustrate this position. Article 7 of the European Convention on Commercial Arbitration provides, *inter alia,* that "Failing any indication by the parties as to the applicable law, the arbitrators shall apply the proper law under the rule of conflict that the arbitrators deem applicable." This provision has inspired similar provisions in the Model Law,[94] the ICC Rules,[95] and the UNCITRAL Rules.[96]

Most arbitrators do not, however, have as their starting point a search for appropriate conflict rules. Rather they examine the parties' contractual provisions to see whether they are sufficient to resolve the dispute. This attitude is consistent with the doctrine of party autonomy, for a contract is after all an embodiment of the parties' expectations on how their transaction should be organized. Contracts contain provisions that seek to express the parties' contractual obligations and the manner and under what conditions these obligations should be enforced. Normally, the more complex a commercial transaction, the more detailed the contractual provisions. This is because the parties' objective is to set out their expectations as clearly as is necessary to dispel possible misunderstanding of their respective contractual duties.[97] Where the provisions of the contract are sufficiently detailed to resolve the dispute at hand and they do not infringe the provisions of relevant mandatory rules,[98] arbitrators usually apply them without having to determine what the applicable law is. This approach was adopted by the arbitral tribunal in *ICC Case No. 1990 of 1977.*[99] Dealing with the question of applicable law, the tribunal stated that "[i]n so far as the questions in dispute are regulated by the parties in their contract and this contractual regulation does not contravene the mandatory rules of the two laws in question, it is permitted to resolve them on the basis of the contract. . . . These can be resolved without a preliminary decision on the applicable law."[100]

The application of contractual provisions has its in-built limitations. First, however widely contracts are drafted, they rarely contain provisions to govern the entire field of potential areas of dispute.[101] Second, some phrases in contractual provisions may need to be defined within the context of a national law. For example, the delimitation of the precise scope and ramifications of *force majeure* may necessitate reference to a national law. Consequently the use of contractual provisions can not be a substitute in all cases for the making of a positive choice of law. In most cases arbitrators would have to exercise their discretion to select a governing law.

In what ways do arbitrators decide on applicable law in the absence of the parties' express choice? There are five common methods adopted by arbitrators: the use of conflict rules of the place of arbitration; the cumulative application of relevant conflict rules; the use of general principles of conflict of laws; direct application of the *lex mercatoria*; and the application of the substantive law suggested by relevant connecting factors.[102] Let us examine each of these methods.

Conflict Rules of the Place of Arbitration

The use of the conflict rules of the seat of arbitration was first urged by the Institute of International Law in its Amsterdam session in 1957. This was a period in which the jurisdictional theory of arbitration dominated international arbitral jurisprudence. There was at the time a general belief in an organic link between an arbitration and the law of its seat. Reflecting the thinking at this period, the Institute adopted a resolution that "The rules of choice in force in the State of the seat of the arbitral tribunal must be followed to settle the law applicable to the substance of the difference."[103]

This theory was based on the assumption that the perceived organic link between an arbitration and its seat bound arbitrators to apply the same conflict rules that were applicable to judicial proceedings.[104] To reach this conclusion, the theory ascribed the same weight to an arbitral seat as it did to a court's forum. Mann, one of the theory's ardent supporters, notes that just as "the judge has to apply the private international law of the forum, so the arbitrator has to apply the private international law of the forum."[105]

This theory has the benefits of uniformity and predictability. If commonly adopted, it would unify the procedure for determining the applicable law where parties fail to express their choice, and it is predictable in that parties would know beforehand what conflict rules the arbitrators would use to determine the applicable law, at least in cases where they know beforehand the intended place of arbitration.

The conflict rules of the arbitral seat have been used in some awards as a means of determining the applicable law. In *ICC Case No. 1598 of 1971*,[106] the tribunal noted that "[i]f a concrete rule of conflict rules has to be applied, the law in force at the seat of the arbitral tribunal must be followed."[107] Similarly, in *ICC Case No. 1455 of 1967*,[108] the arbitral tribunal stated that "the solution which is in practice the most convenient . . . consists in the reference to the conflict of laws rules of the forum."[109]

This writer believes that the forum theory attaches overly great importance on the seat of arbitration, and seeks unfairly to equate the consequences of a choice of arbitral seat with that of the engagement of a judicial forum. Let us take the latter point first. An arbitral seat is simply not the same as a judicial forum. Arbitrators do not owe an allegiance to an arbitral forum in the same way that national judges do, because arbitrators, unlike judges, are not State agents. Their mission is quite different from that of judges:

A national judge must apply the conflict rules of the forum. He applies his own national law to determine the proper choice of law rules. These are the rules of the State upon which his powers depend, and may express the State's policies as to the correct determination of the extent of legislative jurisdiction of other States. The international arbitrator's powers, on the other hand, are derived from an arbitration agreement, and an arbitrator does not exercise public or institutional powers in the name of the State.[110]

Moreover, advocates of the forum theory attach excessive weight to the choice of an arbitral seat. As has been reiterated a number of times in this book, arbitral seats are sometimes chosen for reasons of convenience: the proximity to the arbitrators and the parties, the quality of the facilities in a particular location, and similar reasons. In other cases, the choice of the seat of arbitration is fortuitous because the choice is made on the parties' behalf by an arbitral institution or some other third party. It seems unfair to ascribe undue weight to the seat of arbitration whose choice is merely fortuitous or a product of the dictates of convenience.[111] Moreso as in some cases the seat of arbitration has no connection either to the parties or their transaction.

The weaknesses of the forum theory led to its gradual abandonment. Its decline arose with the inception of the European Convention, which granted arbitrators the power to apply, in the absence of the parties' express choice, the proper law determined by the rule of conflict that they "deem applicable." This provision freed arbitrators from the bind of the conflict rules of the forum. Its implicit repudiation of the resolution of the Institute of International Law motivated arbitrators to look beyond the conflict rules of the forum in searching for the applicable law. The progeny of the European Convention's approach, namely the ICC Rules, the Model Law and the UNCITRAL Rules, further accelerated the process toward the disintegration of the forum theory. For example, before the enactment of the 1975 ICC Rules, there was no provision on the manner of determining the applicable law in the absence of the parties' choice. Consequently, most ICC arbitrators were influenced by the resolution of the Institute of International Law to apply the conflict rules of the seat of arbitration.[112] However, with the enactment of Article 13(3) in the 1975 ICC Rules, a provision that was inspired by the European Convention, the trend changed, and the forum theory became increasingly outdated. This new trend is exemplified by the statement of the tribunal in *ICC Case No. 3540 of 1980*:[113] "[I]n this field the most recent and authoritative doctrine as well as the jurisprudence of arbitrators, especially that of ICC, acknowledge that, in determining the substantive law, arbitrators may avoid the rules of conflict of the forum."[114] In the same vein, the tribunal in *ICC Case No. 2930 of 1982*[115] noted that "the most authoritative present-day doctrine and international arbitration jurisprudence admit that in determining the substantive law, the arbitrator may leave aside the application of the conflict rules of the forum."[116]

The rejection of the forum theory does not mean that the conflict rules of the forum are never considered relevant by arbitrators determining the choice of law. On the contrary, its rejection simply means a repudiation of the view that in all cases the conflict rules of the forum are the sole indicators of applicable law. Today, some arbitrators may perhaps refer to the conflict rules of the forum where, apart from the fact that it is the *situs* of the arbitration, there are other factors that connect it with the dispute, for example, where one of the parties resides in the forum, or the contract was performed in the forum.[117]

Cumulative Application of Relevant Conflict Rules

This method, which emerged from the U.S. conflict of laws methodology,[118] involves the cumulative application of the conflict rules of legal systems connected with the dispute. Its objective is to ascertain whether the relevant conflict rules connected to the dispute all point to the same substantive law. If they do, the arbitrators apply this law without the need to specify which particular national conflict rule they deem applicable. This method is very useful in false conflict situations—that is, cases in which the competing conflict rules all point toward the application of a particular substantive law.

The rationale for this approach was explained by the tribunal in *ICC Case No. 1176*:[119]

> [I]f [arbitrators] can show on the question in issue that the conflict rules of the different States with which the matter submitted to them have any ties that are similar or lead to a same result, they have the power to apply these common conflict rules since they can be sure of satisfying the implicit or supposed intention of the parties from which they derive their power.[120]

This approach was adopted in *ICC Case No. 953 of 1956*,[121] where, in a dispute between a German party and a Greek party, the arbitrators sitting in Switzerland held:

> To resolve whether the substance of the claim is justified, it is necessary to determine initially the substantive law applicable to the dispute. If the agreement of the parties does not express itself on the subject, it is necessary in the first place to research from where to draw the conflict of laws rules to resolve the question. The answer to the question is sensibly facilitated by the fact that the principles of private international law developed in German law, as well as in Greek law and in Swiss law, lead to the same result.[122]

In determining the conflict rules connected with the transaction, arbitrators use a variety of standards, ranging from the conflict rules of the parties' residence, the rules of the seat of arbitration, and those of the country where the contract is to be performed. For example, in *ICC Case No. 953*, cited above, the tribunal made use of German and Greek law (the laws of the parties' respective residences) and Swiss law (the law of the arbitral seat).

This method inspires a certain confidence in the parties regarding the legitimacy of the conflict rules adopted by the arbitrator. The cumulative application of relevant conflict rules demonstrates to the parties that a conscious attempt was made by the arbitrators to link the choice of law process with their contractual arrangement. This method is therefore more firmly rooted in the expectations of the parties than the forum theory that gives predominant effect to the arbitral seat.

The Achilles' heel of the cumulative method is that it cannot be used in cases where there is a true conflict—that is, where the relevant conflict rules point to different substantive laws. In such cases, the arbitrators have to apply some other method in determining the applicable law. However, the cumulative approach represents an attempt to anchor the choice of a substantive law on the firm grounds of its connection to the parties' contractual arrangement. Although imperfect, it represents a considerable improvement on the forum approach.

General Principles of Conflict of Laws

This approach is based on the presumption that certain principles of conflict of laws are common to the world community, or at any rate to a majority of them. It is thus premised on the possibility of distilling common principles from national conflict rules. There is no doubt that if there are indeed such principles that are generally accepted, they should be applied by arbitrators not only because their application would be deemed to be within the expectations of the parties, but also because their general acceptance argues the case for their application in international commercial relations.

Some arbitral tribunals have applied conflict rules that they claimed were generally accepted. For example, in *ICC Case No. 4650*[123] the tribunal held that it "does not deem it necessary to decide on a specific rule of conflict to designate the proper law of the contract in view of the fact that most major rules in some form or other point to the place of the characteristic or dominant work."[124] Similarly, in *ICC Case No 6527 of 1991*, the tribunal found it "more appropriate to apply the general principles of international private law as stated in international conventions."[125] The tribunal relied on the provisions of the Hague Convention on the law applicable to international sales of goods and the EEC Convention on contractual obligations.

This approach is commendable as it seeks to free the determination of applicable law from the conflict rules of any particular national jurisdiction and to locate it in rules that are common to most jurisdictions or embodied in generally accepted conventions and international commercial practice. The harmonization of national conflict rules through the adoption of conventions, such as the EEC Convention on Contractual Obligation, contributes to the evolution of uniform rules and practices in determining applicable law. Nonetheless, it is important that arbitrators do not hide behind the olive branch of general principles to mask their convenient conclusions as principles of general application.

Direct Application of the *Lex Mercatoria*

There is a discernible trend in arbitral practice that supports the proposition that arbitrators, in the absence of a choice of law by the parties, may apply the so-called *lex mercatoria,* without the need to justify this measure by reference to any national conflict rule. Some advocates of this view go as far as suggesting that the parties' consent to arbitration is indicative of their submission to the *lex mercatoria*. Arguing this position, T. Carbonneau states that the parties' "engagement in a transnational commercial venture and invocation of the international arbitral process constitutes an implied submission to the law which governs all transnational commercial venture."[126] This proposition flies in the face of the fact that many parties to international commercial ventures actually choose national law as their governing law, thereby negating any implied submission to the *lex mercatoria*. Moreover, even when parties do not make an express choice of law, the preponderance of arbitral awards apply national laws, a fact that indicates that there is no one law governing transnational commercial relations, as Carbonneau would have us believe.

Lando, speaking along the same line as Carbonneau, argues that the "*lex mercatoria* has the advantage that it does away with the choice-of-law process which many lawyers abhor."[127] This view implies that arbitrators may dispense with conflict rules and directly apply the *lex mercatoria*. More combative advocates of this view go as far as to suggest that arbitrators may apply the *lex mercatoria* if the State to which the applicable conflict rules point does not have a clear answer to the issue in dispute. They further suggest that arbitrators may apply the *lex mercatoria* where the answer suggested by the relevant national law is "clearly out of line with the reasonable expectations of the parties and the business community as a whole" or where "the rule is not fit for international trade".[128] Acceptance of this latter view would make arbitrators judges of the fitness of national laws for international trade and the needs of the business community. This theory would grant arbitrators the power to dictate which rules of national laws would be applied in the international arena, a rather strange prospect.

The so-called *lex mercatoria*, as we have seen, lacks a comprehensive body of rules sufficient to regulate complex commercial transactions. Worse, its legality is disputed in some jurisdictions and arbitrators run the risk of compromising the enforceability of their awards by applying the *lex mercatoria*.[129]

If the argument of the advocates of the *lex mercatoria* had been that arbitrators should take into account trade usages irrespective of the applicable national law, very few people would dispute that. Indeed arbitrators and national courts have always adopted this position. For example, under ICC Rules arbitrators are enjoined to use trade usages and customs as complementary sources of rules that must be considered together with national law.[130] Regrettably, this is not the view adopted by the advocates of the *lex mercatoria*; they rather suggest that an arbitrator could choose the *lex mercatoria* as the governing legal standard independent of the provisions of relevant national laws. This approach has been uncritically adopted in a number of awards, and in some instances sanctioned by some national courts.

In *Pabalk Ticaret* v. *Norsolor*[131] ICC arbitrators sitting in Vienna held a French party liable for breach of a contract with a Turkish party. In deciding the applicable substantive law the arbitrators declined to apply any national law:

> Faced with the difficulty of choosing a national law the application of which is sufficiently compelling, the Tribunal considered that it was appropriate, given the international nature of the agreement, to leave aside any compelling reference to a specific legislation and apply the international *lex mercatoria*.[132]

On appeal, the Court of Appeal of Vienna set aside a portion of the award (dealing with the amount of damages) on the ground that the arbitrators failed to conform with Article 13(3) of the ICC Rules, which, in the court's view, required them to base their decision on a national law determined by conflict of law analysis. On further appeal to the Austrian Supreme Court, the Court of Appeal's decision was reversed on the ground that the arbitrators' application of the *lex mercatoria* did not infringe any mandatory rule of law.[133]

A similar decision was reached in *Compania Portland* v. *Primary Coal Inc.*[134] In that case the ICC arbitrator, in the absence of a choice of law by the parties, chose the *lex mercatoria* as the governing law. Portland sought to set aside the award in France, the seat of arbitration, on the ground that the arbitrator decided in a manner incompatible with his mandate. According to Portland, the arbitrator erred in not selecting the governing law through the conflict of law methodology as, it claimed, the arbitrator was required to do under the ICC Rules. The Cour d'appel of Paris refused to set aside the award because the arbitrator was not required to make use of a conflict rule belonging to any given system in order to determine the applicable law. According to the court, the arbitrator "was free to refer to the principles governing the matter."[135] The court went on:

The arbitrator applied these principles and determined the most characteristic factor connecting the dispute to a body of rules of substantive law, taking into account the nature of the dispute. He examined the connecting factors invoked, rendered a final decision that none of them justified the application of a [national] law, and decided to apply the body of principles and trade usages called *lex mercatoria,* i.e. international norms which can apply to the solution of such a dispute in the absence of a determined [national] jurisdiction.[136]

It is noteworthy that these decisions were made in civil law jurisdictions that have been traditionally liberal in their treatment of the *lex mercatoria.* Regrettably, the courts did not express any opinion on the question whether the *lex mercatoria* is indeed a comprehensive body of law. In view of the dispute about the legal foundation of the *lex mercatoria* (particularly in some common law jurisdictions), and in view of its incomplete nature, it would seem that arbitrators should not apply the *lex mercatoria* unless the parties themselves indicate a preference for it. As one tribunal correctly notes, the choice of the *lex mercatoria* "would require an agreement between the parties."[137]

Direct Application of a Conflict of Law Rule Without Reference to Any National Law

It is becoming increasingly commonplace for arbitrators to apply a conflict rule without grounding its application on a particular national law. Here the arbitrators examine the important factors connecting the contract to a particular jurisdiction, with the aim of determining which country is most closely connected to the transaction. This is akin to the English proper law doctrine, and it has the benefit of circumventing the rigors of the conflict of law methodology.

It should be recalled that the European Convention,[138] the Model Law,[139] and the ICC Rules,[140] among others, require arbitrators to make a choice of law by reference to the "conflict of law rules which [they] deem applicable." This would seem to suggest that arbitrators should anchor their choice of applicable law on the conflict of law rules of a particular jurisdiction. This interpretation is, however, not generally accepted;[141] some commentators argue that an arbitral tribunal need not rely on any national conflict of law rule in determining the governing law. To avoid this controversy, in all common law provinces and the territories in Canada the legislation adopting the Model Law were modified to free arbitrators from the requirement of applying national conflict rules.[142] For example, Article 28(3) of the British Columbia International Commercial Arbitration Act[143] provides that failing an express choice of law by the parties "the arbitral tribunal shall apply the rules of law it considers appropriate given all the circumstances surrounding the dispute." Explaining the rationale behind this provision, J. Blom, a member of the task force that recommended British

Columbia's adoption of the Model Law, notes that "the task force hoped that freeing the arbitral tribunal from having to proceed to a decision via conflict of laws, would allow the tribunal to decide on the merits of the dispute in the most direct manner and with a minimum of artifice."[144] Similarly, in its resolution on The Autonomy of the Parties in International Contracts between Private Persons or Entities, the Institute of International Law[145] stipulated that "[i]n the absence of an express agreement, the choice [of law] shall be derived from those circumstances which indicate clearly the intention of the parties."[146]

Arbitrators often use this direct method in determining the applicable law. In *ICC Case No. 4237*,[147] the tribunal in exercising its discretion to make a choice of law declined to do so through the national conflict of laws methodology:

> In view of the international character of the present arbitration, the arbitrator deems it appropriate to apply those conflict rules which are generally followed in international arbitrations of this kind under consideration. The decided international awards published so far show a preference for the conflict rule according to which the contract is governed by the law of the country with which it has the closest connection. The country with which it has its closest connection is the country where the party who has to carry out the most characteristic performance has its head office.[148]

A similar approach was adopted in *ICC Case No. 3316*.[149] This approach is somewhat similar to the general principles method in that its application presupposes the general application of a norm favoring the law of the place with which the contract is most closely connected. However, there is a significant difference between the direct application method and the application of general principles. Arbitrators using the direct methodology rely on connecting factors in locating applicable law not necessarily because the use of these connecting factors is generally accepted, but because they deem this method appropriate. Arbitrators using the direct approach need not demonstrate that the approach is commonly accepted; all they have to do is to demonstrate their preference for this method. It should be noted that the direct approach, which is essentially an indirect application of the proper law doctrine, is becoming the dominant conflict of law method in modern legislation and court decisions.[150] It was adopted by the European Convention on Contractual Obligations. Article 4(1) of the convention provides, *inter alia*, that in the event of a failure by the parties to make an express choice of law, "the contract shall be governed by the law of the country with which it is most closely connected."[151]

This writer believes that the direct approach is best suited for eradicating the confusion that this area of arbitration has become. If generally accepted, it would enable arbitrators to directly select the applicable law without the rigors of deciding which conflict rule to apply. An arbitrator faced with the problem of determining the governing law in the absence of the parties' agreement would directly apply the law most closely connected to the contract. It is to be hoped that the next international project on arbitration will adopt this straightforward approach to choice of law by arbitrators. Canadian legislations have led the way in this respect.

CONCLUSION

The lesson to be learned from the discussion in this chapter seems to be that parties to international contracts should endeavor to make an express choice of law to govern their contract, preferably national law. Such a choice simplifies matters a great deal: the principle of party autonomy makes such choice binding on arbitrators, subject of course to mandatory provisions of relevant laws.

As we have seen, arbitral practice regarding the determination of an applicable law in the absence of the parties' choice is still in a state of flux, with different arbitrators adopting different approaches. While the method of applying the law most closely connected to the transaction seems to be the emerging common practice in this regard, parties are better advised to put this matter beyond doubt by stipulating their own choice of law.

NOTES

1. P. North and J. Fawcett, *Cheshire and North Private International Law*, 11th ed. (London: Butterworths, 1987) at 449.

2. For example, Article 187(1) of the Swiss Private International Law Statute, 1987, provides that an "arbitral tribunal shall decide the case according to the rules of law agreed upon by the parties." In the same vein Article 1054 of the Netherlands Code of Civil Procedure stipulates that "If parties have made a choice of law, the arbitrator decides in accordance with the rules of law chosen by the parties." See also P. North, "The E.E.C. Convention on the Law Applicable to Contractual Obligations (1980): Its History and Main Features" in P. North, (ed.) *Contract Conflicts: The E.E.C. Convention on the Law Applicable to Contractual Obligations —A Comparative Study* (Amsterdam: North-Holland Publishing Company, 1982) 3 at 12; and G. Wetter, "Choice of Law in International Arbitration Proceedings in Sweden" (1984) *Swedish and Int'l Arb.* 16.

3. O. Lando, "The Law Applicable to the Merits of the Dispute" in P. Sarcevic (ed.) *Essays on International Commercial Arbitration* (London: Graham and Trotman, 1989) 129 at 134.

4. J. Lew, *Applicable Law in International Commercial Arbitration: A Study in Commercial Arbitration Awards* (Dobbs Ferry, NY: Oceana Publications, 1978) at 75.

5. See W. Craig, W. Park, and J. Paulsson, *International Chamber of Commerce Arbitration*, 2d ed. (Dobbs Ferry, NY: Oceana Publications, 1990) at 621.

6. Extracted in S. Jarvin and Y. Derains, *Collection of ICC Arbitral Awards: 1974–1985* (Deventer, The Netherlands: Kluwer Law and Taxation Publishers,

1990) 3 at 4–5. See also the award in *ICC Case No. 5865 of 1989*, extracted in (1990) 1:2 *The ICC Int'l Court of Arbitration Bull.* at 23.

7. See Lord Wright in *Vita Food Products* v. *Unus Shipping Co.* [1939] A.C. 277 at 290.

8. See A. Anton and P. Beaumont, *Private International Law*, 2d ed. (Edinburgh: W. Green, 1990) at 267.

9. See M. Rubino-Sammartano, *International Arbitration Law* (Deventer, The Netherlands: Kluwer Law and Taxation Publishers, 1990) at 252.

10. See A. Redfern and M. Hunter, *Law and Practice of International Commercial Arbitration*, 2d ed. (London: Sweet and Maxwell, 1991) at 101.

11. See section entitled "Implied Choice of Law."

12. This phenomenon is, however, not pervasive in arbitral practice. A former general counsel of the ICC Court of Arbitration notes that the *lex mercatoria* "rarely appears" in ICC awards. See S. Jarvin, Comment (1986) *JDI* 1138.

13. O. Lando, "The Lex Mercatoria and International Commercial Arbitration" (1985) 34 *I.C.L.Q.* 747.

14. A. Redfern and M. Hunter, *Law and Practice of International Commercial Arbitration*, 1st ed. (London: Sweet and Maxwell, 1986) at 92. See also M. Medwig, "The New Law Merchant: Legal Rhetoric and Commercial Reality" (1993) 24 *Law & Policy Int'l Bus.* 589.

15. C. Schmitthoff, *Commercial Law in a Changing Economic Climate*, 2d ed. (London: Sweet and Maxwell, 1981) at 20. The issue whether arbitrators can apply the *lex mercatoria* independent of an express choice by the parties is addressed in the subsection entitled "Direct Application of the *Lex Mercatoria*." The following discussion focuses on cases where the parties themselves expressly chose the *lex mercatoria* as the governing law.

16. L. Trakman, *The Law Merchant: The Evolution of Commercial Law* (Littleton, CO: Fred B. Rothman, 1983) at 7.

17. See C. Schmitthoff, supra note 15 at 2 *et seq*; C. Stoecker, "The Lex Mercatoria: To What Extent Does It Exist?" (1990) 7 *J. Int'l Arb.* 101 at 102 *et seq*; L. Trakman, id. at 7 *et seq*.

18. As Pollock noted with regard to English law:

> Yet the law merchant has not wholly lost its old character. It has not forgotten its descent from the medieval law of nature which claimed to be a rule of universal reason embodied in the various forms of cosmopolitan usage. Conforming to English procedure and legal method, it can still be reinforced by additions from established general custom.

F. Pollock, "Introduction to the Commercial Law of Great Britain and Ireland" in W. Bowstead and Sir Thomas Scrutton (eds.) *Commercial Laws of the World*, vol. XIII (Boston Book Co., 1911) at 11.

19. B. Goldman, "The Applicable Law: General Principles of Law—The Lex Mercatoria" in J. Lew (ed.) *Contemporary Problems of International Arbitration* (London: Centre for Commercial Law Studies, 1986) at 114.

20. O. Lando, supra note 13 at 747.

21. O. Lando, supra note 3 at 144–146. See also M. Chang, *The Autonomy of International Commercial and Maritime Arbitration: International, Canadian and Far Eastern Perspectives* (Seoul: International Legal Studies, 1989) at 154–167.

22. C. Schmitthoff, supra note 15 at 22–23.

23. See Lord Mustill, "The New Lex Mercatoria: The First Twenty-Five Years" in M. Bos and I. Brownlie (eds.) *Liber Amicorum for Lord Wilberforce* (Oxford: Clarendon Press, 1987) 149 at 156.

24. See G. Herrmann, "The Contribution of the ICC to the Development of International Trade Law" in N. Horn and C. Schmitthoff (eds.), *The Transnational Law of International Commercial Transactions* (Deventer, The Netherlands: Kluwer Law and Taxation Publishers, 1982) 35. See also in the same book, R. Dolzer, "International Agencies for the Formulation of Transnational Economic Law" at 61.

25. For the role of ICC in the harmonization of international trade rules, see M. Rowe, "The Contribution of the ICC to the Development of International Trade Law" in N. Horn and C. Schmitthoff, id at 51.

26. Lord Justice Mustill, supra note 23 at 157.

27. J. Robert and T. Carbonneau, *The French Law of Arbitration* (New York: Matthew Bender, 1983) at 11:4–19.

28. See Lord Justice Mustill, supra note 23 at 159.

29. See T. Carbonneau, "Rendering Arbitral Awards with Reasons: The Elaboration of a Commercial Law of International Transactions" (1985) 23 *Col. Journ.* 579; J. Lew, "The Case for the Publication of Arbitration Awards" in P. Sanders (ed.) *The Art of Arbitration: Liber Amicorum for Pieter Sanders* (Deventer, The Netherlands: Kluwer Law and Taxation Publishers, 1982) at 223.

30. See W. Craig et al., supra note 5 at 619.

31. Id. at 621–631.

32. See H. Smit, "Substance and Procedure in International Arbitration: The Development of a New Legal Order" (1991) 65 *Tulane L.R.* 1309 at 1315–1322.

33. See P. North, *Private International Law Problems in Common Law Jurisdictions* (Dordrecht, The Netherlands: Martinus Nijhoff, 1993) at 110–111.

34. O. Lando, supra note 13 at 752.

35. H. Berman and F. Dasser, "The 'New' Law Merchant and the 'Old': Sources, Content, and Legitimacy" in T. Carbonneau (ed.) *Lex Mercatoria and Arbitration* (New York: Transnational Juris Publications, 1990) 21 at 32.

36. O. Lando, supra note 13 at 752–753.

37. M. Reisman, Book Review (1986) 80 *A.J.I.L.* 268 at 271.

38. See F. A. Mann's introduction to the *Lex Mercatoria and Arbitration*, supra note 35 at xxi.

39. On the difference between the application of the *lex mercatoria* and the practice of amiable composition, see D. Rivkin, "Enforceability of Arbitral Awards Based on *Lex Mercatoria*" (1993) 9 *Arbitration Int'l* 67 at 71–72.

40. In the English case of *Hutton* v. *Warren* (1836) 1 M. & W. 466, the court stated:

> It has long been settled that in commercial transactions extrinsic evidence of custom and usage is admissible to annex incidents to written contracts in matters with respect to which they are silent. The same rule has also been applied to contracts in other transactions in life and this has been done upon the principle or presumption that, in such transactions, the parties did not mean to express in writing the whole of the contract by which they intended to be bound, but to contract with reference to those known usages.

A similar principle is embodied in Article 1135 of the French Civil Code: "Contracts give rise not only to the obligations expressed therein, but also to all consequences which equity, usages or the law attach to that obligation in accordance with its nature."

41. Similarly, Article 13(5) of the ICC Rules enjoins arbitrators in all cases to take into account relevant trade usages.

42. See W. Craig et al., supra note 5 at 617.

43. See Id.

44. See B. Goldman, supra note 19 at 122–123.

45. See J. Robert and T. Carbonneau, supra note 27 at 11:4–19. See also *Norsolor* v. *Pabalk Ticaret* (1984) 9 *Y. Comm. Arb.* 159; *Compania Talenciana de Cementos Portland SA* v. *Primary Coal Inc.* (1991) *Mealey's Int'l Arb. Rep* 7.

46. See Lord Justice Mustill and S. Boyd, *The Law and Practice of Commercial Arbitration in England*, 2d ed. (London: Butterworths, 1989) at 81; F. A. Mann, "Private Arbitration and Public Policy" (1985) 4 *Civil Justice Q.* 256 at 264. But see M. Hunter, "Lex Mercatoria" (1987) *L.M.C.L.Q.* 277.

47. On the prospects of enforcing in England an award based on the *lex mercatoria*, see M. Mustill, "Contemporary Problems in International Commercial Arbitration: A Response" (1989) 17 *Int'l Bus. Law* 161 at 162.

48. A. Goldstajn, "The New Law Merchant Reconsidered" in F. Fabricius (ed.) *Law and International Trade* (Frankfurt: Athenaum Verlag, 1973) 171 at 181. The role of mandatory rules of national law in international arbitration is considered in Chapter 6.

49. Lord Mustill, supra note 23 at 174–177. See also M. Blessing, "The New Arbitration Law in Switzerland: A Significant Step Towards Liberalism" (1988) 5 *J. Int'l Arb.* 9 at 61–62.

50. O. Lando, supra note 3 at 110.

51. The precise limits to the powers of an *amiable compositeur* is not entirely free from controversy. This is evidenced in the definition of *amiable compositeur* contained in the *Dictionary of Arbitration*:

> A French phrase for an arbitrator who has great freedom formulating the terms of his award. The concept of *amiable compositeur* is widely used in continental legal system. It has been variously defined as conciliator, arbitrator *de facto*, or in the most extreme sense, an arbitrator under no obligation to observe the rules of law. An *amiable compositeur* is nevertheless subject to the rules of "natural justice" and must observe the fundamental rules governing judicial procedure . . .

(New York: American Arbitration Association, 1970) at 14. See M. Mustill and S. Boyd, supra note 46, at 76; R. Christie, "Amiable Composition in French and English Law" (1992) 58:4 *Arbitration: J. Chartered Inst. of Arbs.* 259; G. Naon, *Choice-of-Law Problems in International Commercial Arbitration* (Tubingen: Mohr, 1992) at 97.

52. *ICC Case No. 4567* (1986) 11 *Y. Comm. Arb.* 143 at 147.

53. D. Thomas, "Commercial Arbitration—Justice According to Law" (1983) 2 *Civil Justice Q.* 166 at 182.

54. E. Cohn, "Commercial Arbitration and the Rules of Law" (1944) 4 *U.T.L.J.* 1.

55. See P. O'Keefe, *Arbitration in International Trade* (Sydney: Prosper Law Publications, 1975) at 193.

56. *ICC Case No. 3755 of 1988*, extracted in (1990) 1:2 *The ICC International Court of Arbitration Bulletin* at 25. The arbitrators in the above case went on to say:

According to a more liberal interpretation, the arbitrators invested with the authority of *amiable compositeurs* have the right to deviate from the applicable positive law according to the rules of international private law, given that they consider it necessary and just, in conformity with the general objective of the contract, and more generally, when it is in view of a solution to the dispute. In this case, the arbitrators do not have to justify their divergence from the law which is normally applicable to the case." Id.

57. R. David, *Arbitration in International Trade* (Deventer, The Netherlands: Kluwer Law and Taxation Publishers, 1985) at 335.

58. According to Christie, "[t]he parties to a long-term contract are often more like partners in joint venture than potential adversaries, and a pragmatic solution achieved by amiable composition is more likely than a strictly legal solution to enable them to continue their association." Supra note 51 at 266.

59. "Analytical Commentary on the Draft Text of a Model Law on International Commercial Arbitration," United Nations, General Assembly, A/CN.(/264, March 25, 1985, at 62–63.

60. The subject of mandatory rules and their effect on international commercial arbitration is discussed in Chapter 6.

61. *ICC Case No. 1677* (1978) 3 *Y. Comm. Arb.* 217. Chapter 6 examines the kinds of mandatory rules that arbitrators must respect.

62. (1982) 7 *Y. Comm. Arb.* 96.

63. Id. at 105.

64. See W. Craig et at., supra note 5 at 137. Article 1497 of the French Code of Civil Procedure allows international commercial arbitrators to rule *"ex aequo et bono* if the agreement of the parties gives it this authority."

65. For example, arbitrators in Quebec, following the French practice, have the power to act as amiable compositors. See J. Brierley, " 'Equity and Good Conscience' and Amiable Composition in Canadian Arbitration Law" (1991) 19 *C.B.L.J.* 461 at 464.

66. See, for example, A. Foustoucos, "Greece" (1980) 5 *Y. Comm. Arb.* 54 at 47; O. Glossner, "Federal Republic of Germany" (1979) 4 *Y. Comm. Arb.* 60 at 73; Y. Derains, "France" (1981) 6 *Y. Comm. Arb.* 1 at 17; J. Trolle, "Denmark" (1980) 5 *Y. Comm. Arb.* 28 at 36; L. Matray, "Belgium" (1980) 5 *Y. Comm. Arb.* 1 at 17.

67. These include several Canadian provinces. See J. Brierley, supra note 65. See also A. McInnis, "Amiable Composition: Whither the Direction of Hong Kong Arbitration Law" (1991) 21 *H.K.L.J.* 343; M. Jacobs, *Commercial Arbitration: Law and Practice* (Sydney: The Law Book Company, 1990) at 5501.

68. *Orion Compania* v. *Belfort* [1962] 2 Lloyd's L.R. 257 at 267. See also W. Gill, "United Kingdom" (1977) 11 *Y. Comm. Arb.* 90 at 107; E. Cohn, "The Rules of Arbitration of the International Chamber of Commerce" (1965) 14 *I.C.L.Q.* 156.

69. *Czarnikow* v. *Roth, Schmidt & Co.* [1922] 2 K.B. 478 at 484.

70. [1978] 1 Lloyd's L.R. 357.

71. Id. at 362.

72. See R. Christie, supra note 51.

73. [1989] 1 Lloyd's L.R. 473.

74. Id. at 485.

75. For a reasoned argument against the present state of English law on the matter, see D. Thomas, supra note 53. See also S. Boyd, " 'Arbitration Not To Be Bound by Law' Clauses" (1990) 6 *Arb. Int'l* 122; K. Bentil, "Commercial Arbitration

Authorised Not to Apply Strict Rules of Law and Judicial Review" (1992) *J. Business Law* 26.

76. See Section 1(1) of the English Arbitration Act, 1979.

77. See Section 3 of the English Arbitration Act, 1979.

78. F. A. Mann, "*Lex Facit Arbitrum*" in P. Sanders (ed.) *International Arbitration: Liber Amicorum for Martin Domke* (The Hague: Martinus Nijhoff, 1967) 157 at 176.

79. D. Thomas, supra note 53 at 182.

80. For a comparative analysis of this theory, see O. Sandrock, "The Place of Arbitration and the Law Applicable to the Merits of the Dispute" in M. Storme and F. Ly (eds.) *The Place of Arbitration* (Ghent: Mys and Breesch, 1992) at 89.

81. [1968] 1 W.L.R. 406.

82. Id. at 413.

83. See O. Lando, supra note 3 at 136.

84. Writing about the Foreign Trade Tribunal in Yugoslavia, A. Goldstajn noted:

> If a dispute has been submitted to the FTA in Belgrade and if there is no specific stipulation on the choice of law it can be assumed, by virtue of generally accepted practice, that the agreement of the parties to submit the case to the standing arbitration tribunal in Yugoslavia, justifies the assumption that it was their will to accept the Yugoslav legal system as competent for the settlement of their relationship . . . i.e. tying up the arbitration award to a specific legal system.

A. Goldstajn, "Submission to Arbitration of Disputes with a Foreign Element" (1959) 5 *Yugos. R. Int'l L.* 118 at 120.

85. (1956) 83 *Clunet* 452.

86. Id. at 453.

87. See J. Lew, "The Place of Arbitration and the Applicable Procedural Law in English Common Law" in M. Storme and F. Ly (eds.), supra note 80 at 80–82.

88. *Compagnie d'Armement Maritime SA* v. *Compagnie Tunisienne de Navigation SA* [1971] A.C. 572. Lord Wilberforce stated that:

> An arbitration clause must be treated as an indication, to be considered together with the rest of the contract and relevant surrounding facts. Always it will be a strong indication; often, especially where there are parties of different nationality or a variety of transactions which may arise under the contract, it will be the only clear indication. But in some cases it must give way where other indications are clear. Id. at 600.

89. See P. North and J. Fawcett, supra note 1 at 459.

90. R. Rooij and M. Polak, *Private International Law in The Netherlands* (Deventer, The Netherlands: Kluwer Law and Taxation Publishers, 1987) at 119.

91. *ICC Case No. 2997 of 1978*, reported in S. Jarvin and Y. Derains, supra note 6 at 61.

92. *ICC Case No. 1512 of 1971*, reported in S. Jarvin and Y. Derains, supra note 6, 3 at 4.

93. P. Lalive affirms this fact as follows:

> The arbitrator exercises a private mission, conferred contractually, and it is only by a rather artificial interpretation that one can say that his powers arise from—and even then very indirectly—a tolerance of the State of the place of arbitration, or rather of the various States involved (States of the parties, of the *siege*, of the probable places of execution of the award), which accept the institution of arbitration, or of the community of nations, notably those which

have ratified international treaties in the matter. Would it not be to force the international arbitrator into a kind of Procrustean bed if he were assimilated to a State Judge, who is imperatively bound to the system of private international law of the country where he sits and from which he derives his power of decision.

Quoted by W. Craig et al., supra note 5 at 265. Similarly, in *Mitsubishi Motor Corp.* v. *Soler Chrysler-Plymouth*, the U.S. Supreme Court noted that "the international arbitral tribunal owes no prior allegiance to the legal norms of particular states; hence it has no direct obligation to vindicate their statutory dictates. The tribunal . . . is bound to effectuate the interests of the parties." 105 S. Ct. 3346 at 3359 (1985). See also A. von Mehren, "Arbitration between States and Foreign Enterprises: The Significance of the Institute of International Law's Santiago de Compostela Resolution" (1990) 5 *ICSID Review* 54 at 56–57.

94. Article 28(2) of the Model Law provides that "Failing any designation by the parties, the arbitral tribunal shall apply the law determined by the conflict of law rules which it considers applicable.

95. Article 13(3) of the ICC Rules provides that "In the absence of any indication by the parties as to the applicable law, the arbitrator shall apply the law designated as the proper law by the rule of conflict which he deems appropriate."

96. Article 33 of the UNCITRAL Arbitration Rules provides that "Failing such designation by the parties the arbitral tribunal shall apply the law determined by the conflict of laws rules which it considers applicable."

97. This is why building contracts can in some cases run into hundreds of pages.

98. The subject of mandatory rules is discussed in Chapter 6.

99. Reported in S. Jarvin and Y. Derains, supra note 6 at 20.

100. Id. at 20.

101. See M. Hunter, J. Paulsson, N. Rawding, and A. Redfern, *The Freshfield Guide to Arbitration and ADR: Clauses in International Contracts* (Deventer, The Netherlands: Kluwer Law and Taxation Publishers, 1993) at 32.

102. See the interim award in *ICC Case No. 5717 of 1988*, extracted in (1990) 1:2 *The ICC Int'l Court of Arbitration Bull.* at 22.

103. The Institute has since reversed its position. In its 1991 Resolution on The Autonomy of the Parties in International Contracts between Private Parties and Entities, the Institute stated: "In the absence of an express agreement [on applicable substantive law by the parties] the choice shall be derived from those circumstances which indicate clearly the intention of the parties." (1991) 64 *Yearbook Institute Int'l Law* 384, Article 3(2).

104. See *B.V. Haegens Bouw* v. *N.V. Theuma Deurenindustrie* (1993) 18 *Y. Comm. Arb.* 612 at 614 (Court of Appeal, Brussels).

105. F. A. Mann, supra note 78 at 167.

106. S. Jarvin and Y. Derains, supra note 6 at 19.

107. Id.

108. Id. at 18.

109. Id. Other awards that have utilized the law of the forum include *ICC Case No. 2637 of 1975*, reported in S. Jarvin and Y. Derains, supra note 6 at 16; *ICC Case No. 5460 of 1987* (1988) 13 *Y. Comm. Arb.* 104 at 106.

110. W. Craig et al., supra note 5 at 285.

111. See S. Baker and M. Davis, *The UNCITRAL Arbitration Rules in Practice: The Experience of the Iran-United States Claims Tribunal* (Deventer, The Netherlands: Kluwer Law and Taxation Publishers, 1992) at 176.

112. As could be seen from the awards cited above, most of the awards that applied the forum theory were decided before 1975.

113. Reported in S. Jarvin and Y. Derains, supra note 6 at 105.

114. Id. at 109.

115. (1984) 9 *Y. Comm. Arb.* 105.

116. Id.

117. See W. Craig et al., supra note 5 at 287.

118. V. Danilowicz, "The Choice of Law in International Arbitration" (1986) 9 *Hastings Int'l & Comp. L.R.* 235 at 265.

119. Cited by Y. Derains, "Possible Conflict of Law Rules and the Rules Applicable to the Substance of the Dispute" in P. Sanders (ed.) *UNCITRAL's Project for a Model Law on International Commercial Arbitration* (Deventer, The Netherlands: Kluwer Law and Taxation Publishers, 1984) at 177.

120. Id.

121. (1978) 3 *Y. Comm. Arb.* 214.

122. Id.

123. (1987) 12 *Y. Comm. Arb.* 111.

124. Id. at 112. See also *ICC Case No. 3043* (1979) Clunet 1001.

125. (1993) *Y. Comm. Arb.* 44 at 46.

126. T. Carbonneau, supra note 29, at 597. In one award, the tribunal in applying the *lex mercatoria* noted that "this practice [common practice in international arbitration particularly in the field of oil drilling], which must have been known to the parties, should be regarded as representing their implicit will." See *ICC Case No. 3572 of 1982* (1989) 14 *Y. Comm. Arb.* 111 at 117.

127. O. Lando, supra note 13 at 754.

128. A. Lowenfeld, "Lex Mercatoria: An Arbitrator's View" in T. Carbonneau, supra note 35 at 37, 51.

129. As W. Craig et al. note, "it would seem futile and imprudent to make abstract declarations to the effect that they [arbitrators] have rendered an award on a legal foundation whose legitimacy may still not be apparent to many national courts." Supra note 5 at 300.

130. See Article 13(5) of the ICC Rules. See also W. Craig, "International Ambition and National Restraints in ICC Arbitration" (1985) 1 *Arb. Int'l* 49 at 67.

131. (1984) 9 *Y. Comm. Arb.* 109.

132. Id. at 110.

133. (1984) 9 *Y. Comm. Arb.* 159.

134. (1991) 16 *Y. Comm. Arb.* 142.

135. Id. at 144.

136. Id.

137. *ICC Case No. 4650* (1987) 12 *Y. Comm. Arb.* 111.

138. Article 7.

139. Article 28(2).

140. Article 13(3).

141. In *Compania*, supra note 134 at 144, the Court of Appeal of Paris held that the ICC Rules did not require an arbitrator "to make use of a conflict rule belong-

ing to a given legal system in order to determine the law applicable to the substance."

142. See J. Castel, "International Commercial Arbitration" in P. Emond, (ed.) *Commercial Dispute Resolution: Alternatives to Litigation* (Ontario: Canada Law Book, 1989) 121 at 142.

143. S.B.C. 1986, c. 14.

144. J. Blom, "Conflict of Laws Aspects of the International Commercial Arbitration Act" in R. Paterson and B. Thompson, (eds.) *UNCITRAL Arbitration Model in Canada* (Toronto: Carswell, 1987) 127 at 131.

145. Supra note 103.

146. Article 3(2).

147. Reported in S. Jarvin and Y. Derains, supra note 6 at 167.

148. Id. at 170–171.

149. Extracted in S. Jarvin and Y. Derains, supra note 6 at 87. See also the interim award in *ICC Case No. 5717 of 1988*, supra note 102 at 22; interim award in *ICC Case No. 5660 of 1990* (1992) 17 *Y. Comm. Arb.* 226.

150. See O. Lando, supra note 3 at 142–143.

151. Article 4(2) of the convention further contains a presumption that a contract "is most closely connected with the country where the party who is to effect the performance which is characteristic of the contract has, at the time of conclusion of the contact, his habitual residence, or in the case of a body corporate or unincorporated, its central administration."

CHAPTER FIVE

Issues in the Law Applicable to State Contracts

INTRODUCTION

The globalization of commercial activities has stimulated the flow of business across national boundaries. A substantial part of these business relations involves foreign private parties and governments. Governments of economically developing countries are especially involved in these transactions because in most of these countries active State participation in foreign trade and investment is considered an essential part of national economic policy. This trend is facilitated by moves toward the creation of a New International Economic Order,[1] by virtue of which States play an active and dominant role in the control of their resources and the regulation of multinational corporations operating in their territories.

Contracts between States, or State agencies, and foreign private parties are called State contracts so as to underscore the fact that a State party is involved in the transaction.[2] State contracts vary from the old-type concession agreements to more recent types, such as joint ventures, turnkey projects, technology transfer agreements, and management agreements.

Providing a suitable conflict resolution machinery in State contracts could pose considerable problems. While the private party may not have confidence in the impartiality of the court of the State party, State parties are in most cases reluctant to submit disputes between them and foreign nationals to the municipal courts of another country. In these kinds of situations "arbitration imposes itself for a lack of an acceptable alternative."[3] The arbitration of State contract disputes is on the increase,[4] and there is a proliferation of investment agreements providing for arbitration of disputes under the auspices of the International Centre for the Settlement of Investment Disputes.[5]

This chapter examines some of the legal issues that arise in connection with the law applicable to the merits of State contract disputes. It focuses on some of the regimes that have been suggested as governing these types of disputes, and concludes with an examination of the role that renegotiation can play in State contract relations.

STABILIZATION CLAUSES

One peculiar characteristic of State contracts is that one of the parties, the State, has the ability to alter its laws in such a manner as to affect the rights and obligations created by the contract. Under the proper law doctrine, by virtue of which the proper law of a contract is determined, in the absence of an express agreement by the parties, by the law with which the contract is most closely connected,[6] the applicable law in a State contract will usually be the law of the State party. This is because in most instances the transactions involved in a State contract would have very significant ties with the territory of the State party. For example, investments contemplated in investment agreements are usually made in the territory of the State party.[7] If the law of the State party is applicable in State contract disputes (either by virtue of the parties' express choice or by operation of choice of law methodology), the State party could effect changes in the rights and liabilities arising under the contract by enacting legislation designed to achieve this purpose.

One of the techniques developed to circumvent the prospect of a State party altering the contractual balance in a State contract is the stabilization of the contract. This is done by the means of stabilization clauses which are designed to freeze the essential provisions of State contracts by prohibiting any legislative or administrative act that derogates from, or is otherwise inconsistent with, the provisions of the contract or the legal environment of the transaction.[8] The aim of these clauses is to insulate the State contract from changes in the law of the State party. Changes in the State law subsequent to the date of the contract become ineffectual in altering the obligations of the parties. It is believed that this insulation from subsequent changes in the law of the State party protects the private party from the risk of adverse changes of that law by the State party.[9]

There are three possible ways of stabilizing a State contract.[10] The first method is by incorporating the State law into the contract and freezing it as of a stipulated date,[11] thereby precluding the application of all subsequent legislation that would otherwise apply to the contract. Another method of stabilization is by stipulating that any enactment or regulation made subsequent to the date of the contract cannot materially affect the rights and obligations of the parties under the contract. This stipulation is coupled with a pledge by the State party that obligations under the contract can be altered only by the mutual agreement of the parties.[12] The third method is by a provision stipulating that any subsequent legislation or regulation shall be inoperative in connection with the contract if the legislation or regulation is inconsistent with contractual provisions, or if the legislation or regulation, although not inconsistent with the contractual provisions, has an material adverse effect on it.[13]

There is considerable doubt as to the validity and efficacy of stabilization clauses.[14] One view is that these clauses inhibit the exercise of the State party's right to permanent sovereignty over its resources.[15] The ascription of binding effect to these clauses, it is said, fails to reckon with the fact that a State "has to take into account not only immediate pecuniary benefits of the agreement as an ordinary party would," but also has to "assess the impact of the agreement on the political, economic and social life" of its community.[16]

On the other hand, some observers argue that by consenting to a stabilization clause a State makes a representation from which it cannot equitably retreat:

> In subscribing to a protection clause, the host government has thus created to the benefit of the other contracting party a legitimate expectation, which the government may not subsequently frustrate without infringing the principle of good faith. Certain authors refer here to the principle of estoppel which forbids the State to take a position contrary to that which it took in the contract and on the faith of which the investor has obligated himself.[17]

It would seem that central to the validity of stabilization clauses is the question whether a State can by contractual arrangement restrict its capacity to exercise its legislative functions. If this is not possible, stabilization clauses can never achieve their objective of insulating State contracts from the legislative activities of the State party.

The sole arbitrator in the *Texaco Arbitration*,[18] Professor Dupuy, entertained no doubt whatsoever that a State can by virtue of a contractual arrangement limit its sovereign powers:

> [T]o decide otherwise would in fact recognize that all contractual commitments undertaken by a State have been undertaken under a purely permissive condition on its part and are therefore lacking of any legal effect. From the point of view of its advisability, such a solution would gravely harm the credibility of States since it would mean that contracts signed by them did not bind them; it would introduce in such contracts a fundamental imbalance because in these contracts only one party—the party contracting with the State—would be bound. In law, such an outcome would go directly against the most elementary principle of good faith and for this reason it cannot be accepted.[19]

The approach adopted in *Texaco* fails to draw a distinction between State contracts and other private contractual arrangements.[20] In the latter case, which involves the private interests of individual contracting parties operating for the purposes of profit maximization, there is a strong case for a rule preventing one of the parties from unilaterally altering the contractual balance of the agreement. This is because the parties represent private interests and they ought to be allowed to operate on an equal footing, with a national legal system ensuring that the contractual system is fair and equitable.

In State contracts, however, the State's interests go beyond the narrow objective of profit maximization and extends to the enhancement of the welfare of its citizenry. To State parties, State contracts are a component of an overall economic policy designed to actualize the needs and demands of their citizens. These contracts are, to States, vehicles for the furtherance of public interests. This fact argues against the application of legal rules specifically designed for commercial transactions involving private parties to State contracts that implicate the national interests of a State.[21] State contracts by virtue of their public interest component "cannot be insulated from the pressures which impinge on public institutions such as political changes in the country, changed economic conditions and the general expectations of the public."[22]

It is noteworthy that under the domestic laws of most economically developed countries, a contractual clause is viewed as incapable of denying the government the right to terminate a contract by a subsequent legislative act.[23] Such clauses are considered an unwarranted limitation on the capacity of the State to discharge its public duties. In *Georgia* v. *City of Chattanooga*,[24] for example, the U.S. Supreme Court stated "[t]he taking of private property for public use upon just compensation is so often necessary for the proper performance of governmental functions that the power is deemed essential to the life of the State. It cannot be surrendered, and, if attempted to be contracted away, it may be resumed at will."[25] This principle is founded on the realization that a State needs its unfettered legislative powers in the discharge of its public duties. A contractual limitation on the legislative powers of a State subjugates the public interests of the State to the needs of a single party, a prospect that the U.S. Supreme Court considered repugnant and untenable. One may then ask why the position should be different in the arena of international commerce?[26] Certainly, a foreign private party's commercial interests are not more valuable than those of nationals of the State party, and the public policy implications of a State contract are no less desirous of recognition simply because a foreign private party is involved. One sees no compelling reason why this principle should not extend to State contracts in international transactions.

Professor Dupuy in his award in *Texaco Arbitration* suggests that a stabilization clause "does not affect in principle the legislative and regulatory sovereignty" of the State party because the State party reserves all its prerogatives to issue laws and regulations "in respect of national and foreign persons with which it has not undertaken such commitment."[27] According to him, the clause only precludes certain acts "as far as the contracting parties are concerned—with respect to whom [the] commitment has been undertaken."[28] Professor Dupuy, however, misses the point: it is not whether the legislative competence of a State can be circumscribed in favor of a single contracting party, but whether such a limitation is valid at all. That a State is only precluded from making legislation affecting a particular contract in no way detracts from the fact that its legislative competence is infringed. Moreover, Professor Dupuy's view does not recognize the fact that a single agreement, especially concession agreements, can be so central to the economic well-being of a nation that the terms of the agreement assume a formidable importance that would not otherwise flow from an individual contract.[29]

An examination of two awards arising from the Libyan oil nationalization arbitrations illustrates the two main ways in which stabilization clauses are viewed in international arbitrations. The *Texaco Arbitration*[30] arose in connection with an oil concession between Libya and Texaco. The concession agreement contained a stabilization clause providing that the agreement could be altered only by the mutual agreement of the parties.[31] When the Libyan government nationalized Texaco's assets relating to the concession, the sole arbitrator held that the act of nationalization was illegal under international law as it breached the stabilization clauses in the concession agreement. Holding that the nationalization remained illegal regardless of the issue of compensation, he ordered *restitutio in integrum*.[32] However, in the *LIAMCO Arbitration*,[33] which had almost identical facts with the *Texaco Arbitration*, the sole arbitrator held that, irrespective of the stabilization clauses, Libya could lawfully terminate the concession by means of a nondiscriminatory nationalization accompanied by compensation. In his view, the nationalization was a legitimate exercise of State power provided appropriate compensation was paid.[34]

The *Texaco* view that a nationalization in contravention of a stabilization agreement remains illegal despite appropriate compensation is generally regarded as going too far, especially in its insistence on *restitutio in integrum*.[35] By contrast, the *LIAMCO* approach finds much support among academic writers who insist that while stabilization clauses may not preclude expropriatory measures, they nevertheless strengthen the legal position of the private party with respect to claims of compensation.[36] Indeed, one writer has suggested that the breach of a stabilization clause entitles the private party to higher compensation.[37]

The controversy as to the need for, and the effect of, stabilization clauses is really a reflection of the tension between stability and flexibility in State contracts. While the private party, on the one hand, aims at keeping the contract beyond the legislative competence of the State party,[38] the State party, on the other hand, desires flexibility so that the contract can be adapted to changing economic pressures. Each party has a legitimate interest to protect, but neither a dogmatic insistence on the right to nationalization nor the assertion of the inalterability of "stabilized contracts" properly responds to the need to cure the inherent instability of State contracts. While insistence on the right to nationalize does not take into account the financial and other contributions of the private party to the investment, investors cannot reasonably expect that in a world in rapid evolution, there may not be circumstances that warrant a reasonable readjustment of a long-term relationship.[39]

Those who advocate for "stabilized contracts" do not fully comprehend the need for the adaptation of State contracts to changing economic, social, and political climates. Rather, they seek unrealistically to create "the palace of the sleeping beauty—*la belle au bois dormant*—in which time stands still."[40] It is the writer's view that stabilization clauses should not be interpreted as limiting a State party's exercise of its governmental powers. It is unreasonable for private parties to assume that stabilization clauses could effectively remove a particular contractual relation from the control of the State in whose territory the business arrangement is conducted. The exercise of the sovereign powers of a State is too important to be subjugated to the provisions of a contract. Nevertheless, where the exercise of a State's sovereign powers adversely affects a private party's contractual rights, the private party ought to be compensated for its loss.

Given the peculiar nature of State contracts and their in-built tensions, it is advocated that renegotiation offers the best possibilities for maintaining a fair contractual balance in such contracts. Renegotiation of State contracts would enable the parties to hold consultations aimed at adapting their contract to changing circumstances. The need for renegotiation clauses in State contracts is examined in more detail in the "Conclusion" to this chapter.

QUASI-INTERNATIONAL AGREEMENTS

Another method by which it has been sought to remove State contracts from the control of the State party is by categorizing State contracts as quasi-international agreements. Under this theory, a State contract is viewed as constituting its own legal order and proper law. The contract is said to embody the totality of the law necessary for the regulation of the relationship between the contracting parties. The contract provides the "essential ingredients necessary to resolve any dispute between contracting parties,"[41] and reference need not be made to any external law except in instances allowed by the contract. The goal of this theory is to place the provisions of the contract beyond the legislative and executive competence of the State party. If indeed a State contract is its own proper law and the exclusive source of contractual obligations, a unilateral act of the State party will be inoperative to alter the provisions of the contract.

The leading proponent of this theory, Professor Verdross, rejected the view that every agreement must be based on the legal order of a preexisting legal community and asserted that State contracts are

> neither governed by some municipal law of some State, nor are they international treaties. . . . Accordingly, these agreements . . . form a third group of agreements, characterized by the fact that the private rights established by them are governed by a new legal order, created by the concurring will of the parties, i.e. the agreed *lex contractus*.[42]

He characterizes the insistence on a municipal legal foundation for State contracts as "positivist prejudice,"[43] and attributes primary importance to the autonomy of the will of the parties by virtue of which parties are free to designate the law governing their contractual relations.

The protection that this theory grants to a private party is far beyond that possible under international law. For, while international law permits nondiscriminatory expropriation accompanied by appropriate compensation, this theory proposes that expropriation can be valid only when carried out within the terms of the State contract.[44]

The theory, however, scarcely finds any support in the real world. The closest semblance of support for it lies in the legal maxim, "The contract is the law of the contracting parties," which is applied by some legal systems in the Middle East as part of the Sharia law.[45] However, under this maxim, contracts "must be in conformity with the general principles of Islamic law as established by the Koran, the Sunna and the writings of Moslem jurists."[46] Thus, this maxim of Sharia law is hardly evidence of the veracity of the quasi-international agreement theory because the autonomous status of the contract is granted by Islamic law, and Islamic law remains the reference point for determining the legality and efficacy of the contract and its provisions.

The quasi-international agreement theory is objectionable on two grounds: one theoretical, the other practical. First, the theory erroneously presumes that a contract determines its own legal effect and is capable of creating legal obligations independent of any municipal or international legal system. This presumption begets some relevant questions. From where do the parties receive the capacity to enter into legal relations? Which law stipulates that the agreement between the parties is capable of producing legal consequences? Finally, by virtue of which law does the expression of a commitment in a contractual document bind the parties? It would be pure fallacy to believe that in the contemporary world parties could on their own accord, acting outside any recognizable legal system, create legal relations that are binding on them, and which national courts or international tribunals might be called upon to enforce. At most, their contract and its performance would constitute little more than a convergence of expectations and conduct that are unenforceable at law. As F. A. Mann tells us, "freedom of contract does not exist independently of the legal systems which grant it or confer any measure of sovereignty upon the contracting parties."[47] This view is reiterated by Professor Sauser-Hall in the *ARAMCO Arbitration*:

> It is obvious that no contract can exist *in vacuo*, i.e. without being based on a legal system. The conclusion of a contract is not left to the unfettered discretion of the parties. It is necessarily related to some positive law which gives legal effect to the reciprocal and concordant manifestations of intent made by the parties. The contract cannot even be conceived without a system of law under which it is created.[48]

Professor Verdross suggested that the reason for the validity of quasi-international agreements lies neither in municipal nor international law, but in the general principles of law and *pacta sunt servanda*, which the concurring parties recognize in entering into the agreement.[49] He went further to add that an agreement need not necessarily be based on a preexisting legal order but the agreement itself may create such a legal order.

To take his last point first, this writer finds it difficult to conceive how an individual agreement is capable of creating its own legal order, except where there is an underlying legal system that not only grants the parties the power to engage in legally binding contractual relations, but also provides the supporting enforcement mechanism.[50] Additionally, *pacta sunt servanda* is applicable in municipal and international legal systems as a result of its express recognition in these systems, but from where does this principle originate in the context of quasi-international agreements? It would seem that the principle *pacta sunt servanda* can grant legal effectiveness to a contract only if the existence of the principle predates the contract. If it does, it follows that the binding effect of the principle is derivable from a system of law outside the contract, that is, either municipal or international law. The above argument also effectively rebuts Verdross' suggestion that the validity of quasi-international agreements flows from general principles.

The second objection to the theory of quasi-international agreements is that no contract, however elaborately drafted, can contain the entire complex body of rules necessary for the resolution of the range of disputes that could arise between the contracting parties. What contract, for example, can contain all the detailed and minute rules governing the formation, breach, and frustration of contracts? In the words of P. Lalive, a contract, even comprising hundreds or thousands of provisions, will never be so exhaustive as to become independent from external law for matters of interpretation and explanation.[51] In most instances, difficult problems arise from unclear contractual provisions, a situation that necessitates reference to the interpretative and substantive rules of an appropriate legal system.

Professor Verdross has sought to meet this argument by suggesting that a quasi-international agreement may provide for a legal system for purposes of filling contractual gaps. According to him, "the *lex contractus* may refer, for its interpretation or the filling of eventual gaps, to the legal order of the contracting State, or of the other Party, or to international law. But these legal orders can only be applied in as much as they are delegated by the *lex contractus*."[52]

But what happens in cases where the parties do not stipulate any law to fill contractual gaps? More important, by virtue of which law are the parties able to select a law to fill contractual gaps, and what makes this selection binding on national courts and international tribunals called upon to enforce the contract?

It is clear that dogmatic insistence on the autonomy of State contracts fails to adequately explain the legal basis for such autonomy. The truth is that the legal effectiveness of a contract is founded on a system of law: national or international; and a State contract, while embodying the essential elements for its interpretation, can never constitute its own legal system and proper law. A State contract is ultimately founded on some system of law.

INTERNATIONALIZATION OF STATE CONTRACTS

During the first decades of this century it was generally accepted that State contracts were governed by municipal law. This position was reflected in the statement of the Permanent Court of International Justice in the *Serbian Loans Case*, where the court stated that any "contract which is not a contract between States in their capacity as subjects of international law is based on the municipal law of some country."[53]

The rationale for this view was that States were the only proper subjects of international law. Therefore, contracts between States and private parties could not be governed by international law. The corollary of this view was that the applicable law in State contracts would normally be that of the State party,[54] the underlying assumption being that a State, by virtue of its position as a sovereign, cannot be taken to consent to the application of the laws of another country.

However, a group of academics, such as Wuarin, Freund, and von Liszt, expressed the idea that State contracts relating to public debts were governed by international law.[55] Articulating this position, E. Borchard suggested that public debts possessed distinctive legal characteristics that justified their treatment as a separate category: "The debt is generally authorised and created by an act of legislation, which escapes all judicial review. . . . Neither contracting party in these cases would be willing to submit to the national municipal law of the other."[56]

This view was soon embraced by other jurists who argued that all State contracts, not just those involving public debts, could be internationalized by subjecting the contract to public international law. One of the strongest advocates of this view is F. A. Mann. He contends that the theoretical justification of internationalization lies in the fact that

> [i]t is no longer attractive to suggest that public international law and private international law respectively have fields of application, which are clearly and perhaps even inflexibly defined and which are determined by *a priori* or conceptualist reasoning, such as the formula that public international law is applicable only as between international persons or that relationships between international persons are necessarily subject to public international law. Both branches of law are branches of the same tree. They apply in conformity with the demands of reasonable justice and practical convenience. They overlap and pervade each other. Both are called upon to contribute to the progressive evolution of the law.[57]

He argues that inasmuch as State contracts could be governed by international law, these contracts should not be considered as treaties or treated as being governed by public international law in the same sense as transactions between States are. According to Mann, what it implies is that in choosing the applicable substantive law the parties could "make public international law the object of the choice."[58]

It seems that the internationalization of State contracts, especially in relation to contracts involving developing countries, arose partly in response to what was perceived as the unsuitability of laws in developing countries to regulate international commerce. This view, which was pervasive in the 1950s and 1960s (a period when most colonies attained independence) was central to the award in the *Abu Dhabi Case*.[59] In that case a contract between the Sheikh of Abu Dhabi and Petroleum Development Limited granted the latter exclusive rights to explore and exploit oil in Abu Dhabi. The agreement, which did not contain a definite choice of law, stated that the parties based their agreement "on goodwill and sincerity of belief and on the interpretation of this Agreement in a fashion consistent with reason."[60] In a dispute between the parties, the arbitrator recognized that if any municipal law was applicable it would, *prima facie*, be that of Abu Dhabi. He, however, concluded that "[n]o such law can reasonably be said to exist. The Sheikh administers a purely discretionary justice with the assistance of the Koran; and it would be fanciful to suggest that in this very primitive region there is any settled body of legal principles applicable to the construction of modern commercial instruments."[61] He went on to hold that the concession agreement's reference to principles of goodwill and sincerity prescribes "the application of principles rooted in good sense and common practice of the generality of civilized nations—a sort of modern law of nature."[62]

This approach was also adopted in *Qatar* v. *International Maritime Oil Company*,[63] where the arbitrator found that the circumstances surrounding the case necessitated the application of Islamic law. Nevertheless, he held that Islamic law as administered in Qatar "does not contain any principles which would be sufficient to interpret this particular contract." He then applied the principles of justice, equity, and good conscience.

Whatever the veracity of the position then adopted in the *Abu Dhabi* and *Qatar* arbitrations, it is certainly no longer the case that the laws in developing countries do not contain adequate provisions to regulate State contract disputes. Most countries of the developing world now have a sophisticated body of rules governing commercial transactions, some of which were enacted as part of sundry international projects aimed at harmonizing national practice relating to commercial transactions.[64] Therefore, the lack of suitable law in developing countries is no longer (assuming it ever was) a tenable ground for internationalization.

The rationale for internationalization has now shifted to other grounds. On one view, the satisfaction of the ever-growing demand for capital in the developing countries requires that the suppliers of capital be afforded the maximum possible protection.[65] The law of the State party is considered inappropriate for this purpose as the State may amend its laws to alter the contractual balance of the agreement. Internationalization is seen as the best solution because it places the contract beyond the reach of the sovereign powers of the State party, and subjects unilateral acts of the State party to international standards.[66] Internationalization is thus a sort of insurance for the "considerable risks [the investor assumes] in bringing finance and technical aid to countries in the process of development."[67] J. Kuusi adds that the "possible submission of the State contract to international law is thus, on the private party's side, a calculated decision in order to reduce the disadvantages which anyone undertakes in establishing a legal relationship with an entity which can ultimately have recourse to its powers as a sovereign."[68]

Some writers, however, reject the application of international law to State contracts on the ground that the application of international law may implicate the international responsibility of States.[69] This fear is unfounded because corporations and natural subjects are not, properly speaking, subjects of international law. They thus lack the requisite standing to engage the international responsibility of a State.[70] The subjection of a State contract to international law by no means entails that the private party thereby becomes a subject of international law who can claim international responsibility; the sole result of such internationalization is that the contract is governed by international law.[71] Consequently, the remedies available to the private party in the event of a State party's breach of the agreement are those flowing from the contract:

> [Internationalization] does not imply that the foreign party can itself invoke the international responsibility of the opposing State. The "international law" to be applied includes, primarily, relevant rules concerning interpretation and, secondly, rules relating to the modalities of contractual performance. The arbitrators need not

and cannot evaluate an "international wrong" when one of the parties has no standing to assert such a wrong.[72]

It is now generally accepted that State contracts could be governed by international law.[73] Let us examine the various factors that have been suggested as evidence of internationalization of State contracts.

Choice of the Parties

The doctrine of party autonomy is widely accepted in international arbitral practice. With respect to the choice of applicable substantive law, this doctrine gives primacy to the will of the parties as expressed in their contractual document. Thus, the will of the parties is the central element in determining the law governing State contracts.[74]

Parties to a State contract are free to—but rarely—choose international law as their governing law as they are not constrained to select a municipal legal system. Parties may decide that the principles of international law are better suited to govern their contractual relationship. For example, a 1933 concession agreement between the Persian government and the Anglo-American Oil Company contained an arbitration clause, which provided that the award shall be based on "the juridical principles contained in Article 38 of the Statute of the Permanent Court of International Justice."[75]

Mann has suggested that in the absence of an express choice by the parties, a State contract should be considered internationalized "if it is so rooted in international law as to render it impossible to assume that the parties intended to be governed by a national system of law."[76] He, however, declined to "lay down any hard-and-fast rule or anything in the nature of a presumption." Apart from contracts between States and international organizations (such as the World Bank and the IMF), one wonders what other contracts could be so strongly rooted in international law as to compel the application of that law. Save for these quasi-public agreements, there is little basis for a tribunal to presume that a State contract is internationalized in the absence of a clear indication to that effect. The restriction that internationalization places on the exercise of State power (for instance in cases of expropriation) requires that internationalization should not be presumed in the absence of a definite and clear indication that the parties intended to impose the restriction.[77]

Some arbitrators hold that State contracts could be internationalized in the absence of an express choice by the parties. A number of them adopt this view even in cases where there are indications that the parties contemplated the application of national law. For example, in *Mobil Oil Iran* v. *Iran*[78] the investment agreement between the parties provided that the agreement "shall be interpreted in accordance with the laws of Iran" and that "the rights and obligations of the Parties shall be governed by and according to the provisions" of the agreement. The arbitration tribunal held that Iranian law governed only the interpretation of the agreement and not the substance of the parties' obligations. The tribunal went on to hold:

> In the absence of contract provisions, the Tribunal must decide what choice of law is applicable by taking into consideration all circumstances that it deems relevant. In view of the international character of [the contract], of the magnitude of the interest involved, of the complex set of rights and obligations which is established . . . , the Tribunal does not consider it appropriate that such an Agreement be governed by the law of one Party. . . . Accordingly, the Tribunal determines that the law applicable to the Agreement is Iranian law for interpretative issues, and the general principles of commercial and international law for all other issues.[79]

It is submitted that the approach adopted by the tribunal is wrong. First, although Iranian law was mentioned specifically in connection to matters of interpretation, that reference negates an intention to internationalize the contract. Had the parties intended to subject their agreement to public international law, nothing prevented them from so doing, especially since they had selected municipal law for the interpretation of their contract. Second, in the absence of an express indication by the parties, the tribunal should have fallen back on ordinary rules of conflict of laws.

Economic Development Agreements

Some writers and arbitrators have suggested that economic development agreements are by nature subject to international law. This proposition is anchored not on the presumed intention of the parties, but on the grounds that the character of these agreements, and their perceived positive contribution to the economic well-being of the recipient countries, compel their internationalization. What are these economic development agreements?

Their origin lies in the old-type concession agreements that embraced all contracts, with the exception of loan agreements, for the investment of foreign capital in developing the resources of a State. D. O'Connell defined economic concession as a license granted by a State to a private party "to undertake works of a public character extending over a considerable period of time, and involving the investment of more or less large sums of capital."[80]

The characterization of these contracts as concession agreements was later viewed as inappropriate because it blurred the bilateral nature of the transaction.[81] The term "economic development agreement" was viewed as more suitable because it underscored the network of reciprocal rights and duties between the foreign investor and the State, and it also clearly expressed the ostensible object of the agreement: the economic development of the recipient country. According to W. Friedmann, economic development agreements are "marked by a series of obligations on the part of the investor and corresponding promises and permissions on the part of the host government" with the objective of fostering "the national development of the host country."[82] The term is now defined to include more modern forms of investments, such as turn-key contracts.[83]

Dupuy identifies three elements of economic development agreements.[84] First, they are not concerned with an isolated purchase or performance, but bring to the host country investments and technical assistance, particularly in the area of research and exploitation of mineral resources. The private party thereby contributes to the economic and social progress of the host country. Second, these contracts, by virtue of their long duration, require permanent installations as well as the acceptance of extensive responsibilities by the investor. Third, due to the investments made by the private party, there is the need not only to ensure the stability of the contractual arrangement, but also to strike a balance between the State party's interest in economic development and the private party's objective of profit maximization.

It is this desire to protect the investments of the private party that has led to the theory that economic development agreements are inherently internationalized. According to Dupuy, "Such a solution seems particularly suitable for giving the guarantees of protection which are indispensable for foreign companies, since these companies undergo very considerable risks in bringing financial and technical aid to countries in the process of development."[85]

In the *Texaco Arbitration*,[86] Dupuy held that the agreement between Texaco and Libya was internationalized because it fell within the "dimension of a new category of agreements between States and private persons: economic development agreements."[87] The same view was adopted in *Revere Copper and Brass Inc.* v. *Overseas Private Investment Corporation*.[88] There the majority of the arbitrators held that a State contract was internationalized on the ground that it involved the exploitation of natural resources, although the contract contained no reference either to international law or the general principles of law:

> We regard [the principles of public international law] as particularly applicable where the question is, as here, whether actions taken by a government contrary to and damaging to the economic interests of aliens are in conflict with undertakings and assurances given in good faith to such aliens as an inducement to their making the investments affected by the action. . . . In such cases, the question of breach is not left to the determination of municipal courts applying municipal law. The reason for this is that such contracts, while not made between governments and therefore wholly international, are basically international in that they are entered into as part of a contemporary international process of economic development.[89]

The categorization of certain State contracts as economic development agreements and the attribution of an internationalizing effect to them seem to be designed specifically for contracts involving developing countries. It appears that only contracts involving developing countries would satisfy the test for designating a contract as an economic development agreement.[90] More instructive, the term is usually defined to exclude contracts involving developed countries.[91] This yields the absurd result whereby the legal implication of a contract would vary depending on whether the contract was entered into with a developed or developing country.[92] This discriminatory effect of the theory renders it objectionable.

A legal adviser to the U.S. Department of State once stated that when a foreign private party invests in the United States "he does so understanding that U.S. laws are going to apply to him just as to any other entrepreneur."[93] One wonders, why should the position be different when a foreign investor invests in a developing country? The view that economic development agreements contribute to the economic development of developing countries is scarcely sufficient justification for the dichotomy in the treatment of investments in developed and developing countries. It cannot be gainsaid that foreign investments in developed countries also contribute to the economic development of these countries.[94] Those writers and arbitrators who propound these theories of internationalization in relation to developing countries are normally understandably reluctant to extend them to developed countries. For example, no arbitrator has suggested that Japanese investments in the United States or Europe are, by virtue of their contribution to the economic well-being of the United States or Europe, governed by international law, in the absence of a clear indication to that effect in the investment contracts.

The theory of economic development agreements places on its head the presumption against limiting the sovereign authority of States. One wonders why this presumption, which is fundamental in international law, can be so easily reversed in favor of inferences supporting internationalization to the benefit of foreign investors.[95] Given the restriction that the international standards imported by internationalization would have on the sovereign powers of a State, the existence of a clear and unequivocal evidence of an intention to internationalize is necessary before international law could be applied to a State contract. C. Greenwood, one of the advocates of internationalization, has cautioned that "[t]he restriction which an internationalized contract may place upon a State's exercise of its sovereignty is such that internationalization should not be presumed in the absence of clear indications that the parties intended to impose such a restriction."[96]

Finally, one may well ask, why aren't these so-called economic development contracts considered internationalized when the investment is made by a local subject (that is, a citizen of the State party)? Are local subjects entitled to less protection than foreign investors? The nonextension of the internationalization theory to contracts involving local subjects would seem to indicate that the theory is merely an indirect means of granting to foreign investors protection that is unavailable to local investors who, it may be added, contribute no less to the economic development of their countries.

There is nothing in the nature of the so-called economic development agreements to make them inherently subject to international law. The parties to a State contract could of course select international law to govern their agreement, but in the absence of such a clear indication, arbitrators should resort to traditional conflict analysis. The pleas of internationalization should especially be rejected where the parties have made an express choice of law. Such an approach was adopted in *Amoco* v. *Iran*,[97] where a joint-venture agreement between the parties provided that the agreement "shall be construed and interpreted in accordance with the plain meaning of its terms, but subject thereto, shall be governed and construed in accordance with the laws of Iran." In a dispute between the parties before the Iran-U.S. Claims Tribunal, Amoco contended that the agreement was an economic development agreement, and therefore was rooted in international law. The company further argued that Iranian law could apply only insofar as it was consistent with the terms of the agreement. In rejecting Amoco's submission, the tribunal held:

> [T]he Tribunal cannot accept that Iranian law plays only a subordinate role, as contended by the Claimant. Nor is the Tribunal convinced that the . . . agreement should be characterized as an agreement governed, by nature, by international law. Such a construction is manifestly contrary to the plain meaning of [the agreement]. It is clear that the parties chose Iranian law as the law of the contract and no reason appears for reaching the provisions otherwise.[98]

Also in *Klockner* v. *Cameroon*, the parties' agreement to construct a fertilizer factory in Cameroon contained no express choice of law. Rejecting the view that a special legal regime applied to the agreement, the tribunal held that the applicable law should be "the civil and commercial law applicable in Cameroon."[99] More significantly, the tribunal emphasized that it would not "apply new or exceptional legal principles to turn-key operations only because they concern projects affecting the economic and social development of a given country."[100] It is hoped that these awards forebode a rejection of the theory of economic development agreement. Collectively, they cast doubts on the view that economic development agreements are by definition subject to international law.

Provision for Arbitration

It is sometimes suggested that a State contract is internationalized if it provides for arbitration.[101] This view originated from the idea that submission to the jurisdiction of a court implies the acceptance of the law of that court as the law governing the dispute in question. By analogy, a submission of a dispute to arbitration, it is argued, "involves the acceptance of such system of law as the arbitrators may decide to be the relevant one."[102]

Some arbitrators suggest that parties' submission of their dispute to arbitration manifests a "negative intention" rejecting the exclusive application of the host State's law.[103] In *Texaco*[104] Dupuy took this theory a step further by holding that a "process of the internationalization of a contract consists in inserting a clause providing that possible differences which may arise in respect of the interpretation and performance of the contract shall be submitted to arbitration."[105] According to him, "It is . . . unquestionable that the reference to international arbitration is sufficient to internationalize a contract, in other words, to situate it within a specific legal order—the order of the international law of contracts."[106]

Dupuy misreads the purpose and effect of arbitration clauses. An arbitration clause in a State contract is designed to remove the settlement of any resulting dispute from the jurisdiction of municipal courts, and to invest the arbitral tribunal with the exclusive jurisdiction to settle the dispute. Thus, an arbitration clause, *prima facie*, deals with the forum for dispute settlement and not choice of law. The objective of such clauses in State contracts is to afford the parties a neutral forum in which to resolve their contractual differences, free from the interference of the national courts of either of the parties.

Arbitration clauses are not signposts indicating the intention of parties to internationalize their agreement. Assuming that arbitration clauses should play a role in determining the choice of law, it is not clear why such clauses should be interpreted as necessitating the application of international rather than municipal law. The fact that parties decide to settle their disputes in an international forum does not necessarily imply that they wish their disputes to be resolved by international law. The position is different in situations where the arbitral tribunal chosen by the parties is assumed to apply international law. An example is the International Convention for the Settlement of Investment Disputes, which authorizes the application of international law under certain circumstances.

Reference to "Good Faith," "Good Conscience," or "Good Will"

Contractual provisions stipulating that parties to a State contract intend to base their relationship on "good faith," "good conscience," or "good will" have been interpreted in some awards as evidence of the intention of the parties to internationalize their agreement.[107] For example, in the *Sapphire Arbitration*[108] the agreement between the National Iranian Oil Company and a Canadian company provided that the parties undertook to carry out their obligations "in accordance with the principles of good faith and good will and to respect the spirit as well as the letter of the agreement." The contract also referred to Iranian law, which was stabilized in some respect. Placing reliance, in part, on the parties' reference to principles of good faith and good will, the tribunal held that the parties had intended to insulate the agreement from Iranian law:

> Such a clause is scarcely compatible with the strict application of the internal law of a particular country. It most often calls for the application of general principles of law, based upon reason and upon the common practice of civilized nations. . . . It is . . . perfectly legitimate to find in such a clause evidence of the intention of the parties not to apply the strict rules of a particular system, but rather to rely upon the rules of law, based upon reason, which are common to civilized nations.[109]

The tribunal reached this conclusion despite the parties' specific reference to Iranian law, and the lack of any explicit reference to international law or general principles of law in the parties' agreement.

Contractual provisions referring to good faith, good will, or similar phrases are no more than an expression of the intention of the parties to discharge their contractual obligations in a manner compatible with fairness and equity, free from the rigors of strict legal principles. These phrases are not exclusive to international law and, following their interpretation in domestic law, they should not be interpreted as importing the internationalization of contracts in which they are contained. These phrases reflect notions well known in domestic law by virtue of which parties wish to perform their agreement in a more flexible manner. This position is affirmed by the award in the *Amoco Arbitration*.[110] In that arbitration, the parties undertook to perform their agreement "in accordance with the principles of mutual good will and good faith and to respect the spirit as well as the letter of the provisions" of their agreement.[111] Amoco contended that the reference to principles of good faith evidenced the intention of the parties to submit their contract to international law. In rejecting this argument, the tribunal rightly noted that

> the principles of good will and good faith apply in practically all systems of law to contracts as well as to treaties. Article 21 [referring to these principles] simply sets forth a principle of interpretation and implementation of the Khemco Agreement which, as a long-term contract, implies a continuous cooperation between the parties and therefore must not be performed in a strict formalistic way.[112]

The ICSID Convention

The Convention on the Settlement of Investment Disputes between States and Nationals of Other States (ICSID) establishes the International Centre for the Settlement of Investment Disputes as an autonomous international arbitration institution. The ICSID provides facilities for conciliation and arbitration of investment disputes involving State contracts.[113] Article 42(1) of the convention, dealing with the applicable substantive law, provides as follows:

> The Tribunal shall decide in accordance with such rules of law as may be agreed by the parties. In the absence of such agreements, the Tribunal shall apply the law of the Contracting State party to the dispute (including its rules of the conflict of laws) and such rules of international law as may be applicable.

Thus, ICSID tribunals must give primacy to the choice of law made by the parties. In the absence of an express choice by the parties, the tribunal is mandated to apply the domestic laws of the State party in conjunction with relevant rules of international law. It would seem that, under the alternative test, the laws of the host State can be displaced only in cases where it does not conform with international law standards.[114]

However, it has been suggested in one arbitration that the ICSID rules embody a principle of wider application that requires the introduction of international standards to State contract disputes arbitrated *outside* the ICSID framework. In *SPP* v. *Egypt*[115] the agreement between the parties, which provided for ICC arbitration, did not stipulate an applicable law. The parties later agreed that in view of the circumstances of the case, the relevant domestic law was Egyptian law. However, during the arbitration proceedings, SPP contended that the applicable law included principles of international law relating to investments. The tribunal held that reference to Egyptian law should be construed so as to include relevant principles of international law, and that Egyptian law was applicable only when it did not contravene these principles. It found support for this conclusion, in part, on Egypt's adherence to the ICSID Convention. The tribunal suggested that Article 42 of the ICSID Convention should be treated as "illustrative of a principle of wider application."[116]

This writer believes that the ICC tribunal clearly went overboard in applying the provisions of the ICSID Convention to an ICC arbitration. The ICSID Convention applies solely to arbitrations conducted under the auspices of ICSID. When a State party adheres to the convention, it implicitly agrees to abide by Article 42 of the convention whenever it is a party to an ICSID arbitration. This presumption by no means extends to arbitrations outside ICSID as the convention's provisions are exclusively relevant to ICSID arbitrations.

Conclusion

In conclusion, parties to a State contract in exercising their autonomy of will are free to select international law to govern their contract, as indeed has been the case in a few instances.[117] Internationalization should not however be presumed in the absence of a clear and unequivocal expression of the parties intention to achieve this result.

Nevertheless, as a practical matter, it is doubtful whether international law contains the essential provisions to govern State contracts. Some of the suggested principles of international law suitable for application to State contracts include *pacta sunt servanda*, *rebus sic stantibus*, respect for acquired rights, unjust enrichment, and abuse of rights. These principles, however, speak on such a high level of abstraction as to be difficult to apply in real cases. In domestic law, the application of these principles or their equivalents is defined and enhanced by supplementary rules that enable courts to apply them to specific cases.[118] International law lacks an elaborate system of rules to graft flesh on these skeletal principles. Affirming the unsuitability of international law for application in State contract disputes, M. Wolff queries: "What is the influence of mistake [in international law]? Does it render the contract void or voidable or neither? Is a set-off allowed and in what circumstances? . . . International law gives no answer to such questions."[119]

In response, Mann opines that guidance should be found in State practice relating to treaties. He adds that a new branch of international law is in the process of formation and that this branch will contain detailed and definite contractual rules regarding the interpretation, performance, and termination of contracts.[120] However, State practice relating to treaties does not comprise sufficient rules to regulate State contracts. What, for example, is the State practice relating to anticipatory breach of a State contract? In addition, Mann's reference to an emerging branch of international law is not helpful to an arbitrator seeking real and definite rules for the resolution of a contractual dispute. Parties to a State contract should not be expected to base their agreement and relationship on rules that are at best abstract and at worse unformulated. National laws remain the more suitable system for the regulation of State contracts.

GENERAL PRINCIPLES OF LAW

Lord McNair in his seminal article on general principles of law suggested that those principles are particularly suitable for application to economic development agreements.[121] He argued that public international law was inapplicable to these agreements because public international law is an "inter-State system" that applies only to inter-State relations.[122] In his view, general principles of law constitute a "legal system" and its principles, which share "a common source of recruitment and inspiration" with public international law, are amenable to State contract disputes. Other writers have also advocated the application of general principles to State contracts.[123]

These principles have sometimes been adopted by parties as their choice of law, and arbitral tribunals have had to apply them in some arbitrations.[124] In some instances, arbitral tribunals have had to apply general principles in situations where the parties did not expressly adopt them. An example is *ICC Case No. 3572 of 1982*,[125] where the agreement between the parties did not contain a choice of law. The arbitral tribunal thus had to determine the applicable law by virtue of Article 13(3) of the ICC Rules of Conciliation and Arbitration, which provides that in the absence of an express choice by the parties, "the arbitrator shall apply the law designated as the proper law by the rule of conflict which he deems appropriate." The tribunal, finding that it was "inappropriate" to apply the law of either of the parties, held:

> The Arbitral Tribunal will refer to what has become common practice in international arbitrations particularly in the field of oil drilling concessions and especially to arbitrations located in Switzerland. Indeed, this practice, which must have been known by the parties, should be regarded as representing their *implicit will*. . . . The Arbitral Tribunal therefore holds internationally accepted principles of law governing contractual relations to be the proper law applicable to the merits of the case.[126] [emphasis added]

This method of imputing an intention to the parties, and the conclusion reached in the case, are clearly unjustified in view of the fact that the parties did not express preference for any system of law or rules to govern their relationship. The attempt to ground the tribunal's conclusion on the fact that the parties must have known that arbitral tribunals apply general principles to oil concessions is unhelpful. First, the range of laws applied by arbitral tribunals to oil concessions ranges from the law of the State party to public international law.[127] One may ask, why shouldn't the parties be presumed to have intended to apply domestic law or, for that matter, international law? Second, the mere fact that a majority of arbitrators apply a given set of law or rules to certain types of cases does not necessarily imply that a particular set of parties must be presumed to have selected that law or those rules. Third, in the instant case, the parties may have expected that the arbitral tribunal would, in accordance with ICC rules, select the appropriate rule of conflict, rather than directly applying general principles of law without reference to any set of conflict rules.

What, indeed, are the general principles of law? One commentator has indicated that "the search for general principles is not easy."[128] The search involves a pragmatic attempt to extract the maximum measure of agreement on the principles of law found in major legal systems.[129] This implies a comparative analysis of laws in all major legal systems with a view to identifying their common ground of agreement,[130] a task that could be very difficult in some instances. As Carbonneau points out, "[a]s more and more States with differing socio-economic systems develop sophisticated yet diverse regimes of contract law, it will become increasingly difficult to elaborate principles that are sufficiently common and sufficiently specific to govern factual situations."[131] The harmonization of State practice in certain areas of law—for example, in response to the projects undertaken by the United Nations Commission on International Trade Law—might lessen the task of identifying general principles. Nonetheless, there will still exist areas in which State practices continue to differ in significant ways,[132] with the result that it is difficult to distill general principles.

Most of the attempts to determine general principles so far have involved the comparative examination of the laws of developed Western countries.[133] The rationale for this may be that laws in most developing countries are largely influenced by those in countries that formerly colonized them. This view contains some element of truth, but there are still large areas in which laws in developing countries take their own individual courses. Thus, the problem of identifying general principles would be further compounded if the comparative methodology involved in this process includes the examination of laws in developing countries, as indeed should be the case.

A commentator has suggested that the problem of identifying general principles may be attenuated by comparing only the principles recognized in the legal systems of the parties involved in the particular dispute.[134] Thus, in a dispute between a Swiss party and a Taiwanese party, the arbitral tribunal, in applying general principles, will apply those principles of law that are common to Switzerland and Taiwan. This is an idea that merits serious consideration, but where the laws of the parties' nationalities differ radically from each other, the process of elaborating general principles would be no less onerous than a project involving a broad selection of legal systems. Even if the principles in both States coincide, they cannot, properly speaking, be labeled general principles as they would not necessarily be general to a broad selection of other States.

The truth is that despite the attraction of the concept of general principles of law to academic writers and some arbitrators, these principles do not constitute a readily identifiable and comprehensive system of rules to regulate the complex contractual relations that are often involved in State contracts. It would seem that any principle that is indeed general to a genuinely representative selection of legal systems would often be too broad as to be unhelpful in specific cases.[135] It is this writer's view that municipal law remains the most appropriate body of law for application to State contracts.

CONCLUSION

At the beginning of the discussion of applicable substantive law to State contracts, it was stated that one of the foremost characteristic of such contracts is their inherent instability. Presumably, all contracts could be viewed as intrinsically unstable because they are based on present material conditions and seek to project prevailing economic and social realities into the unpredictable realm of future activity. Intervening events may make the expectations and obligations of the parties something radically different from what they initially anticipated. State contracts are, however, much more unstable than private contracts because the intervening events that affect the contractual equilibrium include the public interests of the State party and the necessity for it to secure its ability to discharge its public duties. The situation in State contracts is further complicated by the fact that some State contracts—for example, those dealing with the exploration and exploitation of mineral and other resources—may be so central to the economic well-being of a State that the activity contemplated by the contract is considered an integral part of the State party's economic policy. Take the case of States that are members of the Organization of Petroleum Exporting Countries (OPEC). The economies of most OPEC members are often so dependent on the vagaries of the oil market that they take particular interest in the contracts involving the exploitation or sale of their petroleum resources.

The private party, on the other hand, is continuously afraid of being made to bear singly the brunt of a State policy, a policy that may, in furtherance of some public good, result in the frustration of the private party's contractual expectations. It is true that private parties do not enter into contractual arrangements in order to promote the public interests of the State party; their interests are normally that of profit maximization and the furtherance of their individual or corporate interests.

It is then clear that the tension that is evident in State contracts emanates from the conflicting interests of the State party's need for contractual flexibility and the private party's insistence on contractual stability. All the efforts to subject State contracts to international law or general principles of law, or to engraft stabilization clauses into these contracts, are commonly targeted at the same goal: the freeing of the contract from the control and regulation of the State party and its laws.

This writer believes that national law is the most credible standard for regulating State contract disputes. This need not necessarily be the law of the State party. National laws are easily accessible and are comprehensive enough to govern State contracts. On the other hand, international law and general principles are inadequate standards for regulating complex commercial relations: They are incomprehensive and rarely easily ascertainable.

Furthermore, stabilization clauses are not a solution to the instability of State contracts. These clauses seek unfairly to make State contract provisions inalterable. Advocates of these clauses do not give adequate regard to the considerations of public interest that the participation of the State party impresses upon a State contract. A more realistic approach would be to recognize the right of State parties to terminate a State contract, subject to the payment of appropriate compensation.

Regarding the inherent instability of State contracts, renegotiation offers a lot of possibilities. Renegotiation embodies an acknowledgment of the dynamic nature of State contract relations, and it meshes neatly with the tendency of businesspeople to view contractual documents as nothing more than the basic framework of their relationship. In conformity with the need to foster fair and equitable contractual dealing, parties recognize that this framework may be adapted or modified in light of changing business realities.[136] As K. Llewellyn tells us:

> In the self-government of sub-groups contract provides an original framework, a constitution, a source of ultimate sanction in dispute or breakdown. . . . But for the running of affairs [contract terms] say but little. The play of personality, the unrecorded adjustment from day to day, further factual agreement from time to time, informed by usage and by initiative and acquiescence which do not even call for conscious agreeing—these are what fill the contractual framework with a living content; these are what often so stretch and overlay it as to make the initial contract a wholly misleading guide to what occurs.[137]

Studies demonstrate that in a majority of cases the contractual document is not the focal point in the resolution of contractual problems. Conscious of the need to preserve their business relations, parties are more interested in an amicable and cordial resolution of contractual problems than in flailing the technical provisions of the contract before each other's face.[138] This tendency could probably be a recognition of the fact that the changing economic and other conditions could render contractual provisions increasingly unrealistic, especially in long-term relations.[139] In such cases, the renegotiation of the contract would be more equitable than insistence on strict contractual stipulations.

It is suggested that in this attitude to the resolution of contractual problems lies the best possibilities for the maintenance of equilibrium in State contract relations. Renegotiation lends an element of flexibility to State contracts. It allows the parties to consult in an informal setting with an aim to bringing the contractual document in tune with changing business climates. Far from the rigidity of ironclad contracts, the prospect of renegotiation encourages each party to abide by the contract in the realization that in appropriate cases the parties would consult to rectify those portions of their agreement that pose difficulties.

It is increasingly being recognized that renegotiation, as opposed to immutability of contracts, lies at the center of the future of long-term State contracts. When fully accepted, the practice of renegotiation would render such contract no more than an embodiment of the parties' intention to engage in rational commercial dealings, with the possibility for the review and adaptation of the contractual terms to the changing economic environment:

> Instead of a contract in the traditional sense, an investment agreement could be regarded as no more than a broad framework in which the government and the transnational corporation declare their basic commitment to a particular undertaking or project, but a framework which admits of a continuous process of revision and redefinition of their relations when circumstances require.[140]

Renegotiation is increasingly being accepted as a substitute for the perceived need to stabilize the law of the host country. In *Amoco* v. *Iran*,[141] Judge Brower noted that "the protection of some alien investors formerly sought in a stabilization clause is nowadays sometimes provided in a quite different way by a broad renegotiation clause."[142] A broad renegotiation clause, especially one providing for periodic review of the contract, fosters flexibility in State contract relations. Renegotiation clauses would however be more useful in long-term contracts because it is usually in these kinds of commercial relations that changing business and political climate affect the underlying assumptions of the contract. Thus, in joint-venture and management agreements, either of the parties could rely on a renegotiation clause to seek a revision of the contract when the economic climate changes. For example, in cases of economic depression or volatile market conditions, parties may decide to renegotiate. Periodic review offers the parties the opportunity to continually review the state of their relationship in order to identify areas of difficulties and to formulate plans for confronting anticipated problems and changing economic environments.

An example of a periodic renegotiation clause is contained in an agreement between the Republic of Liberia and the Liberia Gold and Diamond Corporation: "Not less than every 4 years after the commencement of commercial production, the parties shall consult in Liberia for the purposes of considering such changes in or clarifications of this Agreement as either party deems to be appropriate."[143]

Renegotiation is normally held in private proceedings and consultations between the parties. There are, however, institutional[144] and procedural[145] facilities that could facilitate the process of renegotiation.

One vital question remains: is there any ground on which renegotiation could be asserted in the absence of an express agreement of the parties to renegotiate? Some commentators have suggested that the right to renegotiate could be presumed independent of contractual provisions. A. Bucher and P. Tschanz suggest that international arbitration practice tends to recognize an obligation to renegotiate "independent from any national law, even the proper law chosen by the parties, in such a way as to meet the needs of international trade."[146] M. Sornorajah further argues that renegotiation clauses should be inferred in all international contracts and that a norm mandating renegotiation of such contracts "is already being developed in international practice."[147]

This writer has searched diligently without success for evidence of a legal obligation to renegotiate independent of contractual stipulation. Evidence of renegotiation in particular cases where renegotiation was sanctioned by the parties hardly congeals into a positive norm because the process in such cases flows from the parties' approval of renegotiation. Despite the obvious benefits of renegotiation, the obligation to renegotiate constitutes an integral part of other obligations flowing from a contractual document. Thus, the obligation to renegotiate is dependent on contractual stipulations and, additionally, on the provisions of the proper law of the contract. Absent an obligation to renegotiate under the terms of the contract or provisions of the proper law, one fails to see the grounds on which a legal obligation to renegotiate can be established.[148] It is the proper law of the contract that verifies the parties' obligation to renegotiate, or, in some cases, mandates renegotiation itself. It is also the proper law of the contract that determines the legal consequences of a refusal to renegotiate.[149]

Thus, while the practice of renegotiation is encouraged, there is at present no inherent obligation of parties to a State contract to renegotiate. Nevertheless, it is instructive to note that parties often agree to renegotiate even in the absence of a prior contractual stipulation, especially in the context of long-term contractual relationships.[150]

If the process of renegotiation fails, parties to a State contract would have to resort to arbitration in cases where they agree to submit their dispute to arbitration. In these instances, the arbitral tribunal would have to apply some law to the merits of the dispute. As argued above, national law offers the most comprehensive and accessible set of rules to govern the complex contractual dealing often involved in State contracts.

International law and general principles of law, which have seduced many a legal scholar, are all too often so abstract and fluid as to be unhelpful in resolving complex disputes. Beneath the veneer of generalities such as good faith and *pacta sunt servanda*, there is an unsettling paucity of concrete and readily identifiable rules in international law or general principles to govern complex commercial relations.

Most legal systems contain sophisticated and comprehensive sets of rules that are continually amended or updated to adapt them to ever-changing developments in the business sector. In contrast, international law and general principles often lack detailed and clear rules. National law therefore affords the best option for parties to a State contract who seek definition and determinacy in their relationship.

NOTES

1. See "Declaration on the Establishment of a New International Economic Order" U.N. Resolution 3201 (S-VI), U.N. doc. A/RES/3201 (S-VI) May 9, 1974.

2. See W. Peter, *Arbitration and Renegotiation of International Investment Agreements* (Dordrecht, The Netherlands: Martinus Nijhoff, 1986) at 85.

3. W. Park, "Arbitration of International Contract Disputes" (1984) 39 *Bus. Law* 1783.

4. See K. Bockstiegel, "The Legal Rules Applicable in International Commercial Arbitrations Involving States or State-Controlled Enterprises" in *International Arbitration: 60 Years of ICC Arbitration—A Look at the Future* (Paris: ICC Publishing, 1984) 117 at 128.

5. See I. Shihata, "The Institute of International Law's Resolution on Arbitration between States and Foreign Enterprises—A Comment" (1990) 5 *ICSID Review* 65 at 67.

6. See A. Dicey and J. Morris, *The Conflict of Law*, 10th ed. (London: Sweet and Maxwell, 1980) at 778–83; *Charron* v. *Montreal Trust Co.* [1958] O.R. 597 (C.A.).

7. See M. Sornarajah, *The Pursuit of Nationalized Property* (Dordrecht, The Netherlands: Martinus Nijhoff, 1986) at 92.

8. See S. Asante, "Stability of Contractual Relations in the Transnational Investment Process" (1979) 28 *I.C.L.Q.* 401 at 409. The author identifies four situations against which stabilization clauses are directed in investment agreements:

1. The raising of taxes beyond the rates operating at the time of the agreement or otherwise stipulated in the agreement.
2. The imposition of any fiscal changes in the General industrial or commercial sectors in excess of the fiscal charges provided in the agreement.
3. The amendment of the laws, such as corporate and tax laws, which were in force on the date of the agreement. . . .
4. Expropriation, nationalization and any other form of intervention in the enterprise.

Id. See also S. Chatterjee, "The Stabilisation Clause Myth in Investment Agreements" (1988) 5:4 *J. Int'l Arb.* 97 at 98; E. Paasivirta, "Internationalisation and Stabilisation of Contracts versus State Sovereignty" (1989) 60 *B.Y.I.L.* 315 at 323; A. Bucher and P. Tschanz, *International Arbitration in Switzerland* (Basel: Helbing and Lichtenhahn, 1989) at 107.

9. This point was made by the sole arbitrator in *Sapphire International Petroleum Ltd.* v. *National Iranian Oil Company* [(1967) 35 I.L.R. 136 at 171]:

> Under the present agreement the foreign company was bringing financial and technical assistance to Iran, which involved it in investments, responsibilities and considerable risks. It therefore seems natural that they should be protected against any legislative changes which might alter the character of the contract, and that they should be assured of some legal security. This could not be guaranteed to them by the outright application of Iranian law, which it is within the power of the Iranian State to change.

See also *ICC Case No. 3380* of 1980, extracted in S. Jarvin and Y. Derains, *Collection of ICC Arbitral Awards: 1974–1985* (Deventer, The Netherlands: Kluwer Law and Taxation Publishers, 1990) 97 at 99.

10. See W. Peter, supra note 2, at 136 *et seq.*

11. An example of this is the "Nchanga" Zambia Agreement of 1970, extracted in W. Peter, supra note 2 at 137–138:

> Any arbitral tribunal . . . shall . . . in interpreting and applying any agreements, documents, legislation, orders, and other instrument with which the dispute is concerned, apply the law of the Republic of Zambia . . . as it existed on the 24th December, 1969, disregarding all

legislation, instruments, orders, directions and court decisions having the force of law in Zambia ... adopted, made, issued or given subsequent to that date, it being the intention of the parties hereto that such decisions shall be made as if decided on that date under Zambian law.

12. This is illustrated by Article 17 of the Oil Concession Agreement of 1948 between the Ruler of Kuwait and the American Independent Oil Company (AMINOIL), which provided:

> The Shaikh shall not by general or special legislation or by administrative measures or by any other act whatever annul this Agreement except as provided in Article 11. No alteration shall be made in the terms of this Agreement by either the Shaikh or the Company except in the event of the Shaikh and the Company jointly agreeing that it is desirable in the interest of both parties to make alterations, deletions or additions to this Agreement.

(1984) 9 *Y. Comm. Arb.* 71 at 81.

13. W. Peter (supra note 2 at 137) gives the example of Article 44 of the agreement between the Republic of Botswana and RST Ltd. which provided:

> [T]he enactment of any amendments to existing laws or regulation or the enactment of any new laws or regulations applicable to the company . . . shall not constitute a breach by Government of this Master Agreement in the event that:
>
> (ii) such laws or regulations do not contravene the terms and conditions of the Master Agreement or any of the scheduled Agreements; unless
>
> (A) the application of such laws or regulations to the Company . . . has or would have a material adverse effect on the net income or financial position of the Company . . . or a financially materially adverse effect on the rights and obligations of their shareholders under the law of Botswana existing as the date hereof.

14. See, for example, S. Zorn, "New Developments in Third World Mining Agreements" (1977) 1 *Nat. Res. F.* 239 at 243.

15. See E. Arechaga, "Application of the Rules of State Responsibility to the Nationalization of Foreign-Owned Property" in K. Hossain (ed.) *Legal Aspects of the New International Economic Order* (New York: Nichols Publishing Company, 1980) 220 at 230.

16. See M. Sornarajah, supra note 7, at 94; "Supremacy of the Renegotiation Clause in International Contracts" (1988) 5 *J. Int'l Arb.* 97 at 106; S. Asante, supra note 8, at 403. See also L. Kissan and E. Leach, "Sovereign Expropriation of Property and Abrogation of Concession Contracts" (1959–60) 28 *Fordham L.R.* 117 at 199; R. Geiger, "The Unilateral Change of Economic Development Agreements" (1974) 23 *I.C.L.Q.* 73 at 77.

17. Per P. Weil, quoted in W. Peter, supra note 2, at 144. See also E. Nwogugu, *The Legal Problems of Foreign Investment in Developing Countries* (Manchester: Manchester University Press, 1965) at 173–174; Z. Kronfol, *Protection of Foreign Investment* (Leiden, The Netherlands: A. W. Sijthoff, 1972) at 85; F. Sheikh, *The Legal Regime of Foreign Investment in the Sudan and Saudi Arabia: A Case Study of Developing Countries* (Cambridge: Cambridge University Press, 1986) at 257.

18. *Texaco* v. *Libyan Arab Republic* (1977) 53 I.L.R. 389.

19. Id. at 496. For a similar view, see the opinion of Sir Fitzmaurice in the *Aminoil Arbitration* (1984) 9 *Y. Comm. Arb.* 71 at 92 *et seq.*

20. For an examination of the underlying reason of this reluctance to distinguish between the two types of contracts, see A. Fatouros, "International Law and the Internationalized Contract" (1980) 74 *A.J.I.L.* 134 at 140.

21. A. Fatouros argues that state contracts should be treated in the same manner as public contracts under municipal law, a treatment that is different from that accorded to municipal private contracts. According to him, as a general rule, "public contracts are subject to the overriding interest of the public, as conceived in good faith by the state," and are accordingly more flexible than private contracts. See A. Fatouros, *Government Guarantees to Foreign Investors* (New York: Columbia University Press, 1962) at 267, 269. See also S. Chatterjee, supra note 8 at 108.

22. S. Asante, supra note 8 at 404.

23. See D. Bowett, "State Contracts with Aliens: Contemporary Developments on Compensation for Termination or Breach" (1988) 59 *B.Y.I.L.* 50 at 57.

24. 464 U.S. 472.

25. Id. at 480. See also *Atlantic Coast Line* v. *Goldsboro* 232 U.S. 558. A similar view was expressed in the English case of *Czarnikow* v. *Rolimpex*, where Lord Denning held that "a government cannot fetter its duty to act for the public good. It cannot bind itself—by an implication in the contract—not to perform its public duties." [1977] 3 W.L.R. 686. See also *Amphitrite* v. *King* [1929] 3 K.B. 500.

26. It should be noted that the unilateral variation or termination of state contracts is done as much by economically developed countries as by their counterparts in the economically developing world. In the case of England and Norway, it has been said that "[i]t will have become clearer to oil companies that the U.K. and Norwegian governments are no more willing than their OPEC counterparts to stick rigidly to contracts that they deem unreasonably disadvantageous and that there is no absolute constitutional protection in either country for the principle *pacta sunt servanda*." T. Daintith and I. Gault, "*Pacta Sunt Servanda* and the Licensing and Taxation of North Seal Oil Production" (1977) 8 *Cambrian L.R.* 28 at 42.

27. Supra note 18 at 478.

28. Id. The same view was expressed in the ICSID Award in *AGIP* v. *Popular Republic of Congo*. The tribunal stated:

> These stabilization clauses, freely accepted by the Government, do not affect the principles of its sovereign legislative and regulatory powers, since it retains both in relation to those, whether nationals or foreigner, with whom it has not entered into such obligations, and changes in the legislative and regulatory arrangements stipulated in the agreement simply cannot be invoked against the other contracting party.

(1982) 21 I.L.M. 726.

29. An example is the Ghana-Valco agreement whose renegotiation is discussed in F. Tsikata (ed.) *Essays from the Ghana-Valco Renegotiations* (Accra: Victoriaborg Press, 1986). See also E. Nwogugu, supra note 17 at 170–72.

30. Supra note 18.

31. Clause 16 of the concession provided:

> The Government of Libya will take all steps necessary to ensure that the Company enjoys all the rights conferred by this Concession. *The contractual rights expressly created by this Concession shall not be altered except by mutual consent of the parties.*
>
> This concession shall throughout the period of its validity be construed in accordance with the Petroleum Law and Regulations in force on the date of execution of the agreement. . . . *Any amendment to or repeal of such Regulation shall not affect the contractual rights of the Company without its consent.* [emphasis added]

32. Supra note 18, at 494–495. Similarly, the Iran-U.S. Claims Tribunal in *Mobil Oil Iran Inc.* v. *Iran* stated that stabilization clauses "preclude a sovereign during the stated period from exercising the rights it otherwise possesses under international law to take an alien's property for a public purpose, and without discrimination and for a just compensation." (1987) 16 *Iran-U.S. C.T.R.* 3 at 65. See F. A. Mann, "The Aminoil Arbitration" (1983) 54 *B.Y.I.L.* 217 at 221.

33. (1981) 6 *Y. Comm. Arb.* 89.

34. For a discussion of the Libyan oil nationalization cases, see C. Greenwood, "State Contracts in International Law—The Libyan Oil Arbitration" (1982) 53 *B.Y.I.L.* 27; A. Varma, "Petroleum Concessions in International Arbitration" (1979) 18 *Colum. J.T.L.* 259; R. White, "Expropriation of the Libyan Oil Concessions: Two Conflicting International Arbitrations" (1981) 30 *I.C.L.Q.* 1; R. von Mehren and P. Kourides, "International Arbitration between States and Foreign Private Parties: The Libyan Nationalization Cases" (1981) 75 *A.J.I.L.* 476.

35. See A. Redfern and M. Hunter, *Law and Practice of International Commercial Arbitration*, 2d ed. (London: Sweet and Maxwell, 1991) at 105.

36. L. Bouchez, "The Prospects for International Arbitration: Disputes between States and Private Enterprises" (1991) 8:1 *J. Int'l Arb.* 81; W. Peter, supra note 2, at 145; A. Bucher and P. Tschanz, supra note 8 at 111. There are, however, those who contend that stabilization clauses lack any legal effectiveness. See S. Zorn, supra note 14 at 243.

37. E. Arechaga argues that "[a]n anticipated cancellation in violation of a [stabilization clause] would give rise to a special right to compensation; the amount of indemnity would have to be much higher than in normal cases since the existence of such a clause constitutes a most pertinent circumstance which must be taken into account in determining the appropriate compensation." Supra note 15 at 230. One wonders why the existence of a stabilization clause should increase the amount of damages payable in the event of expropriation. Stabilization clauses are designed to address the issue of the validity of expropriatory measures and not to regulate or influence the calculation of damages.

38. It is instructive to note that stabilization clauses are rarely found in state contracts involving developed countries. As M. Faber and R. Brown note, "it has to be recognized that [stabilization clauses] cannot be negotiated with any of the industrialized countries of the West. A mining or oil company would get short shrift if it sought from the British Government contractual guarantees binding Parliament for the future in terms of a specific fiscal package." M. Faber and R. Brown, "Changing the Rules of the Game: Political Risk, Instability and Fair Play in Mineral Concession Contracts" (1980) 2 *Third World Q.* 101 at 113.

39. G. Delaume, *Transnational Contracts* (Dobbs Ferry, NY: Oceana Publications) Chapter 2, para. 2.07 at 23: Issued December, 1989.

40. A. Redfern & M. Hunter, supra note 35 at 106.

41. J. Lew, *Applicable Law in International Commercial Arbitration: A Study in Commercial Arbitration Awards* (New York: Oceana Publications, 1978) at 494.

42. A. Verdross, "The Status of Foreign Private Interests Stemming from Economic Development Agreements with Arbitration Clauses" (1958) 18 *ZaoRV* 449 at 451–452.

43. A. Verdross, "Quasi-International Agreements and International Economic Transactions" (1964) 18 *Yearbook W.A.* 230 at 231.

44. Id. at 235 *et seq.*

45. See Z. Kronfol, supra note 17 at 71; J. Anderson and N. Coulson, "The Moslem Ruler and Contractual Obligations" (1958) 33 *N.Y.U.L.R.* 917; P. Kourides, "The Influence of Islamic Law on Contemporary Middle Eastern Legal Systems: The Formation and Binding Force of Contracts" (1970) 9 *Colum. J.T.L.* 384.

46. F. Sheikh, supra note 17 at 239.

47. F. A. Mann, "The Proper Law of Contracts Concluded by International Persons" (1959) 35 *B.Y.I.L.* 34 at 49. See also S. Asante, supra note 8 at 406.

48. *Saudi Arabia* v. *Arabian American Oil Co.* 27 I.L.R. 117. Lord McNair has also stated that a contract that seeks to have a legal as opposed to a social operation and effect "cannot exist in a vacuum but must have a place within a legal system." Lord McNair, "The General Principles of Law Recognized by Civilized Nations" (1957) 33 *B.Y.I.L.* 1 at 7.

49. A. Verdross, supra note 43 at 231.

50. Professor Friedman views as "frightening" the prospect of "groups of governments and private parties establishing autonomous legal orders of their own." W. Friedman, *The Changing Structure of International Law* (New York: Columbia University Press, 1964) at 128. H. Cattan expresses doubts as to the existence of a legal order outside municipal and international law:

> I have always known . . . of the existence of an international legal order, and side by side with it, a series of municipal legal systems. But the existence of a third kind of legal system distinct from both the former and the latter and existing, as it were, mid-way between the two—rather like the basket in which Aristophanes placed Socrates mid-way between the ceiling and the floor—the existence of a third system of this kind is, I must confess, entirely unknown to me.

The Law of Oil Concession in the Middle East and North Africa (New York: Oceana Publications, 1967) at 114.

51. See W. Peter, supra note 2 at 92, for a translation of the relevant portion of Lalive's article.

52. Supra note 43 at 230.

53. PCIJ Series A. No 20 at 41. This view was affirmed by a Committee established by the League of Nations for the Study of International Loan Contracts. The committee expressed the view that every contract "which is not an international agreement—i.e., a treaty between states—is subject (as matters now stand) to municipal law." Report of the Committee for the Study of International Loan Contracts, League of Nations Publication 11, *Economic and Financial*, 1939, at 21. See also E. Borchard, *The Diplomatic Protection of Citizens Abroad* (New York: The Banks Law Publishing Co., 1915) at 281–291.

54. See R. Jennings, "Rules Governing Contracts between States and Foreign Nationals" in *Rights and Duties of Private Investors Abroad* (New York: Matthew Bender, 1965) 123 at 124.

55. See F. Garcia-Amador, L. Sohn and R. Baxter, *Recent Codification of the Law of State Responsibility for Injuries to Aliens* (Dobbs Ferry, NY: Oceana Publications, 1974) at 63.

56. E. Borchard, supra note 53 at 303.

57. F. A. Mann, supra note 47 at 56. See also F. A. Mann, "State Contracts and International Arbitration" (1967) 42 *B.Y.I.L.* 1.

58. F. A. Mann, "The Theoretical Approach Towards the Law Governing Contracts between States and Private Persons" (1975) *Rev. Belge D.I.* 562 at 564. See

also E. Nwogugu, supra note 17 at 249; P. Bondzi-Simpson, *Legal Relationships between Transnational Corporations and Host States* (Westport, CT: Quorum Books, 1990) at 68.

59. (1951) 18 I.L.R. 144.

60. Id. at 148.

61. Id. at 149.

62. Id.

63. (1953) 20 I.L.R. 534.

64. See A. Agyemang, "The Applicability of Host Developing Countries' Laws to Investment Contracts—The African Case" [1989] *Australian Int'l Law News* 2 at 8–9.

65. See Dupuy in *Texaco*, supra note 18 at 456. See also J. Hyde, "Economic Development Agreements" (1962) 106 *Hague Recueil* 271.

66. D. Suratgar, "Considerations Affecting Choice of Law Clauses in Contracts between Governments and Foreign Nationals" (1962) 2 *Indian J.I.L.* 273 at 302.

67. *The Sapphire Arbitration*, supra note 9 at 175-176. See also F. Feliciano, "Legal Problem of Private International Business Enterprise: An Introduction to International Law of Private Business Association and Economic Development" (1966) 118 *Hague Recueil* 209.

68. J. Kuusi, *The Host State and the Transnational Corporation: An Analysis of Legal Relationships* (Hampshire: Saxon House, 1979) at 99.

69. See S. Toope, *Mixed International Arbitration: Studies in Arbitration between States and Private Persons* (Cambridge: Grotius, 1990) at 78.

70. Id. at 88.

71. See C. Okeke, *Controversial Subjects of Contemporary International Law* (Rotterdam: Rotterdam University Press, 1973) at 214.

72. S. Toope, supra note 69 at 87. See also C. Amerasinghe, "State Breaches of Contracts with Aliens and International Law" (1964) 58 *A.J.I.L* 881 at 897. This point was acknowledged by Dupuy in *Texaco* where he said that the "private person has only a limited capacity and his quality as a subject of international law does enable him *only* to invoke, in the field of international law, the rights which he derives from the contract." Supra note 18 at 458 (Emphasis added). See also I. Seidl-Hohenveldern, "The Theory of Quasi-International and Partly International Agreements" (1975) *Rev. Belge D.I.* 567 at 570.

73. See, for example, C. Greenwood, supra note 34 at 48–53; R. Jennings, "State Contracts in International Law" (1961) 37 *B.Y.I.L.* 156 at 181; A. Redfern and M. Hunter, supra note 35 at 106; L. Sohn and R. Baxter, "Responsibility of States for Injuries to Economic Interests of Aliens" (1961) 55 *A.J.I.L.* 545.

74. For example, the resolution of the Institute of International Law on Arbitration between States, State Enterprises, or State Entities, and Foreign Enterprises (September 12, 1989) provides that "[t]he parties have full autonomy to determine the procedural and substantive rules and principles that are to apply in the arbitration." Article 6, reproduced in (1990) 63 *Yearbook Institute Int'l Law* 325. See also G. Schwarzenberger, "The Protection of British Property Abroad" (1952) 5 *Current L.P.* 315; A. Farmanfarma, "The Oil Agreement between Iran and the International Oil consortium: The Law Controlling" (1955) 34 *Texas L.R.* 287.

75. See D. Suratgar, supra note 66 at 285. Also the 1935 Qatar-Anglo Persian Oil Company Agreement provided that disputes arising from the agreement should be settled by arbitration and that the award of the arbitration should be consistent with "legal principles familiar to civilised nations." (1951) 18 I.L.R. 162.

76. F. A. Mann, "The Law Governing State Contracts" (1944) 21 *B.Y.I.L.* 11 at 21.

77. See A. Fatouros, supra note 21 at 135.

78. Supra note 32.

79. Id. at 27–28.

80. D. O'Connell, *The Law of State Succession* (Cambridge: Cambridge University Press, 1956) at 106.

81. See Lord McNair, supra note 48 at 1.

82. W. Friedmann, "The Relevance of International Law to the Process of Economic and Social Development" (1966) 60 *Proc. A.S.I.L.* 8 at 13.

83. S. Pogany, "Economic Development Agreements" (1992) 7 *ICSID Review* 1 at 4.

84. See Dupuy in *Texaco*, supra note 18 at 456. See also Lord McNair, supra note 48 at 3–4.

85. See the *Sapphire Arbitration*, supra note 9 at 175.

86. Supra note 18.

87. Id. at 455.

88. (1978) 17 I.L.M. 1321. For a discussion of the award, see D. Joy, "Arbitration of Economic Development Agreements: The Impact of Revere v. OPIC" (1980) 20 *Va. J.I.L.* 861.

89. Id. at 1331.

90. See A. Fatouros, supra note 20 at 136.

91. According to S. Pogany, "[i]n essence, EDAs [Economic Development Agreements] may be regarded as contractual agreements between less developed countries (LDCs) and foreign parties which are generally long-term in character and which often involve the exploitation of natural resources." Supra note 83 at 3.

92. Teson illustrates the uncanny effect of the theory of economic development agreements as follows: "It implies that an oil concession contract between, for example, a Saudi investor and the British government would be subject to British law, while a similar contract between the Saudi government and a British investor would benefit from the protection of international law." F. Teson, "State Contracts and Oil Exploration: The Aminoil-Kuwait Arbitration" (1984) 24 *Virg. J.I.L.* 323 at 332.

93. United States Senate Committee on Foreign Relations (1966) 5 I.L.M. 649 at 666 (per Leonard Meeker).

94. An explanation for the divergence in treatment could be found in the admission by I. Shihata, of the World Bank, that international arbitration "is still largely dominated by individuals whose cultural backgrounds and values may bring them closer to foreign enterprises [from developed countries] than to host governments *in developing countries*." Emphasis added. I. Shihata, supra note 5 at 68.

95. A. Fatouros, supra note 20 at 136.

96. C. Greenwood, supra note 34 at 53. A similar view in connection with stabilization clauses was expressed in *Aminoil Arbitration*: "No doubt contractual

limitations on the state's right to nationalise are juridically possible, but what that would involve would be a particularly serious undertaking which would have to be expressly stipulated." (1982) 21 I.L.M. 1023 at para. 95.

97. (1987) 15 Iran-U.S. C.T.R. 189.

98. Id. at 236.

99. See J. Paulsson, "The ICSID *Klockner* v. *Cameroon* Award: The Duties of Partners in North-South Economic Development Agreements" (1984) 1 *J. Int'l Arb.* 145, for extracts from the award.

100. The award was subsequently annulled on the grounds, *inter alia*, that the tribunal failed to apply the law of Cameroon. See (1986) 1 *ICSID Review* 89. This ground for the annulment of the award implicitly supports the view that so-called economic development agreements are not inherently governed by international law.

101. See F. Sheikh, supra note 17 at 248; R. Jennings, supra note 73 at 156. A. Fatouros in his book *Government Guarantees to Foreign Investors* published in 1962 (supra note 21 at 293–294) endorsed this view, however, in a later article ("International Law and the Internationalized Contracts," supra note 20 at 136) he retreats and suggests that arbitration clauses can hardly be "construed as necessarily a sign of internationalization."

102. Lord McNair, supra note 48 at 6.

103. See *Sapphire Arbitration*, supra note 9 at 172.

104. Supra note 18.

105. Id. at 454–455.

106. Id. at 455.

107. See the *Lena Goldfield Case* (1950) 36 *Cornell L.Q.* 42; *Petroleum Development* v. *Sheikh of Abu Dhabi* (1951) 18 I.L.R. 144; *Qatar* v. *International Maritime Oil Co.* (1953) 20 I.L.R. 534.

108. Supra note 9.

109. Id. at 173.

110. Supra note 97.

111. Id. at 173.

112. Id.

113. See Report of the Executive Directors on the Convention on the Settlement of Investment Disputes between States and Nationals of Other States (1965) 4 I.L.M. 524 at 525.

114. In *Indonesia* v. *Amoco Asia Corp.* (1987) 12 *Y. Comm. Arb.* 129 at 132, an ICSID arbitration tribunal noted that "Art. 42(1) of the Convention authorizes an ICSID tribunal to apply the rules of international law only to fill up *lacunae* in the applicable domestic law and to ensure precedence to international law norms where the rules of the applicable domestic laws are in collision with such norms." See also *SPP* v. *Egypt* (1993) 32 I.L.M. 933; *Klockner* v. *Cameroon* (1986) 2 *Y. Comm. Arb.* 159 at 170.

115. (1983) 22 I.L.M. 752.

116. Id. at 769.

117. See supra note 74.

118. See J. Kuusi, supra note 68 at 81.

119. M. Wolff, "Some Observations on the Autonomy of Contracting Parties in Conflict of Laws" (1950) 35 *Grotius Transactions* 143 at 152. See also J. Lew, supra note 41 at 403.

120. F. A. Mann, "Reflections on a Commercial Law of Nations" (1957) 33 *B.Y.I.L.* 20 at 22–23, 48. See also G. Haight, "The Choice of Public International Law as the Applicable Law in Development Contracts with Foreign Governments" in J. McDaniels (ed.) *International Financing and Investment* (Dobbs Ferry, NY: Oceana Publications, 1964) 554 at 557.

121. Lord McNair, supra note 48 at 6.

122. Id. at 10. This argument is no longer tenable. See subsection in this chapter entitled "Choice of the Parties."

123. See J. Lalive, "Contracts between a State or State Agency and a Foreign Company" (1964) 13 *I.C.L.Q.* 987 at 992; NOTE, "General Principles of Law in International Commercial Arbitration" (1988) 101 *Harvard L.R.* 1816; D. O'Connell, *International Law*, 2d ed. (London: Stevens, 1970) at 983.

124. Examples of contracts providing for the application of general principles are found in Lord McNair, supra note 48 at 7–9. Arbitration awards where general principles were applied include *The Lena Goldfield Arbitration*, supra note 107; *Qatar* v. *International Maritime Oil Company*, supra note 63. For the role of general principles in the context of arbitrations conducted under the auspices of the Iran-U.S. Claims Tribunal, see J. Cook, "Applicable Law in International Arbitration: The Iran-U.S. Claims Tribunal Experience" (1989) *Am. J.I.L.* 292–296.

125. (1989) 14 *Y. Comm. Arb.* 111.

126. Id. at 117.

127. For a discussion of the distinction between general principles of law and public international law, see W. Peter, supra note 2 at 113.

128. J. Lalive, supra note 123 at 1010.

129. See F. Friedman, supra note 50 at 194.

130. In connection with the Iran-U.S. Claims Tribunal, T. Carbonneau urges the tribunal to utilize comparative methodology to produce "a corpus of commercial law principles from the statutory and decisional law of various national legal systems, allowing it to resolve disputes according to a principled substantive consensus among legal systems." T. Carbonneau, "The Elaboration of Substantive Legal Norms and Arbitral Adjudication: The Case of the Iran-United State Claims Tribunal" in R. Lillich (ed.) *The Iran-United States Claims Tribunal: 1981–1983* (Charlottesville: University of Virginia Press, 1984) 104 at 105.

131. S. Toope, supra note 69 at 71.

132. See Id.

133. See, for example, the discussion by W. Peter, supra note 2 at 113–121.

134. W. Peter, supra note 2 at 113.

135. A. Redfern and M. Hunter caution that "[n]o private lawyer could hope to stay in business if he advised his client merely on the basis of general principles. He need not know merely the principles, but also the detailed rules which govern the application of those principles to the problem before him." Supra note 35 at 114.

136. There is at present a movement in contract law to study how extracontractual considerations influence the conduct of businesspeople. See, for example, S. Macaulay, "Non-Contractual Relations in Business" (1963) 28 *Am. Sociological R.* 55; C. Dalton, "An Essay in the Deconstruction of Contract Doctrine" (1985) 94 *Yale L.J.* 997; I. Macneil, *The New Social Contract: An Inquiry into Modern Contractual Relations* (New Haven: Yale University Press, 1980).

137. K. Llewellyn, "What Price Contract? An Essay in Perspective" (1931) 40 *Yale L.J.* 704 at 730.

138. As one businessperson aptly puts it, "if something comes up, you get the other [person] on the telephone and deal with the problem. You don't read legalistic contract clauses at each other if you ever want to do business again. One doesn't run to a lawyer if he wants to stay in business because one must behave decently." See S. Macaulay, supra note 136 at 62.

139. W. Stoever, *Renegotiation in International Business Transactions* (Toronto: Lexington Books, 1981) at 315.

140. S. Asante, supra note 8 at 418.

141. Supra note 97.

142. Id. at 297. See also T. Walde, "Revision of Transnational Investment Agreements: Contractual Flexibility in Natural Resources Development" (1978) 10 *Lawyers of the Americas* 265; I. Macneil, "Contracts: Adjustment of Long-Term Economic Relations under Classical, Neoclassical, and Relational Contract Law." (1978) 72 *Northwestern U.L.R.* 854; H. Zakariya, "Changed Circumstance and the Continued Validity of Mineral Development Contracts" in K. Hossain, supra note 15 at 263.

143. See M. Bartels, *Contractual Adaptation and Conflict Resolution* (Deventer, The Netherlands: Kluwer Law and Taxation Publishers, 1985) at 65. See also W. Peter, "Arbitration and Renegotiation Clauses" (1986) 3 *J. Int'l Arb.* 29, for guidelines on drafting renegotiation clauses.

144. See J. Marcantonio, "ICSID as a Forum for the Renegotiation and Adaptation of Contracts" in N. Horn (ed.) *Adaptation and Renegotiation of Contracts in International Trade and Finance* (Deventer, The Netherlands: Kluwer Law and Taxation Publishers, 1985) at 235.

145. See F. Metzger, "The ICC Rules for Adaptation of Contracts" in N. Horn, id. at 205; G. Hermann, "The UNCITRAL Conciliation Rules: An Aid also in Contract Adaptation and Performance Facilitation" in N. Horn, id. at 217.

146. A. Bucher and P. Tschanz, supra note 8 at 151.

147. M. Sornorajah, supra note 16 at 109.

148. See W. Peter, supra note 2 at 153.

149. Id. at 86.

150. See D. Baird, "Self-Interest and Cooperation in Long-Term Contracts" (1990) 19 *J. Legal Studies* 583 at 595–596.

CHAPTER SIX

Mandatory Rules of Law in International Commercial Arbitration

INTRODUCTION

One of the recurring themes in international commercial arbitration is the tension between the will of the arbitrating parties and the ability of States to regulate the conduct and status of arbitration proceedings. The general trend in international commercial arbitration is to respect, within limits, the will of the parties regarding the choice of law and the procedure for carrying out their arbitration. Thus, party autonomy is recognized as one of the cardinal elements of international commercial arbitration.

This past decade has witnessed an expansion in the scope of arbitrable matters. This trend is exemplified by *Mitsubishi Motors Corp.* v. *Soler*[1] in which the United States Supreme Court held that antitrust disputes arising from international contracts are arbitrable. The court reached this conclusion against the background of a long line of U.S. cases that considered antitrust law fundamental to the ideological and economic integrity of the United States.[2] Underlying the Supreme Court's decision in *Mitsubishi* was the presumption that the arbitrators in the case would respect the imperative provisions of the U.S. Sherman Act (which embodies U.S. antitrust principles), despite the fact that the applicable law in the case was Swiss Law.

It thus seems that the increasing acceptance of international arbitration as a legitimate alternative to litigation implies an expectation on the part of States that arbitrators will, like judges, respect the basic notions of justice and in appropriate cases apply the mandatory provisions of relevant laws. It is one thing to grant parties the power to organize their dispute resolution process in a manner compatible with their objectives; it is a different matter to suggest that parties to an international arbitration are entirely free from the demands of public policy and fundamental provisions of relevant laws.[3] The integrity of international arbitration and its endurance as a viable alternative to litigation would seem to rest on arbitrators' continual respect for public policy of States whose legitimate interests are implicated in arbitration disputes. Arbitrators therefore have to balance their respect for the autonomy of the parties' will with the need to apply mandatory provisions of laws that are relevant to the dispute.

In this chapter, we will examine the impact of mandatory rules in resolving the merits of a dispute before international arbitrators. The problem posed by mandatory rules in international arbitration will be put in perspective by contrasting the position of international arbitrators with those of national judges called upon to enforce imperative laws. Thereafter, the discussion will focus on the discernible trends in the application of mandatory rules in international arbitration. This is done by examining the treatment of mandatory rules of the *lex contractus* and mandatory rules of laws external to the *lex contractus*. The chapter concludes with an examination of the role of transnational public policy (which, in a sense, is the mandatory rule of the international legal order) on the determination of the merits of a dispute. But first, what are mandatory rules?

MANDATORY RULES DEFINED

Traditional conflict theory postulates that a statute is inapplicable to a contract unless the statute forms a part of the proper law of the contract or is otherwise applicable as part of the procedural laws of a forum court. However, it has long been accepted that this proposition is subject to the qualification that imperative laws of the forum may apply to a contract irrespective of the proper law of the contract. Thus, one of the limitations on party autonomy within a national legal system is that overriding laws of the forum may override the law chosen by the parties.[4]

It is these rules of law that are capable of overriding the will of parties that are labeled "mandatory rules."[5] Mandatory rules denote those rules of law from which the parties cannot derogate, rules that in appropriate cases supersede the proper law, thereby substituting their provisions for the will of the parties:

> [A] mandatory rule is a rule which overrides the normally applicable law (or . . . the proper law of the contract) whether that applicable (proper) law is ascertained by reference to an express stipulation or by reference to the closest connection. In short it is a law which applies irrespective of or despite the proper law of a contract.[6]

These rules embody the fundamental policy of a given State and are therefore applicable by virtue of their imperative nature. They typically regulate matters in which the "interest of the State is too important for them to be in competition with foreign laws"[7] or the will of the parties.[8] Thus, there is a close relationship between the concept of public policy and that of mandatory rules. Mandatory rules would include those aspects of public policy and rules of national law that are couched in an imperative manner because they embody the vital socioeconomic policies of the State involved. These includes currency and exchange regulations, boycotts and blockades, embargoes, and environmental protection laws.[9]

Examples of mandatory rules abound in national laws. In Australia, for example, the Consumer Transaction Act applies to a consumer contract involving the delivery of goods in South Australia irrespective of the proper law of the contract.[10] Similar provisions are to be found in the English Employment Protection (Consolidation) Act,[11] the English Uniform Contract Terms Act,[12] and the German Regulation of Standard Contract Terms Act.[13] Occasionally statutory provisions that do not appear mandatory on their face are construed as mandatory by virtue of judicial interpretation.[14]

TREATMENT OF MANDATORY RULES IN NATIONAL COURTS

A national court is obliged to apply the relevant fundamental public policy of its legal system to disputes before it because its adjudicatory competence is founded on the law of that particular system. Thus, a national court would, in appropriate cases, apply the public policy and mandatory rules of its *situs* regardless of the proper law of the contract involved. The court system is one of the vehicles through which a society expresses and protects those fundamental values that underlie its social fabric; thus national courts generally apply imperative rules that invariably represent the essential values of their societies, even in cases where the forum's law does not govern the contract.

Fundamental public policy has a dual aspect in its impact on judicial proceedings. The first, and perhaps the more common, aspect is that it compels a national court to deny recognition to an applicable foreign law that contravenes the stringent public policy of the forum.[15] Second, it mandates the national court to give effect to those national legislations that, by their provisions, govern all contacts regardless of the proper law of the contract. An example of this kind of legislation is the Australian Consumer Transactions Act cited above.[16]

Under the first aspect, the applicability of foreign governing laws is determined by their conformity with the stringent public policy of the forum.[17] This rule was stated by Lord Justice-Clerk Patton in *Connal & Co. v. Loder*:[18]

> Everybody knows that the fundamental principle upon which we introduce foreign law as law affecting the rights of contracts or otherwise, is only to the effect of introducing such law when it is not in direct contradiction to the principle upon which our law is governed, and according to which the rights of the subjects in this country must be determined.[19]

It is generally accepted that this use of public policy should be highly circumscribed. Specifically, public policy is viewed as disabling the application of otherwise applicable law only in cases where the foreign law offends the forum's essential and basic policy interest. As the court in *Loucks* v. *Standard Oil Co.*[20] put it:

> The courts are not free to refuse a foreign right at the pleasure of the judges, to suit the individual notion of expediency or fairness. They do not close their doors unless help would violate some fundamental principle of justice, some prevalent conception of good morals, some deep-rooted tradition of the common weal.[21]

Under the second aspect of public policy, in dealing with a contract containing a foreign choice of law, a national court will apply those laws of the forum that by their provisions are designed to apply to all disputes litigated in the forum that fall within their scope. Here the court has no discretion whether or not to apply the mandatory rule because, as a creature of the national legal system, its jurisdiction and powers are regulated by national law: it is constrained to apply imperative laws of its forum. To illustrate, a court in South Australia dealing with a contract for delivery of goods in South Australia must apply the Consumer Transaction Act, whatever the contractual stipulations of the parties or the provision of the proper law chosen by them.

THE PARTICULAR POSITION OF ARBITRATORS

Unlike national courts, international arbitral tribunals do not owe strict allegiance to the laws of the place of arbitration, neither are they constituted by the laws of the arbitral seat. Indeed, they do not have a forum in the same way as national courts do. An arbitral tribunal could decide to conduct the arbitration proceedings in different countries, in which case it is unrealistic to categorize the stringent public policy of any of the fora as applicable to the merits of the dispute. Even in cases where the proceedings are held in one country, international arbitrators still do not, as a theoretical matter, owe strict allegiance to the laws of that *situs*,[22] in the sense that they are not constrained to apply all the imperative rules of the forum in the same way that national courts are.

It is said that an arbitrator's responsibility is to the arbitrating parties in particular and the international business community in general.[23] This view originates from the fact that the power and authority of arbitrators are primarily derived from the agreement of the parties. As their authority is derived from the will of the parties, arbitrators are said to have a duty, first, to affirm the will of the parties, and, second, to further the interests of international commerce. This implies that arbitrators have to give primacy to the will of the parties while respecting the basic philosophy and principles of international commerce:

[International commercial arbitrators] are the guardians of the international commercial order: they must protect the rights of participants in international trade, give effect to the parties' respective obligations under the contract; imply the presence of commercial *bona fides* in every transaction; respect the customs followed in international trade practice and the rules developed in relevant international treaties; uphold the commonly accepted views of the international commercial community and the policies expressed and adopted by appropriate international organizations; and enforce the fundamental moral and ethical values which underlie every level of commercial activity.[24]

Does this mean that arbitrators are free to ignore the mandatory rules of relevant national laws? While it is true that the jurisdiction of international arbitrators depends on the agreement of the parties, it is also true that arbitration would lose its respect and legitimacy as a dispute resolution system if arbitrators continually ignore the mandatory national laws that are connected with arbitral disputes. States that allow the arbitration of sensitive matters, such as antitrust disputes, do so on the assumption that arbitrators arbitrating antitrust disputes that are substantially connected to their jurisdictions would apply the relevant mandatory antitrust rules of these jurisdictions. If arbitrators reject the application of these mandatory rules, there is little doubt that these States would move to make such sensitive matters nonarbitrable. It is therefore widely acknowledged that arbitrators ought to apply relevant national laws to ensure the continued survival of arbitration:

Every arbitrator has to consider the importance of preserving commercial arbitration as an instrument for settling international disputes. Today commercial arbitration is highly regarded in most countries. Governments have not interfered with its operation and, indeed have encouraged its establishment in their countries. If, however, arbitration is used as a means of evading the relevant policies of countries which have an interest in the subject matter of the dispute, the reputation of arbitration will suffer.[25]

Thus, while arbitrators should respect the will of the parties, they should also ensure that recourse to arbitration does not become a means of avoiding fundamental principles of public policy.[26] Consequently, arbitrators have a responsibility to apply the mandatory rules of those jurisdictions whose national interests are substantially involved in the matter under arbitration.

Two kinds of mandatory rules are potentially involved in arbitration proceedings: those of the *lex contractus*, and those external to the *lex contractus*. Let us examine these two strands of mandatory rules.

MANDATORY RULES OF THE *LEX CONTRACTUS*

Arbitrators generally apply the law chosen by the arbitrating parties;[27] when the parties have made an express choice of law, arbitrators apply that law, together with its mandatory rules. In most awards in which the applicability of the mandatory rules of the law chosen by the parties arose, arbitrators applied those rules as a matter of fact.[28]

However, it is possible to conceive of a situation where an arbitrator need not apply the mandatory rules of the law chosen by the parties. An example would be cases where the underlying purpose and objective of the rule indicate that it is aimed at purely domestic situations as opposed to cases involving international disputes. Additionally, an arbitrator may decline to apply a mandatory rule of a law chosen by the parties in the unlikely event that the rule is contrary to "transnational public policy."[29]

An interesting issue in this area of arbitration is whether arbitrating parties can legitimately exclude the application of the mandatory rules of the law that they choose to govern their agreement. In effect, can the parties slice off unacceptable portions of the governing law of their contract? In theory, it could be argued that since the parties selected the governing law, they could as well determine which parts of that law would govern their agreement; after all they could very well have chosen another law as the governing law. And since the arbitrators are bound to apply the law chosen by the parties, they should have no choice but to respect the will of the parties.

This theoretical argument, however, ignores the basic fact that as hackneyed as the concept of party autonomy is, it has its limitations. Maniruzzaman reminds us that "[a]lthough the parties' freedom of choice (autonomy of will) is a general principle of private international law and is to be respected in principle, it should operate within the limits imposed by such equally important general principles of law or subject to any restraint of public policy."[30] The will of the parties is not sacrosanct; the parties' will prevails so far as it is consistent with relevant public policy. Consequently, since mandatory rules are designed to apply regardless of the parties' choice of governing law, arbitrators may legitimately refuse to recognize the parties' exclusion of mandatory rules of the *lex contractus* in cases where the parties' transaction is very closely connected with the jurisdiction whose law is the *lex contractus*, and the mandatory rules were designed to regulate such transactions. For example, if a Canadian company enters into a distribution agreement with a Japanese auto company for the distribution of cars in Ontario (and the parties choose Ontario law as the applicable law), an arbitral tribunal may refuse to apply a contractual provision excluding Canadian competition laws. To respect the parties' will in such a case would be tantamount to the subjugation of Canada's legitimate interest in regulating its business environment to the interest of private contracting parties. On the other hand, in cases where the jurisdiction whose law was chosen as the proper law by the parties has no connection with the underlying contractual arrangement, the parties could legitimately exclude its mandatory rules. In such cases, the interests of that jurisdiction are not implicated in the parties' commercial relations. The relevant consideration should be the connection between the jurisdiction and the parties' commercial relations.

What about cases where the *lex contractus* is chosen by the arbitrators in the absence of an express choice by the parties? Since the conflict rules used in determining the applicable law in the absence of the parties' express choice usually focuses on the law of the country with which the contract is most closely connected, there are grounds for an arbitral tribunal to apply the mandatory rules of the law of such a country. This is because the transaction would invariably have a notable impact on that country. Even then, the tribunal might have to balance the interests of this country with those of other countries that are equally connected with the transaction. The tribunal's objective should be to determine which of them has a greater claim to the application of its mandatory rules by virtue of its connection with the dispute.

MANDATORY RULES FOREIGN TO THE *LEX CONTRACTUS*

Mandatory rules foreign to the *lex contractus* are those of jurisdictions other than that whose law governs the merits of a dispute. Thus, if Italian law governs a dispute, the mandatory rules of jurisdictions other than Italy are classified as foreign mandatory rules.

In examining the treatment of mandatory rules foreign to the *lex contractus*, it is useful to draw from the experience of national judicial systems, as the issue has more commonly arisen before them. The attitude in most common law jurisdictions is that a mandatory rule shall not be applied unless it is part of the laws of the forum or forms part of the governing law of the contract. Stating the law in England, the editors of *Dicey and Morris Conflict of Laws* note that "Where [a mandatory law] is neither legislation of the forum nor of the applicable law it has no application in England."[31] This position is the same in Australia,[32] but unclear in Canada.[33] The U.S. position is somewhat more liberal in its treatment of foreign mandatory rules in that the American Restatement of Conflict of Laws allows for the application of the mandatory rules of a State "which has a materially greater interest than the chosen State in the determination of the particular issue" and which, under the forum's law, would have been the applicable law in the absence of an express choice by the parties. The reluctance of most common law jurisdictions to fully accept the application of foreign mandatory rules is often based on the ground that recognition of such rules would cause uncertainty in that the parties would not be able to determine beforehand the rules that might affect their transaction.[34]

Civil law jurisdictions, on the other hand, are more receptive to the application of foreign mandatory rules. The civil law approach is exemplified by Article 19 of the Swiss Federal Statute on Private International Law, which provides, *inter alia*:

1. A provision of a law, other than the one designated by this statute, that is meant to be applied mandatorily may be taken into account if interests of a party that are, according to Swiss views, legitimate and clearly overriding so require, and the case is closely connected to that law.[35]

Similarly, Dutch law recognizes the possibility of applying the mandatory law of a third State irrespective of the parties' choice if "it is in the interest of [the] foreign State that some of its rules be observed outside its territory."[36] German courts also acknowledge the possibility of applying foreign mandatory law. In one case, the German BGH applied a Nigerian mandatory law prohibiting the exportation of art objects to a dispute involving the export of Nigerian art objects, even though Nigerian law did not govern the contract.[37]

Thus, while civil law jurisdictions are generally receptive to the application of foreign mandatory rules, common law jurisdictions are often reluctant to apply such rules. However, it should be noted that even in those countries in which the application of foreign mandatory rules is not fully acknowledged, it is generally accepted that "the mode of performing a contract, as distinct from the substance of the obligation, is governed by the law of the place of performance [the *lex loci solutionis*]."[38] Illustrating this principle, Lord Normand remarked in *Kahler* v. *Midland Bank*[39] that: "The courts of this country will not compel the fulfilment of an obligation when performance includes the doing in a foreign country of something which the laws of that country make it illegal to do."[40] This rule is justified by the assumption that the parties must have "intended to incorporate in their contract those parts of [the law of the place of performance] which refer to the manner in which the contractual obligations are to be discharged."[41] Thus, where, for example, an Australian company has a contractual obligation to build an industrial complex in Nigeria, the parties are assumed to understand that Nigerian mandatory rules would determine the formalities required for the erection of such a complex, and other issues such as building codes and employment standards.

Arbitral practice follows this dichotomy between the civil and common law jurisdictions in regard to the application of foreign mandatory rules. In arbitral practice there are both hostile and favorable approaches toward the application of foreign mandatory rules,[42] although there is common acceptance of the role of the *lex loci solutionis* in determining the mode of performance.

The hostile approach is premised on the ground that arbitrators are bound by the will of the parties and are therefore obligated to apply only the law chosen by the parties or, in the absence of such a choice, the law chosen on their behalf by the arbitrators.[43] Consequently, the advocates of this approach contend that arbitrators are barred from applying laws outside the *lex contractus*. They further suggest that as arbitrators are not custodians of public interests (their obligation is to the parties), they should not apply foreign mandatory rules[44] that reflect the public policy of the enacting States. A more common reason for the rejection of foreign mandatory rules (a reason borrowed from common law jurisprudence) is that their application would lead to uncertainty as the parties would not know beforehand which mandatory rules the arbitrators may decide to apply to their case.

This writer believes that the hostile view gives an overly important weight to the will of the parties. As stated above, the will of the parties is not sacrosanct; it may in appropriate cases give way to the legitimate concerns of those States whose interests are implicated by the dispute. To adapt an earlier example, where Canadian competition policy is central to the determination of a dispute involving the importation of automobiles into Canada, it would be unreasonable, indeed an abdication of responsibility, for an arbitrator to refuse to apply that policy on the flimsy ground that the governing law of the contract at hand is, say, Japanese law. The principle of party autonomy ought not to override Canada's cogent public interests in such a case.

One commentator queries whether the principle of party autonomy is "so hallowed that in all cases it should be limited only by the law of the parties' selection?"[45] The answer is certainly no, for "justice is not always to be controlled by the individual as distinct from the community of which the individual is a part."[46]

Furthermore, the application of foreign mandatory rules is not invariably antithetical to the wishes of the parties. As Derains rightly points out, the choice of one law does not necessarily imply an intention to exclude all relevant mandatory rules that are external to the chosen *lex contractus*.[47] It could legitimately be argued that the parties intended their agreement to conform to the mandatory rules of those countries upon which their transactions have a significant impact. For example, in the above illustration, the parties may have selected Japanese law to govern their agreement on the understanding that despite this selection Canadian competition laws would be respected. More important, the will of the parties cannot be used as a ground for refusing to apply the mandatory rules of foreign law as the parties in many cases do not express any view on the applicability of foreign mandatory rules. The choice of a governing law should not be interpreted as implying the exclusion of other relevant laws, unless the parties expressly exclude them. Even then, the arbitrator would have to determine whether the will of the parties can legitimately override the public interests of a country whose jurisdiction is substantially connected to the underlying transaction.

Finally, the plea of uncertainty as a justification for nonapplication of foreign mandatory rules sits a little ill when it is remembered that other principles of law are no less certain. For example, in the absence of an express choice by the parties, arbitrators usually apply the law most closely connected to the contract. Certainly, this process of determining applicable law does not afford complete certainty of application. Moreover, one wonders why the need for certainty should supersede the necessity of respecting the mandatory rules of foreign laws that are substantially connected to the dispute. The application of foreign mandatory rules should involve a balancing of the public interests of the enacting State with the private interests of contracting parties.

In contrast, the favorable approach to the application of mandatory rules recognizes that foreign mandatory rules may be so connected with the dispute as to compel their application, even though they are not part of the governing law. This approach, acknowledging the fact that the will of the parties has to be reconciled with the interests of those States that are closely connected to the dispute, entertains the possibility of applying foreign mandatory rules in appropriate cases.

The favorable approach is accepted in most of the recent conventions dealing with contractual relations. An example is Article 7 of the European Convention on the Law Applicable to Contractual Obligations (the Obligations Convention),[48] which provides that:

> When applying under this Convention the law of a country, effect may be given to the mandatory rules of the law of another country with which the situation has a close connection, if and in so far as, under the law of the latter country, those rules must be applied whatever the law applicable to the contract. . . .[49]

A similar approach is also adopted in Article 16 of the Hague Convention on the Law Applicable to Agency:

> In the application of this Convention effect may be given to the mandatory rules of any State with which the situation has significant connection, if and in so far as, under the law of that State, those rules must be applied whatever the law specified by its choice of law rules.

These conventions are of course not directly applicable to arbitration proceedings, but they represent an emerging consensus on the need to respect the imperative rules not only of the proper law but also other laws that are significantly connected to the transaction. O. Lando rightly sees in the Obligation Convention the embodiment of a reasonable principle that is extendable to international commercial arbitration:

Article 7(1) of the [Obligation] Convention is expressive of international solidarity. States should help each other in the enforcement of relevant government policies. The arbitrators should contribute to this solidarity by giving effect to mandatory provisions claiming application, provided that those rules are enacted by a State having a close relationship with the contract and that it is fair and reasonable to give effect to them.[50]

In applying foreign mandatory rules, arbitrators should, first, weigh the connection of the rules to the dispute, with the aim of determining if the parties' transaction is substantially connected to the country that enacted the mandatory rules. Second, they should ascertain that the policy behind the rules demonstrate that the rules are applicable to international commercial transactions.[51] Arbitrators should place particular emphasis on the policy rationale for the rules because in many cases mandatory rules are designed solely for domestic application. The Obligation Convention endorses this approach by stating that in deciding whether to apply mandatory rules, "regard shall be had to their nature and purpose and to the consequences of their application or non-application."[52] Similarly, Swiss judges applying foreign mandatory rules examine their "policy and [their] consequences for a judgment that is fair according to Swiss views."[53]

The utilization of the nature and purpose of a mandatory rule as a guide in determining its application would invariably lead to the application of the law of the place of performance. This is because the parties should be presumed to act on the understanding that the contract would be performed in accordance with the rules of the country where performance is required. Arbitrators will doubtless be reluctant to require a party to perform a contract, or pay damages for nonperformance, where the mandatory rules of the place of performance make it impossible to do so.[54] The attitude of arbitrators to the mandatory rules of the place of performance is illustrated by the award in *ICC Case No. 1859* where the tribunal stated:

Since the contract must be performed in Lebanon, Syria and Jordan, it is a sure fact that the Lebanese importer was obliged to comply with the mandatory rules of the countries of importation and that the Japanese party cannot now claim that those rules cannot be raised against him.

Any merchant of a country who attempts to sell his products in another country is bound to respect the mandatory rules of the country of reception and cannot claim to be unaware of or not respect police laws or the regulation governing the importation of his goods, particularly when this law or regulation existed at the time of the performance of the contract.[55]

Also, in *ICC Case No. 761*[56] one of the parties argued that the contract was contrary to public policy, and therefore void, according to French law, the law of the place of performance. The tribunal held that insofar as the contract was to be performed in France, French public policy was relevant to the case, although it found that the instant contract did not violate French public policy.

The case is somewhat more delicate when the foreign mandatory rule involved is not that of the place of performance. In such instances, the purpose of the rule and its connection to the dispute are very helpful indicators of the legitimacy of its claim to application. Assume that a Canadian party enters into a contract with a U.S. citizen for the building of a casino in Bermuda. The contract is governed by English law. In proceedings before arbitrators, the Canadian party pleads Ontario's prohibition of gambling as vitiating the contract. Here, the arbitrators should be guided by the nature and purpose of the mandatory rule in question and the extent of its connection to the case. In the instant case, the only connection of Canada to the case is that it is the residence of one of the parties. On the other hand, the place of performance and the governing law have no connection with Canada. Clearly, Canadian laws do not have any legitimate claim to application in the case. Additionally, a finding that Ontario's prohibition of gambling is aimed at domestic situations would fortify the decision not to apply Ontario law.

The application of foreign mandatory rules is particularly crucial in cases involving sensitive State policy, such as competition laws or environmental laws. Here arbitrators should ensure that arbitration does not become a vehicle for avoiding the application of the mandatory rules of countries significantly connected to the underlying transaction. Nonetheless, the application of foreign mandatory rules should be rejected in cases where they lack a substantial connection with the underlying transaction or where their nature and purpose argue against their application to the international arena. *ICC Case No. 4132*[57] illustrates the application of this principle. In a dispute between an Italian party and a Korean party (governed by Korean law), the arbitrators declined to apply European competition law because the contract did not have a significant effect in Europe. According to the tribunal, "[s]ince the Agreement is a contract between an Italian and a Korean undertaking and was for a larger part performed in Korea, this Tribunal is not satisfied that the Agreement may affect trade between Member States [of the European Community]."[58]

Similarly, in a 1982 award of the Amsterdam Grain Trade Association,[59] the arbitral tribunal noted that the application of a foreign mandatory rule depends on its "nature and extent" and the "consequences of its application or inapplication." It held inapplicable the mandatory rule of one of the parties' nationality on the ground of lack of substantial contact with the agreement. The relevant connecting factors in the case pointed to the Netherlands and Germany, and the party's Austrian nationality was, on its own, insufficient to warrant the application of Austrian mandatory rules.

Also in *ICC Case No. 1512*,[60] in an action to enforce a guarantee issued by a Pakistani bank in favor of an Indian company, the Pakistani bank pleaded as a defense some Pakistani decrees making illegal any payment to an Indian party. As the guarantee provided that payment under the guarantee should be made in India, the tribunal held that "Pakistani law, the law of the place of the debtor's residence, should not intervene." The arbitrators focused on the particular issue raised in the case, namely, that of payment under the guarantee; since that particular element was not connected to Pakistan, the Pakistani prohibition could not affect the performance of the contract in Indian territory.

A consideration of the purpose and scope of a mandatory rule with the aim of determining its applicability was made by the sole arbitrator in *ICC Case No. 6379 of 1990*.[61] In a case between an Italian and a Belgian party (in which Italian law was the governing law), the arbitrator refused to apply a Belgian mandatory rule because, *inter alia*, it "does not aim at binding the international arbitrator."[62] The arbitrator found that the rule was designed for application by Belgian courts.

In conclusion, it could be seen that the major trend in arbitral practice is to apply foreign mandatory rules in appropriate cases. The application of these rules in individual cases depends on their connection with the dispute and their nature and purpose.

THE ROLE OF TRANSNATIONAL PUBLIC POLICY

The preceding discussion has focused on the restriction that mandatory rules of national law (rules that are reflective of the public policy of the enacting States) place on the application of the governing substantive law. However, while mandatory national rules may operate to dislodge the applicable substantive law, there is in international commercial practice a public policy superior to national public policy.

This preeminent public policy is sometimes labeled transnational public policy or truly international public policy.[63] Like the concept of public policy in national law, the concept of transnational public policy presupposes the existence of "a certain community and of certain fundamental values."[64] Unlike national public policy, the relevant community here is not a national community but the international community.

While the public policy of a State embodies the moral and ethical philosophy of the State, transnational public policy performs the same role for the international business community. There is a certain similarity between the two: principles that embody the fundamental and ethical values of a national community would in most cases be equally fundamental in the international community. For example, the requirement of fair hearing and due process is considered a basic element of justice in both national and international communities. However, so long as national public policy represents particular and narrow national interests, while transnational public policy represents the values of the world community, the two strands of public policy can not be identical. Thus, while the act of gambling is against public morals in some societies, it can hardly be said that the abhorrence of gambling is part of the fundamental values of the world community.

Transnational public policy represents the fundamental values, the basic ethical standards, and the enduring moral consensus of the international community. Its principles are derived from "the fundamental rules of natural law, the principles of universal justice, *jus cogens* in public international law"[65] and the public policy accepted in a generality of nations.[66] These principles, which include the abhorrence of racial, religious, and sexual discrimination and the repudiation of corrupt practices, are in a sense the mandatory rules of international commercial relations that must be respected in all arbitrations.

The application of transnational public policy is seen as crucial to the maintenance of minimum standards of conduct and behavior in international commercial relations. As the Cour d'Appel of Paris points out, "The security of international commercial and financial relations requires the recognition of a public policy that is, if not universal, at least common to the various legal systems."[67]

Arbitrators are particularly suited to apply the principles of transnational public policy because they have a responsibility to maintain a certain element of equity and fair play in the international commercial arena, and they are not guardians of the public policy of any particular State. This responsibility is partly discharged by their balancing the will of the parties with the legitimate interests of the international community in preserving the basic notions of contractual morality and justice.

Arbitrators, as guardians of the international commercial order, refuse to enforce a contact if it contravenes transnational public policy. This was the result in *ICC Case No. 1110*.[68] In that case, the claimant claimed some money as commission for his efforts in helping the respondent procure an Argentinian government contract. Having determined that the commission amounted in effect to a bribe, the sole arbitrator held the contract in violation of transnational public policy:

> [I]t cannot be contested that there exists a general principle of law recognized by civilized nations that contracts which seriously violate *bonos mores* or international public policy are invalid or at least unenforceable and that they cannot be sanctioned by courts or arbitrators. This principle is especially apt for use before international arbitration tribunals that lack a "law of the forum" in the ordinary sense of the term.[69]

The arbitrator declined to proceed with the arbitration, holding that the corruption involved in the transaction was "an international evil; it is contrary to good morals and to an international public policy common to the community of nations."[70] Also in *ICC Case No. 2730*[71] the tribunal held that an agreement designed to contravene Yugoslav exchange control law was void because the contract was contrary "not only to Yugoslav law but also to morality and *bonos mores*."

Transnational public policy could also be a ground for an arbitrator's refusal to apply the mandatory rule of a relevant national law. Transnational public policy represents values that are superior to those of particular national systems. Therefore, when a mandatory national rule is in conflict with a transnational policy, the latter prevails, at least in an international arbitral forum.[72] This is because arbitrators owe a paramount duty to the international community. Illustrating this principle, P. Mayer gives as an example certain boycott laws that establish restrictions on the grounds of race and religion. He rightly argues that an arbitrator should in the name of transnational public policy refuse to enforce such mandatory laws because they seek to institute racial or religious discrimination which contravenes transnational public policy.

It is useful to enter a caveat regarding the use of transnational public policy in refusing to apply national mandatory rules. If the use of this doctrine is not placed under careful and continual scrutiny, it may become a ready tool at the hands of some jurists who wish to utilize this theory in refusing to recognize or apply those national laws that they deem unsuitable to their regional interests. Now and again one hears all sorts of rules being pleaded as part of transnational public policy, rules that often do not embody generally accepted principles. For example, the doctrine of *pacta sunt servanda* and the principle of good faith are often pleaded in support of an alleged principle of transnational policy that ordains the immutability of State contracts in the absence of a common agreement of the parties to alter the contractual provisions. This argument is made despite clear and readily accessible evidence that State practices in many jurisdictions (for example, State practices in France and those jurisdictions whose legal systems are modeled on the French) adopt the theory of administrative contracts whereby the State in municipal relations has, under certain conditions, extracontractual powers to alter the provisions of a government contract.[73] The type of transnational public policy that could exclude the application of mandatory rules of national law should be interpreted as including only those policies, standards, and principles that truly represent a consensus of the world community and that are necessary for securing contractual morality in international commercial relations.

In sum, the theory of transnational public policy originates from an attempt by arbitrators to enforce those fundamental ethical and moral values that are necessary for the security of international commercial relations. It is the case that the concept of transnational public policy is rarely raised before arbitrators as a ground for invalidating a contractual obligation. Nevertheless, its presence in arbitral practice is a constant reminder to potential arbitrating parties that the relative independence of the arbitral process does not imply that the process could be used to circumvent the application of basic concepts of morality and justice.

CONCLUSION

Mandatory rules are one of the ways in which the doctrine of party autonomy is adapted to the legitimate interests of States in ensuring that the arbitral process affirms the basic elements of contractual morality. Of course, arbitrators are not expected to apply each and every mandatory rule that is pleaded as relevant to the case. Their mission in this regard is to examine the nature and purpose of relevant mandatory rules and ascertain whether the enacting State's connection with the parties' transaction warrants the application of such rules. Where the connection is limited or merely speculative, the arbitrator should decline to apply such rules.[74]

Arbitrators should also ensure that disputes before them conform to the requirements of truly transnational public policy.

The enforcement of appropriate mandatory rules by arbitrators would send a signal to prospective arbitrating parties that the arbitral process is certainly not a device for circumventing imperative laws of States with which their transaction is substantially connected. This attitude will justify the confidence of those States that believe arbitrators are well suited to adjudicate claims involving sensitive matters of State policy.

NOTES

1. 105 S. Ct 3346; 444 U.S. 614.

2. See *United States* v. *Aluminum Co. of America (Alcoa)* 148 F.2d 416. Indeed the court in *American Safety Equipment Corp.* v. *J.P. Maguire and Co.*, 391 F. 2d 821 at 827–828, held that antitrust disputes were nonarbitrable in view of "the pervasive public interest in enforcement of the antitrust laws."

3. A. Bucher and P. Tschanz remind us that

> States that favour international arbitration as a means of resolving international commercial disputes do not by the same token forego compliance with principles and rules which are fundamental for the economic and social system. The fact that arbitral tribunals are allowed to adjudicate disputes instead of courts does not mean that arbitration can enerve the legislative power of States.

International Arbitration in Switzerland (Basel: Helbing and Lichtenhahn, 1989) at 103.

4. As A. Maniruzzaman puts it: "Although the parties' freedom of choice (autonomy of will) is a general principle of private international law and is to be respected in principle, it should operate within the limits imposed by such other equally important general principles of law or subject to any restraints of public policy." "International Arbitrator and Mandatory Public Law Rules in the Context of State Contracts: An Overview" (1990) 7:3 *J. Int'l Arb.* 53 at 63.

5. See *Award of 27 May 1991*, reported in (1992) 17 *Y. Comm. Arb.* 11 at 27–29.

6. See M. Pryles, "Reflection on the E.E.C. Contractual Obligations Convention—An Australian Perspective" in P. North (ed.) *Contract Conflicts: The E.E.C. Convention on the Law Applicable to Contractual Obligations—A Comparative Study* (Amsterdam: North-Holland Publishing Company, 1982) 323 at 331.

7. Y. Derains, "Possible Conflict of Law Rules and the Rules Applicable to the Substance of the Dispute" in P. Sanders (ed.) *UNCITRAL's Project for a Model Law on International Commercial Arbitration* (Deventer, The Netherlands: Kluwer Law and Taxation Publishers, 1984) 169 at 179.

8. Article 3(3) of the EEC Convention on the Law Applicable to Contractual Obligation defines mandatory rules as "rules of law of a country which cannot be derogated from by contract." For a discussion of the Convention, see P. North, supra note 6.

9. Speaking about the European Community Regulation No. 2340 of August 8, 1990, which imposed embargo against Iraq, an arbitral tribunal noted: "These provisions not only cannot be derogated from, they must be necessarily applied; that is, they are provisions which must be necessarily applied in the EC, whichever law applies to the contract, as it appears from their purpose and public law character." *Final Award of 20 July 1992, No. 1491*, reported in (1993) 18 *Y. Comm. Arb.* 80 at 85.

10. M. Pryles, supra note 6 at 331.

11. See A. Anton and P. Beaumont, *Private International Law*, 2d ed. (Edinburgh: W. Green, 1990) at 343.

12. S. 27(2) of the act provides that the provisions of the act apply, notwithstanding the choice of a foreign governing law, if either the choice of law appears to have been imposed wholly or mainly for the purpose of enabling the party imposing it to evade the operation of the act, or, in the making of the contract one of the parties dealt as consumer and he or she was then habitually resident in the United Kingdom and the essential steps necessary for the making of the contract were taken there.

13. See V. Triebel, "The Choice of Law in Commercial Relations: A German Perspective" (1988) 37 *I.C.L.Q.* 935 at 939.

14. See *The Hollandia* [1983] 1 A.C. 565.

15. See F. Juenger, *Choice of Law and Multistate Justice* (Dordrecht, The Netherlands: Martinus Nijhoff, 1993) at 79; P. Carter, "The Role of Public Policy in English Private International Law" (1993) 42 *I.C.L.Q* 1.

16. Supra note 10.

17. See *Ross* v. *McMullen* (1971) 21 D.L.R. (3d) 228; *Oppenheimer* v. *Cattermole* [1976] A.C. 249 at 278.

18. (1868) 6 M. 1095.

19. Id. at 1110. This principle is contained in Rule 2 of *Dicey and Morris Conflict of Laws*: "English courts will not enforce or recognize a right, power, capacity, disability or legal relationship arising under the law of a foreign country, if the enforcement or recognition of such right, power, capacity, disability or legal relationship would be inconsistent with the fundamental public policy of English law." L. Collins (ed.) *Dicey and Morris Conflict of Laws* 11th ed. (London: Stevens and Sons, 1987) at 92. Stating the Canadian position on the issue, J. Castel notes that Canadian courts will not recognize or enforce a right or power that is "contrary to the forum's stringent public policy or essential public or moral interest."

Canadian Conflict of Laws, 2nd ed. (Toronto: Butterworths, 1986) at 153. In a similar vein, Article 17 of the Swiss Federal Statute of Private International Law provides that "The application of provisions of a foreign law is excluded if the outcome is incompatible with Swiss public policy."

20. (1918) 224 N.Y. 99.

21. Id. at 111. See also *Block Bros. Realty Ltd.* v. *Mollard* [1981] 4 W.W.R. 65. There is a trend toward drawing a distinction between domestic public policy and international public policy in the recognition of foreign law. In this respect, non-recognition of foreign law on grounds of public policy would be based not on the internal rules of public policy in the forum, but on the foreign law's inconsistency with the forum court's view of public policy in international matters.

22. See M. Bogdan, "Some Arbitration-Related Problems of Swedish Private International Law" [1990] *Swedish and Int'l Arb.* 70 at 76.

23. See J. Lew, *Applicable Law in International Commercial Arbitration: A Study in Commercial Arbitration Awards* (Dobbs Ferry, NY: Oceana Publications, 1978) at 536. This principle may well be overstated in that an arbitral tribunal still owes a duty to the various national legal systems: a duty to ensure that arbitration proceedings conform with basic notions of justice and fairness.

24. Id. at 340.

25. O. Lando, "The Law Applicable to the Merits of the Dispute" in P. Sarcevic (ed.) *Essays on International Commercial Arbitration* (London: Martinus Nijhoff, 1989) 129 at 158. See also F. Klein, "The Law to be Applied by Arbitrators to the Substance of the Dispute" in J. Schultsz and A. van den Berg (eds.) *The Art of Arbitration: Essays on International Commercial Arbitration, Liber Amicorum for Pieter Sanders* (Deventer, The Netherlands: Kluwer Law and Taxation Publishers, 1982) 189 at 204. Speaking in the same vein, P. Mayer argues that although arbitrators are neither "guardians of the public order nor invested by the State with a mission of applying its mandatory rules," they should nevertheless respect relevant mandatory rules "out of a sense of duty to the survival of international arbitration as an institution." P. Mayer, "Mandatory Rules of Law in International Arbitration" (1986) 2 *Arb. Int'l* 274 at 285–286.

26. W. Craig, W. Park, and J. Paulsson, *International Chamber of Commerce Arbitration*, 2d ed. (Dobbs Ferry, NY: Oceana Publications, 1990) at 307–308.

27. See discussion in Chapter 4.

28. See, for example, *ICC Case No. 1397* (1966) *Clunet* 878. See also *Final Award of 20 July 1992, No. 1491*, supra note 9.

29. The concept of "transnational international public policy" and its effect on the application of mandatory rules of national law is discussed in the section of this chapter entitled "The Role of Transnational Public Policy."

30. A. Maniruzzaman, supra note 4 at 54.

31. L. Collins, supra note 19 at 23. See also *Kleinwort, Sons & Co.* v. *Ungarische Baumwolle Industrie A.G.* [1939] 2 K.B. 678. It should however be noted that in England, as in most common law jurisdictions, there is a requirement that the parties' choice of applicable law must be made in good faith. See *Vita Food Products* v. *Unus Shipping* [1939] A.C. 277. This requirement is aimed at stopping cases of evasion of law, although it is rarely applied. See generally J. Fawcett, "Evasion of Law and Mandatory Rules in Private International Law" (1990) 49 *Cambridge L.J.* 44.

32. See E. Sykes and M. Pryles, *Australian Private International Law*, 2d ed. (Sydney: The Law Book Company, 1987) at 546. See also M. Pryles, supra note 6 at 330.

33. See J. Castel, supra note 19 at 155.

34. See, for example, A. Anton and P. Beaumont, supra note 11 at 344.

35. P. Karrer and K. Arnold, *Switzerland's Private International Law Statute, 1987* (Deventer, The Netherlands: Kluwer Law and Taxation Publishers, 1989) at 44–45.

36. R. Rooij and M. Polak, *Private International Law in the Netherlands* (Deventer, The Netherlands: Kluwer Law and Taxation Publishers, 1987) at 129.

37. See E. Jayme, "The Rome Convention on the Law Applicable to Contractual Obligations (1980)" in P. Sarcevic (ed.) *International Contracts and Conflict of Laws* (London: Graham and Trotman, 1990) 36 at 46–47.

38. L. Collins, supra note 19 at 1236.

39. [1950] A.C. 24.

40. Id. at 36. See also *Libyan Arab Bank* v. *Bankers Trust Co.* [1989] 2 W.L.R. 314 at 328; M. Pryles, supra note 6 at 330; G. Morse, "England" in M. Rubino-Sammartano and G. Morse, *Public Policy in Transnational Relationships* (Deventer, The Netherlands: Kluwer Law and Taxation Publishers, 1991) at England 69–70.

41. L. Collins, supra note 19 at 1238.

42. See P. Mayer, supra note 25 at 283.

43. This approach is illustrated by some awards. In *ICC Award No. 1399*, the arbitrators, considering the validity of a contract that had the indirect object of circumventing Mexican customs law, held that the proper law of the contract (French law) could not be displaced by Mexican law, the law of the place where the goods in dispute where to be imported. See J. Lew, supra note 23 at 550–551. Similarly, in an award rendered by the arbitration court of the Chamber of Foreign Trade of the defunct German Democratic Republic [(1979) IV *Y. Comm. Arb.* 197], the arbitrators, in determining the validity of a license agreement between firms in the GDR and the Federal Republic of Germany, held that the competition laws of the FRG were inapplicable because the contract was governed by the laws of the GDR.

44. Mandatory rules outside the *lex contractus* are here designated as foreign mandatory rules because they are external to the governing law.

45. D. Jackson, "Mandatory Rules and Rules of 'Ordre Public' " in P. North, supra note 6 at 76.

46. Id.

47. Y. Derains, "Public Policy and the Law Applicable to the Dispute in International Arbitration" in P. Sanders (ed.) *Comparative Arbitration Practice and Public Policy in Arbitration* (Deventer, The Netherlands: Kluwer Law and Taxation Publishers, 1987) 227 at 249.

48. Opened for signature in Rome on June 19, 1980. The Convention does not, however, apply to "arbitration agreements": Article 1(2)(d).

49. This provision is considered imprecise, vague, and controversial by those who favor the English approach of not applying foreign mandatory rules. See I. Fletcher, *Conflict of Law and European Community Law* (Amsterdam: North-Holland, 1982) at 170. According to Article 22(1)(a) of the convention, a Contracting State may reserve the right not to apply Article 7(1). Exercising this right, the United

Kingdom and Germany excluded Article 7(1). See L. Collins, supra note 19 at 23; A. Jayme, supra note 37 at 46.

50. O. Lando, supra note 25 at 159.

51. The Institute of International Law has expressed a similar view. Article 9(2) of the Institute's resolution on The Autonomy of the Parties in International Contracts Between Private Persons or Entities (August 31, 1991) provides that foreign mandatory rules can preclude the application of the governing law only "if there is a close link between the contract and the country of that law and if they further such aims as are generally accepted by the international community." (1991) 64 *Yearbook Institute Int'l Law* 384.

52. Article 7(1).

53. Article 19(2) of Switzerland's Private International Law Statute, 1987.

54. W. Craig et al., supra note 26 at 304.

55. 1973 *Rev. Arb.* 122.

56. Reported in J. Lew, supra note 23 at 542.

57. S. Jarvin and Y. Derains, *Collection of ICC Arbitral Awards: 1974–1985* (Deventer, The Netherlands: Kluwer Law and Taxation Publishers, 1990) at 164.

58. Id. at 166.

59. (1983) 8 *Y. Comm. Arb.* 158.

60. (1976) 1 *Y. Comm. Arb.* 128.

61. (1992) 17 *Y. Comm. Arb.* 212.

62. Id. at 218.

63. For a very helpful discussion of the role of transnational public policy in international commercial arbitration, see P. Lalive, "Transnational (or Truly International) Public Policy and International Arbitration" in P. Sanders, supra note 47 at 257.

64. Id. at 315.

65. Lew, supra note 23 at 534.

66. According to J. Robert and T. Carbonneau, transnational public policy incorporates "principles sufficiently general to be recognized by a number of legal systems representing a *bona fide* community of civilized nations." *The French Law of Arbitration* (New York: Matthew Bender, 1983) at 11:9–11. While the concept of civilized nations as used by the authors is not free from controversy, the general idea is that transnational policy includes the synthesis of the public policy of a representative selection of nations.

67. See P. Lalive, supra note 63 at 278.

68. Reported by J. Lew, supra note 23 at 553.

69. Id. at 554.

70. Id. at 555.

71. (1984) *Clunet* 914.

72. See P. Mayer, supra note 25 at 291; J. Lew, supra note 23 at 104.

73. See C. Turpin, "Public Contract" in *International Encyclopedia of Comparative Law*, vol. 7 *Contracts in General*, chapter 4 (Tubingen: J.C.B. Mohr, 1982). See also J. Mitchell, *The Contracts of Public Authorities: A Comparative Study* (London: G. Bell and Sons, 1954).

74. J. Enterria, "The Role of Public Policy in International Commercial Arbitration" (1990) 21 *Law & Policy Int'l Bus.* 389 at 438.

CHAPTER SEVEN

Conclusion

INTRODUCTION

The objective of this book was to examine the choice of law problems faced by international commercial arbitrators and to analyze the solutions adopted by arbitrators, international conventions, national legal systems,and jurists in tackling these problems. The purpose of this concluding chapter is not to recapitulate all the conclusions that were made in the body of the book. Rather this chapter is a reflection on the major trends in choice of law issues in international commercial arbitrations.

PARTY AUTONOMY

One common denominator in arbitral and national legislative practices relating to choice of law problems in arbitration is the preeminent role played by the will of the parties. In deciding the applicable substantive and procedural law to an arbitration, arbitral tribunals, international conventions, and national laws accord a primary place to the will of the parties.

The high place accorded to the will of the parties is in large part a reflection of the fact that arbitration is a private system of dispute resolution. The system is organized to effectuate the parties' desire for a private and self-designed process of dispute resolution. Parties who contract to arbitrate do so on the understanding that they would design the proceedings to suit their particular needs. Arbitrators therefore respect the will of the parties in approaching choice of law issues.

There are, however, three instances in which the will of the parties does not predominate. First, when there is a dispute as to the very existence of the arbitration agreement (for example, where it is argued that one of the parties lacked the capacity to enter into an arbitration agreement), the will of the parties cannot be a useful guide. This is because issues such as capacity are not determined according to a party's will, for no one can confer capacity on him or herself independent of a national legal system. Second, when the issue concerns the arbitrability of a particular subject matter, the will of the parties is clearly irrelevant as the parties' will cannot supplant the legitimate interest of relevant national legal systems in removing some subject matters from the scope of private arbitration. Third, when the will of the parties comes into conflict with the vital interests of a national legal system (for example, where the parties' contract violates some mandatory national law), the former would, in appropriate cases, give way, depending on the connection between the legal system and the dispute at hand.

The primacy given to party autonomy in the determination of arbitral procedure and applicable substantive law has given rise to two developments, both aimed at freeing arbitration from the peculiarities of national laws. The first is the movement toward delocalization of arbitral procedure, and the second is the trend toward delocalization of applicable substantive law. Both of these trends have been discussed in the body of the book; nevertheless, given the controversy that has surrounded them, it is useful to make some final comments.

In regard to delocalization of arbitral procedure, the objective is to remove arbitration proceedings from the peculiarities of the place of arbitration. The ultimate goal is to prevent the law of the place of arbitration from placing undue burden on the arbitration proceedings. Part of the reason why the movement toward delocalization of arbitral proceedings arose was due to the nonharmonization of rules governing international arbitration in national jurisdictions. The result was that each jurisdiction set up its own framework of rules, some of which were not particularly amenable to the process of international arbitration. Added to this was the fact that the setting aside of an award at the place of arbitration could have a potentially global effect on the enforcement of the award. The trend toward delocalization of arbitral procedure was therefore aimed at restricting the role played by the law of the place of arbitration to that allowed by international agreements on arbitration. This way an arbitration could be freed from the peculiarities of the law of its seat.

However, the present move toward the modernization and harmonization of national laws on arbitration, a move exemplified by the Model Law, would make delocalization of arbitration proceedings increasingly unnecessary. This is because under the scheme of the Model Law, the regulatory framework for international arbitration is standardized. This standardization would ultimately reduce the impact of the adverse peculiarities of the place of arbitration on the conduct of arbitration proceedings.

In regard to delocalization of substantive law, the objective is to subject the parties' contract to nonnational standards, such as the *lex mercatoria* and international law. The former is mostly used in private contractual arrangements, the latter is commonly found in State contract disputes.

Regarding the *lex mercatoria*, one sees the rationale for the recognition of trade usages and practices and their application to contractual disputes. These usages and practices are after all the product of the experiences of commercial people and they embody principles and rules that are grounded on the legitimate expectations of the participants and the needs of the particular trade. Indeed, it is the unquestioned utility of trade usages and practices in commercial relations that explains the role they play in contract law doctrine in various jurisdictions. However, these trade usages and practices, even when coupled with general principles of law, are not comprehensive enough to constitute an autonomous system of law for the resolution of complex commercial relations. Parties who choose the *lex mercatoria* to govern their contract therefore run the risk of their arbitrators rendering an award that is based largely on their personal notions of justice and equity, as opposed to any recognizable principle of law. Admittedly, there is nothing wrong in principle with arbitrators basing their decision on considerations of justice and equity if the parties grant them the authority to do so. But parties who grant arbitrators the power to apply the *lex mercatoria* may be unaware that they are actually granting the arbitrators the power to act as "social engineers" in cases where there are conflicting trade usages and practices or where, as in most instances, there are no identifiable usages and practices to apply to a particular case scenario. If the intention of the parties is to enable their arbitrators to decide according to notions of equity and fairness, they may well directly grant them the power of amiable composition.

The attempt to delocalize the law governing State contract disputes poses its own problems. If the parties to a State contract are imprudent enough to select international law—unsupplemented by a particular national law—to govern their agreement, they would soon realize that international law, apart from its proclamations of *pacta sunt servanda* and similar generalities, is incomprehensive for the regulation of complex commercial relations. More worrying, however, is the attempt by some arbitrators to delocalize the applicable substantive law to State contracts independent of the wishes of the parties. As we have seen, attempts have been made to develop a rule by which so-called economic development agreements are inherently internationalized and by which other State contracts are automatically internationalized by the presence of an arbitration agreement. These attempts, as argued in Chapter 5, are very artificial and seek unrealistically to immunize State contracts from changing business environments.

In both private and State contracts, national laws remain the most comprehensive and appropriate governing standard. National laws are readily accessible and are continually updated to meet the changing economic and social environment. In contrast, the *lex mercatoria* and international law are, at best, incomprehensive and do not constitute a self-sufficient body of principles for the regulation of contractual arrangements. They can, however, play a supplementary role to national law.

PLACE OF ARBITRATION

This book has argued that the place of arbitration should not be considered of overwhelming importance in the resolution of choice of law problems in international commercial arbitration. This is because the place of arbitration is in some instances unconnected with the dispute being arbitrated, and in other instances is chosen for reasons of convenience. Thus, the law of the place of arbitration should not be a vital element in determining the applicable substantive law or in determining the validity of an arbitration agreement, unless there is some connection between the place of arbitration and the underlying agreement.

On the other hand, as argued in Chapter 3, the place of arbitration should play a role in ensuring the fairness of the arbitral procedure and in guaranteeing its conformity with the basic dictates of justice. The place of arbitration is most suited for this role because the arbitration is conducted in its jurisdiction. In return for the privilege of conducting an arbitration in a particular jurisdiction, and in return for the assistance that the courts of the place of arbitration render to the arbitral process, the courts of that jurisdiction should ensure that the proceedings are fair and equitable. This role should, however, be played in accordance with the international standards enshrined in the New York Convention, the Model Law, and other international agreements on arbitration.

PUBLIC POLICY AND PRIVATIZED JUSTICE

One of the enduring areas of tension in arbitral practice is how to strike a balance between arbitral autonomy and vital juridical interests. True, arbitration is a private system of dispute resolution, but does this imply that the arbitral process is to remain totally unregulated by national laws? Is arbitration in essence a system of private justice unfettered by national interests?

The perspective informing this book has been eclectic; it stressed the reciprocal and dynamic interaction between the will of the arbitrating parties and the interest of various national legal systems in ensuring the fairness of the arbitral process and its respect of vital national interests. The process of arbitration cannot be totally understood without an appreciation of the role that national legal systems play in supporting arbitration at three crucial stages. These are the stages of enforcing the agreement to arbitrate, aiding the conduct of the arbitration proceedings, and recognizing and enforcing arbitral awards. Without this help provided by national legal systems, arbitration would be nothing more than a convergence of conduct and expectations between the parties, totally unenforceable at law.

Arbitrators recognize the central place of national legal systems in the survival of arbitration. They thus respect the public policies of relevant national jurisdictions in determining the arbitrability of subject matters, in the conduct of the arbitration proceedings, and in determining and applying the law governing the merits of the dispute. This is as it should be, for arbitration should not be allowed to become a means for businesspeople to escape the mandatory rules of jurisdictions in which they do business; neither should the fairness and justice of the arbitral process go unsupervised by national law (even if such supervision is done by reference to international standards).

The more contentious issue is: which national public policies should arbitrators respect or enforce? This book has argued that the requisite test should be the connection of the jurisdiction (whose policy is at issue) to the dispute and the nature of the policy involved. An arbitral tribunal should first determine that a particular jurisdiction is so closely connected with the dispute that its public policy ought to be respected or enforced in the proceedings. In addition, the tribunal should determine that the particular policy is designed for application to international commercial relations. It was also argued that an otherwise applicable national public policy could be denied application if it is contrary to transnational public policy (for example, policies that enact discrimination based on race, religion, or ethnic origins).

The role of public policy in arbitration proceedings is buttressed by Article V(2)(b) of the New York Convention, which permits the denial of recognition and enforcement of an award where the recognition and enforcement of the award would contravene the public policy of the enforcing jurisdiction.

FINAL REMARKS

Arbitration is increasingly being accepted by the international business community as an efficient and flexible method of dispute resolution. The increased use of arbitration has led to the publication of awards and the evolution of a considerable body of juridical writing on the subject. The publication of awards would contribute to the systematic elaboration of rules governing choice of law in international commercial arbitrations. Juridical writings, which are often cited in arbitral awards, would also play a useful role in this regard.

The primacy accorded to party autonomy in the determination of applicable substantive and procedural law meshes neatly with the private nature of arbitration. Nevertheless, it should always be remembered that arbitration can never be entirely privatized, for it must continually respond to the policy demands of those jurisdictions whose legitimate interests are implicated in the proceedings.

It would seem that the survival of international commercial arbitration as a legitimate system of dispute resolution depends not only on its responsiveness to the needs of the participants but, perhaps more crucially, on its respect for vital juridical interests.

Selected Bibliography

Allison, J. "Arbitration of Private Antitrust Claims in International Trade: A Study in the Subordination of National Interests to the Demands of a World Market." (1986) 18 *N.Y.J. Int'l L. & Pol.* 361.

Anton, A. and Beaumont, P. *Private International Law*. 2d ed. Edinburgh: W. Green, 1990.

Asante, S. "Stability of Contractual Relations in the Transnational Investment Process." (1979) 28 *I.C.L.Q.* 401.

Atterbury, W. "Enforcement of A-National Arbitral Awards under the New York Convention of 1958." (1992) 32 *Virginia J. Int'l L.* 471.

Avanessan, A. "The New York Convention and Denationalized Arbitral Awards: With Emphasis on the Iran-United States Claims Tribunal." (1991) 8 *J. Int'l Arb.* 5.

Baird, D. "Self-Interest and Cooperation in Long-Term Contracts." (1990) 19 *J. Legal Studies* 583.

Baker, S. and Davis, M. *The UNCITRAL Arbitration Rules in Practice: The Experience of the Iran-United States Claims Tribunal*. Deventer, The Netherlands: Kluwer Law & Taxation Publishers, 1992.

Bartels, M. *Contractual Adaptation and Conflict Resolution*. Deventer, The Netherlands: Kluwer Law and Taxation Publishers, 1985.

Bentil, K. "Commercial Arbitrators Authorised not to Apply Strict Rules of Law and Judicial Review." (1992) *J. Business Law* 26.

Berg, van den A. "The Efficacy of Award in International Commercial Arbitration." (1992) 58 *Arbitration: J. Chartered Inst. Arbs* 267.

______. "The New York Convention of 1958: Consolidated Commentary." (1989) 14 *Y. Comm. Arb.* 528.

______. *The New York Convention of 1958: Towards a Uniform Judicial Interpretation*. Deventer, The Netherlands: Kluwer Law and Taxation Publishers, 1981.

Berman, H. and Dasser, F. "The 'New' Law Merchant and the 'Old': Sources, Content, and Legitimacy." In Carbonneau, T. (ed.) *Lex Mercatoria and Arbitration*. New York: Transnational Juris Publications, 1990.

Blessing, M. "The New International Arbitration Law in Switzerland: A Significant Step Towards Liberalism." (1988) 5 *J. Int'l Arb.* 9.

Blom, J. "Conflict of Laws Aspects of the International Arbitration Act." In Paterson, R. and Thompson, B. (eds.) *UNCITRAL Arbitration Model in Canada.* Toronto: Carswell, 1987.

Bockstiegel, K. "The Legal Rules Applicable in International Commercial Arbitration Involving States or State-Controlled Enterprises." In *International Arbitration: 60 Years of ICC Arbitration—A Look at the Future.* Paris: ICC Publishing, 1984.

______. "Public Policy and Arbitrability." In Sanders, P. (ed.) *Comparative Arbitrative Practice and Public Policy in Arbitration.* Deventer, The Netherlands: Kluwer Law and Taxation Publishers, 1987.

______. "The Relevance of National Arbitration Laws for Arbitration under the UNCITRAL Rules." (1984) 1 *J. Int'l Arb.* 221.

Bogdan, M. "Some Arbitration-Related Problems of Swedish Private International Law." (1990) *Swedish and Int'l Arb.* 70.

Bondzi-Simpson, P. *Legal Relationships between Transnational Corporations and Host States.* Westport, CT: Quorum Books, 1990.

Bouchez, L. "The Prospects for International Arbitration: Disputes between States and Private Enterprises." In Soons, A. (ed.) *International Arbitration: Past and Prospects.* Dordrecht, The Netherlands: Martinus Nijhoff, 1990.

Bowett, D. "State Contracts with Aliens: Contemporary Developments on Compensation for Termination or Breach." (1988) 59 *B.Y.I.L.* 50.

Boyd, S. " 'Arbitration Not To Be Bound by Law' Clauses." (1990) 6 *Arb. Int'l* 122.

Broches, A. *Commentary on the UNCITRAL Model Law on International Commercial Arbitration.* Deventer, The Netherlands: Kluwer Law and Taxation Publishers, 1990.

Buchanan, M. "Public Policy and International Commercial Arbitration." (1988) 26 *Am. Bus. L.J.* 511.

Bucher, A. and Tschanz T. *International Arbitration in Switzerland.* Basel: Helbing and Lichtenhahn, 1989.

Burger, W. "Using Arbitration to Achieve Justice." (1986) 40 *Arb. J.* 4.

Carbonneau, T. *Alternative Dispute Resolution: Melting the Lances and Dismounting the Steeds.* Urbana: University of Illinois Press, 1989.

______. "Arbitral Adjudication: A Comparative Assessment of Its Remedial and Substantive Status in Transnational Commerce." (1984) 19 *Texas Int'l L.J.* 33.

______. "The Elaboration of Substantive Legal Norms and Arbitral Adjudication: The Case of the Iran-United States Claims Tribunal." In Lillich, R. (ed.) *The Iran-United States Claims Tribunal: 1981–1983.* Charlottesville: University of Virginia Press, 1984.

______. "Rendering Arbitral Awards with Reasons: The Elaboration of a Commercial Law of International Transactions." (1985) 23 *Col. Journ.* 579.

Carter, P. "The Role of Public Policy in English Private International Law." (1993) 42 *I.C.L.Q.* 1.

Castel, J. *Canadian Conflict of Laws.* 2d ed. Toronto: Butterworths, 1986.

______. "International Commercial Arbitration." In Emond, P. (ed.) *Commercial Dispute Resolution: Alternatives to Litigation*. Ontario: Canada Law Book, 1989.

Chang, M. *The Autonomy of International Commercial and Maritime Arbitration: International, Canadian and Far Eastern Perspectives*. Seoul: International Legal Studies, 1989.

Chatterjee, S. "The Stabilisation Clause Myth in Investment Agreements." (1988) 5:4 *J. Int'l Arb.* 97.

Chen, L. *An Introduction to Contemporary International Law: A Policy-Oriented Perspective*. New Haven: Yale University Press, 1989.

Cherian, J. *Investment Contracts and Arbitration*. Leyden, The Netherlands: A. W. Sijhoff-Leyden International Publishers, 1975.

Christie, R. "Amiable Composition in French and English Law." (1992) 58 *Arbitration: J. Chartered Inst. Arbs.* 259.

Chukwumerije, O. "ICSID Arbitration and Sovereign Immunity" (1990) 19 *Anglo-American L.R.* 166.

______. "Is an Arbitration Award 'Made' Where It Is Signed?" (1992) 20 *Canadian Bus. L.J.* 305.

Cohn, E. "Commercial Arbitration and the Rules of Law." (1944) 4 *U.T.L.J.* 1.

Collins, L. (ed.) *Dicey and Morris on Conflict of Laws*. 11th ed. London: Stevens and Sons, 1987.

Cook, J. "Applicable Law in International Arbitration: The Iran-U.S. Claims Tribunal Experience." (1989) *Am. J.I.L.* 292.

Craig, W., Park, W., and Paulsson, J. *International Chamber of Commerce Arbitration*. 2d ed. Dobbs Ferry, NY: Oceana Publications, 1990.

Cremades, B. *Arbitration in Spain*. London: Butterworths, 1991.

Cross, P. "Competence of Competence." (1992) 8 *Arb. Int'l* 205.

Dalton, C. "An Essay in the Deconstruction of Contract Doctrine" (1985) 94 *Yale L.J.* 997.

Danilowicz, V. "The Choice of Law in International Arbitration." (1986) 9 *Hastings Int'l & Comp. L.R.* 235.

David, R. *Arbitration in International Trade*. Deventer, The Netherlands: Kluwer Law and Taxation Publishers, 1985.

Delaume, G. "ICSID and the Transnational Financial Community." (1986) 1 *ICSID Review* 237.

______. "ICSID Arbitration: Practical Considerations." (1984) 1 *J. Int'l Arb.* 101.

______. "State Contracts and Transnational Arbitration." (1981) 75 *A.J.I.L.* 784.

Derains, Y. "Possible Conflict of Law Rules and the Rules Applicable to the Substance of the Dispute." In Sanders P. (ed.) *UNCITRAL's Project for a Model Law on International Commercial Arbitration*. Deventer, The Netherlands: Kluwer Law and Taxation Publishers, 1984.

______. "Public Policy and the Law Applicable to the Dispute in International Arbitration." In Sanders P. (ed.) *Comparative Arbitration Practice and Public Policy in Arbitration*. Deventer, The Netherlands: Kluwer Law and Taxation Publishers, 1987.

Eisemann, F. "The Revised Rules of Arbitration of the International Chamber of Commerce." (1976) 1 *Y. Comm. Arb.* 167.

Enterria, J. "The Role of Public Policy in International Commercial Arbitration." (1990) 21 *Law & Policy Int'l Bus.* 389.

Faber, M. and Brown, R. "Changing the Rules of the Game: Political Risk, Instability and Fair Play in Mineral Concession Contracts." (1980) 2 *Third World Q.* 101.

Fatouros, A. *Government Guarantees to Foreign Investors.* New York: Columbia University Press, 1962.

———. "International Law and the Internationalized Contract." (1980) 74 *A.J.I.L.* 134.

Fawcett, J. "Evasion of Law and Mandatory Rules in Private International Law." (1990) 49 *Cambridge L.J.* 44.

Ferrante, M. "About the Nature (National or A-National, Contractual or Jurisdictional) of ICC Awards under the New York Convention." In Schultsz, J. and Berg, van den A. (eds.) *The Art of Arbitration: Essays on International Arbitration, Liber Amicorum Pieter Sanders.* Deventer, The Netherlands: Kluwer Law and Taxation Publishers, 1982.

Fletcher, I. *Conflict of Laws and European Community Law.* Amsterdam: North-Holland, 1982.

Fouchard, P. *L'arbitrage Commercial International.* Paris: Dalloz, 1965.

Friedman, W. *The Changing Structure of International Law.* New York: Columbia University Press, 1964.

———. *Law in a Changing Society.* London: Stevens and Sons, 1959.

Gaillard, E. "A Foreign View of the New Swiss Law on International Arbitration." (1988) 4 *Arb. Int'l* 25.

Gaja, G. *The New York Convention.* Dobbs Ferry, NY: Oceana Publications, 1978.

Geiger, R. "The Unilateral Change of Economic Development Agreements." (1974) 23 *I.C.L.Q.* 73.

Goldman, B. "The Applicable Law: General Principles of Law—The Lex Mercatoria." In Lew, J. (ed.) *Contemporary Problems of International Arbitration.* London: Centre for Commercial Law Studies, 1986.

Goldstajn, A. "The New Law Merchant Reconsidered." In Fabricius, F. (ed.) *Law and International Trade.* Frankfurt: Athenaum Verlag, 1973.

Goodman, R. "UNCITRAL Model Law on International and Commercial Arbitration: Divergent Approaches in England and Scotland—A Question of Appeal?" (1990) 18 *Int'l Bus. Law* 250.

Greenwood, C. "State Contracts in International Law—The Libyan Oil Arbitration." (1982) 53 *B.Y.I.L.* 27.

Hermann, G. "The Contribution of the ICC to the Development of International Trade Law." In Horn, N. and Schmitthoff, C. (eds.) *The Transnational Law of International Commercial Transactions.* Deventer, The Netherlands: Kluwer and Taxation Publishers, 1982.

———. "The UNCITRAL Model Law—Salient Features and Prospects." In Antaki, N. and Prujiner, A. (eds.) *Proceedings of the First International Arbitration Conference.* Montreal: Wilson and Lafleur, 1986.

———. "The UNCITRAL Model Law on International Commercial Arbitration: Introduction and General Principles." In Sarcevic, P. (ed.) *Essay on International Commercial Arbitration.* London: Graham and Trotman, 1989.

Hirsch, A. "The Place of Arbitration and the Lex Arbitri." (1979) 34:3 *Arb. J.* 43.

Hogg, P. *Liability of the Crown in Australia, New Zealand and the United Kingdom.* Melbourne: The Law Book Company, 1971.

Holtzman, H. and Neuhaus, J. *A Guide to the UNCITRAL Model Law on International Commercial Arbitration: Legislative History and Commentary.* Deventer, The Netherlands: Kluwer Law and Taxation Publishers, 1989.

Horen, van den H. "Commercial Disputes and Their Settlement: A Factor in Business Planning." In *International Arbitration: 60 Years of ICC Arbitration—A Look at the Future.* Paris: ICC Publishing, 1984.

Hunter, M. "UNCITRAL Model Law: Which Road Should London Take?" (1984) 49 *Arbitration* 295.

_____. "Lex Mercatoria." (1987) *L.M.C.L.Q.* 277.

Hunter, M., Paulsson, J., Rawding, N., and Redfern, A. *The Freshfield Guide to Arbitration and ADR: Clauses in International Contracts.* Deventer, The Netherlands: Kluwer Law and Taxation Publishers, 1993.

Hyde, J. "Economic Development Agreements." (1962) 106 *Hague Recueil* 271.

Jacobs, M. *Commercial Arbitration: Law and Practice.* Sydney: The Law Book Company, 1990.

_____. *International Commercial Arbitration in Australia: Law and Practice.* Sydney: The Law Book Company, 1992.

Jarvin, S. "The Place of Arbitration." (1990) *Swedish and Int'l Arbitration* 85.

_____ and Derains, Y. *Collection of ICC Arbitral Awards: 1974–1985* (Deventer, The Netherlands: Kluwer Law and Taxation Publishers, 1990).

Juenger, F. *Choice of Law and Multistate Justice.* Dordrecht, The Netherlands: Martinus Nijhoff, 1993.

_____. "The EEC Convention on the Law Applicable to Contractual Obligations." In North, P. (ed.) *Contract Conflicts: The E.E.C. Convention on the Law Applicable to Contractual Obligations—A Comparative Study.* Amsterdam: North-Holland, 1982.

_____. "The Lex Mercatoria and the Conflict of Laws." In Carbonneau, T. *Lex Mercatoria and Arbitration.* New York: Transnational Juris Publication, 1990.

Kanowitz, L. "Alternative Dispute Resolution and the Public Interest: The Arbitration Experience." (1987) 38 *Hastings L.J.* 239.

Karrer, P. and Arnold, K. *Switzerland's Private International Law Statute, 1987.* Deventer, The Netherlands: Kluwer Law and Taxation Publishers, 1989.

Kellor, F. *American Arbitration: Its History, Functions and Achievements.* New York: Harper and Brothers, 1948.

_____. *Arbitration in Action.* New York: Harper and Brothers, 1941.

Kerr, Mr. Justice. "International Arbitration v. Litigation." (1980) *J. Bus. L.* 164.

Kourides, P. "International Arbitration between States and Foreign Private Parties: The Libyan Nationalization Cases." (1981) 75 *A.J.I.L.* 476.

Kuhn, W. "Arbitrability of Antitrust Disputes in the Federal Republic of Germany." (1987) 3 *Arb. Int'l* 226.

Kuusi, J. *The Host State and the Transnational Corporation: An Analysis of Legal Relationships.* Hampshire: Saxon House, 1979.

Lalive, P. "The New Swiss Law on International Arbitration." (1988) 4 *Arb. Int'l* 2.

_____. "Transnational (or Truly International) Public Policy and International Arbitration." In Sanders, P. (ed.) *Comparative Arbitration Practice and Pub-*

lic Policy in Arbitration. Deventer, The Netherlands: Kluwer Law and Taxation Publishers, 1987.

Lando, O. "The Law Applicable to the Merits of the Dispute." In Sarcevic, P. (ed.) *Essays on International Commercial Arbitration*. London: Graham and Trotman, 1989.

Langrod, G. "Administrative Contracts." (1955) 4 *Am. J.C.L.* 325.

Lew, J. *Applicable Law in International Commercial Arbitration: A Study in Commercial Arbitration Awards*. Dobbs Ferry, NY: Oceana Publications, 1978.

______. "Arbitration Agreements: Form and Character." In Sarcevic, P. (ed.) *Essays on International Commercial Arbitration*. London: Martinus Nijhoff, 1989.

______. "The Case for Publication of Arbitration Awards." In Schultsz, J. and Berg, van den A. (eds.) *The Art of Arbitration: Liber Amicorum for Pieter Sanders*. Deventer, The Netherlands: Kluwer Law and Taxation Publishers, 1982.

Lionnet, K. "Should the Procedural Law Applicable to International Arbitration be Denationalised or Unified?: The Answer of the UNCITRAL Model Law." (1991) 8 *J. Int'l Arb.* 5.

Lipstein, K. "International Arbitration between Individuals and Governments and the Conflict of Laws." In Cheng, B. and Brown, E. (eds,) *Contemporary Problems of International Law*. London: Stevens and Sons, 1988.

Llewellyn, K. "What Price Contract? An Essay in Perspective." (1931) 40 *Yale L.J.* 704.

Macneil, I. "Contracts: Adjustment of Long-Term Economic Relations under Classical, Neoclassical, and Relational Contract Law." (1978) 72 *Northwestern U.L.R.* 854.

Maniruzzaman, A. "International Arbitrator and Mandatory Public Law Rules in the Context of State Contracts: An Overview." (1990) 7:3 *J. Int'l Arb.* 53.

Mann, F. A. "England Rejects 'Delocalised' Contracts and Arbitration." (1984) 33 *I.C.L.Q.* 193.

______. "*Lex Facit Arbitrum*." In Sanders, P. (ed.) *International Arbitration: Liber Amicorum for Martin Domke*. The Hague: Martinus Nijhoff, 1967.

______. "The Law Governing State Contracts." (1944) 21 *B.Y.I.L.* 11.

______. "The Proper Law of Contracts Concluded by International Persons." (1959) 35 *B.Y.I.L.* 34.

______. "Private Arbitration and Public Policy." (1985) 4 *Civil Justice Q.* 256.

______. "State Contracts and International Arbitration." (1967) 42 *B.Y.I.L.* 1.

Mayer, P. "Mandatory Rules of Law in International Arbitration." (1986) 2 *Arb. Int'l* 274.

McClendon, J. "Subject-Matter Arbitrability in International Cases." (1986) *N.C.J. Int'l L. & Comm. Reg.* 81.

McInnis, A. "Amiable Composition: Whither the Direction of Hong Kong Arbitration Law." (1991) 21 *H.K.L.J.* 343.

McLaughlin, J. "Arbitration and Developing Countries." (1979) 13 *Int'l Law.* 211.

McNair, Lord. "The General Principles of Law Recognised by Civilized Nations." (1957) 33 *B.Y.I.L.* 1.

Medwig, M. "The New Law Merchant: Legal Rhetoric and Commercial Reality." (1993) 24 *Law & Policy Int'l Bus.* 589.

Mehren, von A. "Arbitration between States and Foreign Enterprises: The Significance of the Institute of International Law's Santiago de Compostela Resolution." (1990) 5 *ICSID Review* 54.

———. "Draft Report on Arbitration between States and Foreign Enterprises." (1989) 63 *Yearbook Institute Int'l Law* 100.

Mewett, A. "The Theory of Government Contracts." (1959) 5 *McGill L.J.* 222.

Miller, E. "The Adversary System: Dinosaur or Phoenix?" (1984) 69 *Minn. L.R.* 1.

Mitchell, J. *The Contracts of Public Authorities: A Comparative Study*. London: G. Bell and Sons, 1954.

Mustill, M. "Arbitration: History and Background." (1989) 6:2 *J. Int'l Arb.* 43.

———. "Contemporary Problems in International Commercial Arbitration: A Response." (1989) 17 *Int'l Bus. Law* 161.

———."The New Lex Mercatoria: The First Twenty-Five Years." in Bos, M. and Brownlie, I. (eds.) *Liber Amicorum for Lord Wilberforce*. Oxford: Clarendon Press, 1987.

——— and Boyd, S. *The Law and Practice of Commercial Arbitration in England*. 2d ed. London: Butterworths, 1989.

Naon, G. *Choice-of-Law Problems in International Commercial Arbitration*. Tubingen: Mohr, 1992.

Neslor, I. "Problems Concerning the Application and Interpretation of Existing Multilateral Conventions on International Commercial Arbitration and Related Matters." (1972) 3 *UNCITRAL Yearbook* 193.

North, P. (ed.) *Contract Conflicts: The E.E.C. Convention on the Law Applicable to Contractual Obligations—A Comparative Study*. Amsterdam: North-Holland, 1982.

———. *Private International Law Problems in Common Law Jurisdictions*. Dordrecht, The Netherlands: Martinus Nijhoff, 1993.

——— and Fawcett, J. *Cheshire and North Private International Law*. London: Butterworths, 1987.

Nwogugu, E. *The Legal Problems of Foreign Investment in Developing Countries*. Manchester: Manchester University Press, 1965.

O'Keefe, P. *Arbitration in International Trade*. Sydney: Prosper Law Publication, 1975.

Paasivirta, E. "Internationalisation and Stabilisation of Contracts versus State Sovereignty." (1989) 60 *B.Y.I.L.* 315.

Park, W. "Arbitration of International Contract Disputes." (1984) 39 *Bus. Law* 39.

———. "Judicial Supervision of Transnational Commercial Arbitration: The English Arbitration Act." (1980) 21 *Hastings Int'l L.J.* 87.

———. "The Lex Loci Arbitri and International Commercial Arbitration." (1983) *I.C.L.Q.* 21.

———. "National Law and Commercial Justice: Safeguarding Procedural Integrity in International Arbitration." (1989) 63 *Tulane L.R.* 647.

Paulsson, J. "Arbitration Unbound: Award Detached from the Law of Its Country of Origin." (1981) 30 *I.C.L.Q.* 358.

———. "Delocalisation of International Commercial Arbitration: When and Why It Matters." (1983) 32 *I.C.L.Q.* 53.

———. "The Extent of the Independence of International Arbitration from the Law of the Situs." In Lew, J. (ed.) *Contemporary Problems in International Arbitration*. London: Centre for Contemporary Law Studies, 1986.

______. "The ICSID *Klockner* v. *Cameroon* Award: The Duties of Partners in North-South Economic Development Agreements." (1984) 1 *J. Int'l Arb.* 145.

______. "May a State Invoke Its Internal Law to Repudiate Consent to International Commerical Arbitration?" (1986) 2 *Arb. Int'l* 90.

Peter, W. "Arbitration and Renegotiation Clauses." (1986) 3 *J. Int'l Arb.* 29.

______. *Arbitration and Renegotiation of International Investment Agreements*. Dordrecht, The Netherlands: Martinus Nijhoff, 1986.

Phillip, A. "The Significance of the Place of Arbitration in International Arbitration." (1985) *Swedish and Int'l Arb.* 37.

Pogany, S. "Economic Development Agreements." (1992) 7 *ICSID Review* 1.

Redfern, A. "Arbitration: Myth and Reality." (1976) 4 *Int'l Bus. L.* 450.

______. "International Commercial Arbitration: Jurisdiction Denied, The Pyramid Collapses." (1986) *J. Bus. L.* 15.

______ and Hunter, M. *Law and Practice of International Commercial Arbitration*. 2d ed. London: Sweet and Maxwell, 1991.

Rivkin, D. "Enforceability of Arbitral Awards Based on *Lex Mercatoria*." (1993) 9 *Arbitration Int'l* 67.

Robert, R. and Carbonneau, T. *The French Law of Arbitration*.New York: Matthew Bender, 1983.

Rooij, R. and Polak, M. *Private International Law in The Netherlands*. Deventer, The Netherlands: Kluwer Law and Taxation Publishers, 1987.

Roskill, Lord. "Arbitration." (1984) 3 *A.C.L.R.* 25.

Rubino-Sammartano, M. *International Arbitration Law*. Deventer, The Netherlands: Kluwer Law and Taxation Publishers, 1990.

______ and Morse, G. *Public Policy in Transnational Relationships*. Deventer, The Netherlands: Kluwer Law and Taxation Publishers, 1991.

Samuel, A. *Jurisdictional Problems in International Commercial Arbitration: A Study of Belgian, Dutch, English, French, Swiss, U.S. and West German Law*. Zurich: Schulthess Polygraphischer Verlag, 1989.

Sanders, P. "A Twenty Years' Review of the Convention on the Recognition and Enforcement of Foreign Arbitral Awards." (1979) 13 *Int'l Law.* 269.

Schindler, A. "Arbitration Still Bound." (1986) *L.Q.R.* 500.

Schlosser, P. "The Competence of Arbitrators and of Courts." (1992) 8 *Arb. Int'l* 189.

Schmitthoff, C. *Commercial Law in a Changing Economic Climate*. 2d ed. London: Sweet and Maxwell, 1981.

Schwebel, S. *International Arbitration: Three Salient Problems*. Cambridge: Grotius, 1987.

Seidl-Hohenveldern, I. "The Theory of Quasi-International and Partly International Agreements." (1975) *Rev. Belge D.I.* 567.

Sheikh, F. *The Legal Regime of Foreign Investment in the Sudan and Saudi Arabia: A Case Study of Developing Countries*. Cambridge: Cambridge University Press, 1986.

Shihata, I. "The Institute of International Law's Resolution on Arbitration between States and Foreign Enterprises—A Comment." (1990) 5 *ICSID Review* 65.

______. "Towards a Greater Depoliticization of Investment Disputes: The Role of ICSID and MIGA." (1986) 1 *ICSID Review* 1.

Smit, H. "A-National Arbitration." (1989) 63 *Tulane L.R.* 629.
———. "Substance and Procedure in International Arbitration: The Development of A New Legal Order." (1991) 65 *Tulane L.R.* 1309.
Sornarajah, M. *The Pursuit of Nationalized Property*. The Hague: Martinus Nijhoff, 1986.
———. "Supremacy of the Renegotiation Clause in International Contracts." (1988) 5 *J. Int'l Arb.* 97.
———. "The UNCITRAL Model Law: A Third World Perspective." (1989) 6:4 *J. Int'l Arb.* 7.
Stoecker, S. "The Lex Mercatoria: To What Extent Does It Exist?" (1990) 7 *J. Int'l Arb.* 101.
Stoever, W. *Renegotiation in International Business Transactions.* Toronto: Lexington Books, 1981.
Storme, M. and Ly, F. (eds.) *The Place of Arbitration*. Ghent: Mys and Breesch, 1992.
Suratgar, D. "Considerations Affecting Choice of Law Clauses in Contracts between Governments and Foreign Nationals." (1962) 2 *Indian J.I.L.* 273.
Svernlov, C. "The Evolution of the Doctrine of Separability in England." (1992) *J. Int'l Arb.* 115.
Szasz, I. "Introduction to the Model Law of UNCITRAL on International Commercial Arbitration." In Sanders, P. (ed.) *UNCITRAL's Project for a Model Law on International Commercial Arbitration*. Deventer, The Netherlands: Kluwer Law and Taxation Publishers, 1984.
Szurski, T. "Arbitration Agreement and Competence of the Arbitral Tribunal." In Sanders, P. (ed.) *UNCITRAL's Project for a Model Law on International Commercial Arbitration*. Deventer, The Netherlands: Kluwer Law and Taxation Publishers, 1984.
Teson, T. "State Contracts and Oil Exploration: The Aminoil-Kuwait Arbitration." (1984) 24 *Virg. J.I.L.* 323.
Thomas, D. "Commercial Arbitration—Justice According to Law." (1983) 2 *Civil Justice Q.* 166.
Titagawa, K. "Contractual Autonomy in International Arbitration." In Sanders, P. (ed.) *International Arbitration: Liber Amicorum for Martin Domke*. The Hague: Martinus Nijhoff, 1967 at 133.
Toope, S. *Mixed International Arbitration: Studies in Arbitration between States and Private Persons*. Cambridge: Grotius, 1990.
Trakman, L. *The Law Merchant: The Evolution of Commercial Law*. Littleton, CO: Fred B. Rothman, 1983.
Tribel, V. "The Choice of Law in Commercial Relations: A German Perspective." (1988) 37 *I.C.L.Q.* 935.
Varma, A. "Petroleum Concessions in International Arbitration." (1979) 18 *Colum. J.T.L.* 259.
Verdross, A. "Quasi-International Agreements and International Economic Transactions." (1964) 18 *Yearbook W.A.* 230.
———. "The Status of Foreign Private Interests Stemming from Economic Development Agreements with Arbitration Clauses." (1958) 18 *ZaoRV* 449.
Wetter, G. "Choice of Law in International Arbitration Proceedings in Sweden." (1984) *Swedish and Int'l Arb.* 16.

White, R. "Expropriation of the Libyan Oil Concessions: Two Conflicting International Arbitrations." (1981) 30 *I.C.L.Q.* 1.

Wilner, I. "Determining the Law Governing Performance in International Commercial Arbitration: A Comparative Study." (1965) 19 *Rutgers L.R.* 646.

Index

About the Author

OKEZIE CHUKWUMERIJE lectures at the University of Sydney Law School, Australia. He specializes and publishes in international commerical and trade law.